Time and Learning
in the
Special Education Classroom

SUNY Series in Special Education

David A. Sabatino, Editor

Time and Learning
in the
Special Education Classroom

Libby Goodman

State University of New York Press

Published by
State University of New York Press, Albany

For information, address State University of New York
Press, State University Plaza, Albany, N.Y., 12246

Library of Congress Cataloging-in-Publication Data

Goodman, Libby, 1947-
    Time and learning in the special education classroom / Libby
Goodman.
        p.   cm. — (SUNY series in special education)
    Includes bibliographical references.
    ISBN 0-7914-0371-8. — ISBN 0-7914-0372-6 (pbk.)
    1. Special education. 2. Teachers—Time management.   I. Title.
II. Series.
LC3965 . G58   1990
371.9—dc20

10 9 8 7 6 5 4 3 2 1

For my mother and father,
Rose and Jack

Contents

Preface

The genesis of this book lies in two conflicting perceptions about the current state of education for mildly handicapped children. On the one hand, the data on program effects and statistics on the numbers of referrals to and placements in special education portray a disturbing picture of children with learning problems deriving little benefit from special education programs and services. On the other hand, the literature is full of reports and data proclaiming that effective schools and effective education are within our reach. Numerous articles in professional journals delineate the components of effective instruction for both regular and special student. We are told that teachers can make a significant difference in children's academic lives. There is a need to reconcile the "what is" with "what can be."

Special education can justifiably take pride in many important accomplishments. The sheer growth of programs and services within our public schools which has guaranteed access to and appropriate education for all handicapped children is an immense accomplishment. Many legal and legislative milestones have greatly advanced the standing and opportunities for handicapped students. Advances in education for the severely and moderately impaired have been truly remarkable and have expanded horizons for all disabled persons. But the severe, moderately, or multiply impaired, *i.e.*, low incidence handicapping conditions, comprise only a small portion of our total special education population. The accomplishments attained for 10 percent of our students, as laudable as they may be, are not sufficient for all of special education. High incidence handicaps account for approximately 90 percent of our handicapped children and for these students the accomplishments are equivocal. The high numbers of new placements versus low number of students exiting from special education; disappointing data on achievement, social gains and post school adjustments; comparison over time of learning outcomes for similarly functioning students, *e.g.*, learning disabled and underachieving, in dissimilar placements (special classes versus regular classes) which show that underachievers in regular classes frequently learn more and do better than learning disabled students in special classes, etc. is evidence that special education is failing large numbers of mildly handicapped children. What's to be done? Where do the solutions lie?

This author does not presume to have all of the answers. But the author has long harbored the belief that successful education for the mildly handicapped happens, if it happens at all, in the classroom interactions between teacher and student. Therefore, the ferment in regular education about effective schools and effective teaching and the accompanying literature which focuses attention on instructional processes, identifies effective methods and strategies for basic skill instruction and reaffirms the role of teachers is of immense interest and immediately relevant to special education. Yet special educators have little knowledge of this literature and less understanding of its applicability to their classrooms. Extensive time spent in public school classrooms over the last few years and many interactions with special education teachers pursuing higher level degrees in university classes have brought home to me the degree of isolation which characterizes special education teachers. One is also struck by the enthusiastic and eager response of the special education teacher when presented with information about effective classroom teaching methods.

Regular education is the source for much information on instructional processes and on the time and learning relationship. There is much that is relevant and valuable in the special education literature as well. But, regular education has undoubtedly taken the lead in research on time and learning. There is a need to bridge the informational chasm, to synthesize information and research findings from disparate sources. The common denominators for all teachers are the instructional processes and the efficient and effective use of time in the classroom. Teachers fully appreciate the constraints of time, they do not yet fully appreciate or understand how to make the best use their time resources to improve teaching and learning and maximize student learning. Each chapter in the text addresses the issue of instructional time. Some chapters deal with historical perspective and theory, others stress classroom applications. Time is the thread which binds the separate chapters together. It is left to the reader to decide if the right balance has been achieved between theory and practice.

Some comments are in order about what this text does not attempt to do. The text does not contain a comprehensive in depth review of the literature. I am indebted to the educators and researchers who have taken on this arduous and difficult task; I have benefited from their labors. Research reviews were an invaluable resource. An effort was made to cull from the vast literature that which was most relevant to the issues, topics and instructional methods discussed. The topics, for the most part, are no longer controversial. They may have been the object of debate or controversy at some time. But the basic themes and the methodologies discussed rest on firm empirical bases.

There is certainly a need for more research to expand, to refine, and to extend some of these methods further into special education class-rooms. The major task at hand is to encourage and help special educators to analyze their own teaching and reach out for methods of proven effectiveness in the teaching of basic skills. The topic of time and learning is a vehicle which can help special educators do just that.

Chapter 1

Time and Learning: An Overview

Introduction

Throughout the twentieth century, educators have acknowledged the existence of a relationship between time and learning. We *know* that time and learning are interrelated variables fundamental to the learning process. We *know* that students must devote time to their studies if they are to be successful achievers. But our beliefs about the relationship between time and learning rest, in large part, upon assumptions or "common sense" notions rather than solid empirical evidence. Our understanding of the underlying dynamics of the relationship has been limited. More recent research efforts have begun to reveal the nature of the relationship and, as a result our understanding of time and learning is being expanded and refined. Research findings have confirmed some long standing beliefs and assumptions, but more importantly, recent research findings have shed considerable light on the nature of instructional processes.

Now, more than ever, the classroom and the behavior of children and teachers have become the focal points for research. The use of time—particularly instructional time—has become a key concern. Educators are being sensitized to the relationship between time and learning and the critical importance of the efficient and productive use of time in order to enhance learning outcomes. But this was not always the case.

Early Research on Time and Learning

Early in the twentieth century, research into the relationship between time and learning reflected an administrative point of view and was concerned with accurately describing the status quo, that is, the allocation of school time to various disciplines and other school activities. Recommendations which evolved from these research endeavors pointed toward administrative or structural change as a means of improving public education. Borg (1980) cites the works of Thompson, Holmes, and Mann published during the early decades of the twentieth century to illustrate the point. Thompson reviewed a number of school programs and offered suggestions for administrative changes, *e.g.*, demarcation between the junior and senior high school programs, grading and promotion practices, and elimination of certain subject matter which he felt would lead to the more efficient use of school time. Holmes' research involved a survey of how time was allocated across the various disciplines in American elementary schools. He surveyed 50 school systems and found great divergence in the amount of time allocated to various school subjects (a finding which holds true to this day). Mann's study was also concerned with documenting the allocation of school time to various school subjects (Borg, 1980).

The second half of the twentieth century has witnessed an increase in research activity, innovative research designs, and new and different research questions. Time, previously treated as merely a background variable, has become a focal point for research into instructional processes. Time is now recognized as a mediating variable between instruction and performance. There is a growing appreciation for time as an essential component of, and conduit for, effective instruction. Sufficient learning time and appropriate instruction, in tandem, impact greatly on student learning outcomes.

As our view of time and time use in the classroom was changing so was our perception of teacher effectiveness. Medley (1980) tells us that the twentieth century has seen an evolution in the definition and related research on teaching effectiveness. He describes this evolutionary process in terms of sequential phases of development. The first phase, early in the century, was concerned with identification of personality characteristics and/or stylistic qualities which distinguished the effective teacher from the ineffective teacher. For example, teaching effectiveness was equated with qualities such as leadership, loyalty, good judgement, self-control, considerateness, cooperation, etc. At the present time, teaching effectiveness is defined in terms of teaching competencies which translate into specific teaching behaviors in the classroom. Whereas one would have expected the teacher in the early part of the twentieth century to demonstrate "clarity" in his or her presentation, the present day observer would expect the teacher to "ask higher order questions" in his or her classroom presentations. Medley uses the above example to illustrate the evolution from characteristics to specific teaching behaviors; "clarity" defies definition, "asking higher order questions" can be defined, observed, and measured. Intervening phases of development focused upon different methods of instruction, classroom climate and finally specific teaching competencies.

Our perspective of teaching effectiveness has also been influenced by the emergence of process-product research from the 1960s onward. Under this research paradigm the investigation is concerned with identifying the "relationship between teachers' behaviors and students' learning outcomes" (Doyle, 1979, p. 184); that is, "the relationship between what the teacher does and what the student learns" (Waxman & Walberg, 1982, p. 103). The researcher's goal is to identify various facets of the instructional process and to determine how these factors enhance or impede learning. Effectiveness is defined in terms of measurable student outcomes. Effective teachers are those who arrange and manage the learning environment and instructional activities to promote the greatest achievement for their students. Process-product research helped to focus attention on time as a pivotal variable in the learning equation and an instructional variable under the teacher's control. It is interesting that the time factor is employed in current research as both a mediating and outcome variable. Numerous correlations studies have established that the amount of time available for instruction is related to student achievement. And experimental studies have used the time variable, *e.g.*, time on-task or attending behavior, as a measure of student behavior and instructional effectiveness.

The convergence of new definitions and perspectives of teaching effectiveness, the widespread use of innovative and empirically powerful research paradigms, and a reawakening of the interest in time usage in the classroom has been auspicious. The effective use of instructional time and teaching effectiveness are compatible concepts that work together to enhance student performance. But not all professionals share this positive view of the time and learning relationship.

The resurgence of interest in the time variable and research on the relationship between time and learning has not been hailed by all. We are faced with an interesting, if not unusual dilemma, in which different authorities, viewing the same data, reach very different conclusions. For some, the research findings are most promising; others find little in the research findings to warrant much enthusiasm. No one denies the existence of a persistent statistical relationship between instructional time and achievement. Rather, professional disagreement has coalesced around two main issues: (1) the strength of the relationship; and (2) the educational implications for the practitioners. A closer look at both of these issues is warranted.

The Statistical Relationship

Frederick and Walberg (1980) conducted an extensive review of correlational studies pertaining to instructional time and learning outcomes. Studies were grouped into 4 categories based upon the time measures used: years, days, hours, or minutes. A variety of learning outcomes were encompassed in the numerous studies reviewed. Overall, the authors found a moderate and persistent relationship between various outcome measures and time when time was equated with years of schooling and hours or minutes of instruction. Studies involving days of instruction yielded mixed results. Five of nine studies in this category yielded positive correlations ranging in magnitude from .32 to .69. Overall the correlation coefficients for the time variables and outcomes measures ranged from a low of .13 to a high of .71. Frederick and Walberg note that "refining the measure of time to reflect actual time devoted to the outcome being measured was successful in increasing the association" (1980, p. 190). They concluded that "time devoted to school learning appears to be a modest predictor of achievement" (p. 193). Other researchers share this point of view (Burns, 1984; Anderson, 1984).

In a second review, Caldwell, Huitt, and Graeber (1982) categorized studies according to the availability of time for instruction (school year, school day, allocated time), involvement in instruction (attendance year, engagement rate, student engaged time), and academic learning time (children working on appropriate tasks in which they enjoy a high rate of success). Nevertheless, Caldwell *et al.* reached substantially the same conclusion as Frederick and Walberg, namely that time is moderately related to student achievement. They too found that the relationship between time and learning becomes stronger as the measure of time becomes more specific to what students actually do in the classroom. Of all the time measures reviewed, the specific measures of the actual amount of time that children are productively involved in appropriate tasks (academic learning time) showed the strongest relationship to achievement.

Caldwell *et al.* (1982) utilized the data at their disposal to project the cumulative impact of differences in attendance, length of school day, and amount of engaged time for hypothetical high, average, and low attendance students. Their projections were based upon 160 days of school and 4.5 hours of instruction per day for low average students; 160 days per year and 5 hours of instruction per day for average students; 170 days of school and 5.5 hours of instruction per day for the high average students. The projections were adjusted (reduced in effect) to reflect the patterns of allocated and engaged time characteristic for each of the three student groups. The outcome of the projections revealed that the low average student had 30 hours of academic learning time for reading and language arts and 10 hours of academic learning time for math over the entire school year. In contrast, high average students had 224 hours of academic learning time in reading and language arts and 90 hours of academic learning time in mathematics during a comparable school year—6 times the academic learning time of the low average student. The figures paint a vivid picture of the instructional impact that differences in school time, whether due to institutional or individual factors, can make.

Wiley (1973) also studied the relationship between school time and student learning outcomes. His study involved a reanalysis of selected data from the classic study by Coleman, Campbell, Hobson, McPartland, Mood, Weinfeld, and York (1966) titled *Equality of Educational Opportunity*. As a result of their findings, Coleman and his colleagues had concluded that education made very little difference in the lives of children. However, Wiley pointed out that the Coleman study did not "analyze or interpret the data with the objective of determining the impact of the quantity of schooling on pupil achievement" (1973, p. 230). Wiley's reanalysis of the data for a sample of 6th grade students representing inner city Detroit schools yielded evidence of a significant relationship between quantity of schooling and student learning outcomes.

Based on the relationships revealed by his analysis, Wiley projected the effects on achievement which would result from increases in quantity of schooling. He projected that an increase in average daily attendance (ADA) from 88 percent to 95 percent would produce an 11.75 percent increase in verbal ability; a 23 percent increase in reading comprehension, and an 11.83 percent increase in mathematics achievement. If days of school per year, hours of school per day, and ADA are altered upward simultaneously, Wiley projects a 24 percent overall increase in quantity of school over the course of the school year. The accompanying increases in verbal ability, reading comprehension, and mathematics achievement would be 33.58 percent, 65.50 percent, and 33.92 percent respectively.

The projections of Caldwell *et al.* (1982) and Wiley (1973) and others (Leinhardt, Zigmond, and Cooley, 1981; Haynes and Jenkins, 1986) underscore the importance of quantity of schooling, in particular that portion of the school day in which children are actively involved in academic instruction. But we must bear in mind that these projections have yet to be realized. No one has yet demonstrated an ability

to produce the requisite changes in learning time and the accompanying increases in student achievement. But the projections certainly are
an inducement to educators to try to make the predictions a reality.

The Critics' Views

In contrast to the above, there are other learned professionals and
researchers who are far less encouraged by the research findings
(Doyle, 1979; Frymier, 1981; Karweit, 1983-84). The critics point out
that the relationship between instructional time and learning produce
correlation coefficients of only low to moderate value. Many believe
that the relationship between time and learning is overshadowed by
the far stronger relationships between achievement and a variety of
non-school-based variables, *e.g.*, socioeconomic status and ethnic background (Averch, Carroll, Donaldson, Kiesling, Pincus, 1974; Heath and
Nielson, 1974; Jencks, 1972). Some researchers question the inherent
credibility and validity of the data base. Serious methodological and
design flaws within the research studies have been discussed at length
by Heath and Nielson (1974), and Shavelson and Atwood-Dempsey
(1970). Heath and Nielson after reviewing the research on the relationship of specific teaching behaviors and achievement concluded that
the literature "fails to reveal an empirical basis for performance-based
teacher education" (1974, p. 463). And Shavelson and Atwood-
Dempsey (1976) point out that there are methodological and conceptual problems yet to be resolved within the literature on teaching behavior and student outcomes. They hold that the research findings on
teaching effects on pupil outcomes are unstable and unreliable.

To be sure, the methodological problems of concern to the critics
are very real. More than a decade has passed since the publication of
these critical reviews. More recent research on teacher behaviors and
student learning is providing evidence of stable and functional relationships. In response to the critics, Gage (1978) reminds us that there
are no perfect naturalistic research studies and that individual studies
are easy targets for criticism. The analysis of clusters of results from
many related studies often "acquire sufficient power to dispel the false
impression created when the statistical significance of weak single
studies is taken seriously" (Gage, 1978, p. 30). Gage goes on to say that
"if the studies tend to yield the same implications from many different
approaches, our confidence in their implications can be maintained"
(1978, p. 31). Waxman and Walberg (1982) echo this point of view in
their review of process-product research on instructional variables.
They too maintain that consistent results which emerge again and
again across studies with varied student samples and under many dif-

ferent conditions, in which the "usual measurement and statistical problems abound" (Waxman and Walberg, 1982, p. 104), must be taken seriously. The weight of evidence clearly supports the relationship between the time variable and student learning outcomes. The criticism should not sidetrack further investigation of the time and learning relationship; rather, the criticism can be constructive in that the challenge posed by some "methodological" problems increases our understanding of the underlying instructional process. And the problems which limit research outcomes may be functioning within the classrooms to limit instructional outcomes as well.

Karweit and Slavin (1981, 1982) have identified some of the factors that impact upon the strength and consistency of the relationship between time-on-task and achievement. Karweit and Slavin (1981) found that proximate measures of time, that is, measures which accurately reflect actual student use of time (*e.g.*, engaged time) show a stronger relationship to achievement than more general time measures (*e.g.*, allocated time). The reader will recall that Caldwell *et al.* (1982), and Frederick and Walberg (1980) reached the same conclusion. Therefore, the definition and quantification of the time variable will influence the outcome of the research endeavor. In a 1982 study, Karweit and Slavin found that a study's results are affected, sometimes adversely, by the number and length of observation sessions. In general more observation sessions of longer duration rather than fewer and shorter observation sessions ought to be the goal. Karweit and Slavin (1982) are in step with the earlier work of Rowley (1976) regarding the desirability of increased numbers of observations for greater lengths of time. A study of the relationship between time-on-task and achievement which is too sparse, both in number of observations and overall observation time, may very well undermine the research effort from the outset. A third source of inconsistency and weakness in research findings may be the lack of attention to the interaction of student characteristics and time-on-task. Karweit and Slavin (1981) found that additional instructional time does not have equal impact on students of unequal abilities. Their analysis revealed that students below the class mean in entering achievement level produced strong effects for time-on-task; the effect for students above the class mean were far weaker. Therefore, the impact of time spent in learning is a reflection of the amount of time needed to learn. Researchers have paid too little attention to student factors thus far. The implications for special populations have also not been fully explored. The findings of Karweit and Slavin (1982) with regard to the interaction of student characteristics and the impact of time-on-task, highlights the necessity of understanding the context within which learning is taking place and exactly how time is being used for instruction. Frederick and Walberg's (1980) observation that we need to clarify the conditions under which more time spent does indeed produce more learning is amply justified.

Practical Implications

The notion that more time equals more learning may indeed be misleading in its simplicity. The many statistical projections that have been made about the amount of increased achievement that will result from increases in instructional time have yet to be realized in the real world of the classroom. Karweit and Slavin (1981) stress that such extrapolations can be fallacious and/or unrealistic and that, in order to significantly increase students' time-on-task, one must either improve the efficiency of the classroom or increase scheduled instructional time. Rosenshine (1981) and others have expressed reservations about the feasibility of changing the balance between academic and nonacademic activities in the classroom. Increasing the amount of time that students are engaged in academic pursuits through increases in allocated instructional time may be more difficult than it would, at first glance, appear to be. Suffice it to say that "it remains an open question whether it is practically possible for teachers to recover enough lost time to witness the achievement gains predicted" (Karweit and Slavin, 1981, p. 166).

Both avenues to increased learning time—increasing the efficiency of the classroom and increasing scheduled instructional time—will be explored in great detail in up-coming chapters. There are many authors who believe that teachers can and must do a better job of utilizing the time resources under their control. There is a substantial body of literature which speaks directly to the critical issue of effective use of instructional time in the classroom. Special educators have not had sufficient exposure to this literature nor have they made adequate use of this rich source of empirical and applied research.

A Common Concern

It is the decided opinion of this author that special educators have had limited exposure to this important literature on the relationship between time and learning and, as a consequence, are unaware of the implications and applications of important research findings to special education programs and the teaching of handicapped students. The literature pertaining to the relationship between time and learning is a rich source of research supported instructional practices for the successful instruction of basic skills. It is important and relevant for any teacher engaged in the instruction of basic skills, and in this regard regular and special education teachers share a common responsibility and concern.

Regular education has been in the throes of the "effective schools movement" for a decade and more; only recently has the special education community taken notice and begun to discuss the relevance of the effective schools literature and research to the special education classroom (Bickel and Bickel, 1986; Goodman, 1985; Zigmond, Sansone, and Miller, 1986). Yet there are many and compelling reasons why special educators should be attuned to what is happening in regular education and should be familiar with the research literature dealing with instructional processes and especially the use of instructional time in the classroom.

1. The primary focus of the time and learning research literature is the acquisition of basic skills, *e.g.*, reading, mathematics, language arts, etc. The vast majority of mildly handicapped children demonstrate significant deficiencies in basic skills. Remediation of and compensation for basic skills deficits is still the primary purpose of remedial and special education programs. Effective practices for basic skills instruction apply to many types of students in varied educational settings.

2. The target population employed in most of the relevant research to date is comprised of elementary aged children. Special education's primary thrust for the mildly handicapped student is still focused at the elementary level (the need for secondary level transitional programs not withstanding). Intervention at the elementary level carries the hope of significantly altering the child's academic experience from one of failure and frustration to one of success and accomplishment.

3. Many instructional themes of the research literature parallel existing special education practices, *e.g.*, student engaged time in regular education and time-on-task in special education are comparable (not identical) concepts. Many of the instructional principles advocated in the effective school literature, *e.g.*, monitoring of student performance, corrective feedback, etc. are familiar to special educators and are well established as basic tenents of special education methodology.

4. The research literature underscores the importance of demonstrating instructional effectiveness in terms of student outcomes. A commitment to program effectiveness as demonstrated by measures of student performance, *e.g.*, achievement gains, successful integration, and return to regular education, has been sorely lacking in special education. For too long, special educators have relied upon evidence of compliance and process rather than hard data on student performance to substantiate the effectiveness of special education programs.

5. The integration of mildly handicapped children into regular education programs is a major thrust of special education. To successfully integrate handicapped children, special educators must have an appreciation and understanding of the regular classroom if they are to prepare students to function successfully within that milieu. Greater knowledge of current instructional practices in regular education will help special educators to better prepare their students for integration into regular education classrooms and programs.

Now, more than ever, special education teachers need to overcome the professional isolation which has characterized special education from its inception. Special educators tend to blame their isolation on the disinterest, negative attitudes, and/or the outright rejection by regular educators. But some of this professional and intellectual isolation may very well be self-imposed. it seems that regular education may now be the source of critical information and practices which can be of great benefit to the special education teacher, and special educators need to take full advantage of this wealth of information.

Time—The Critical Resource

For the classroom teacher, time is a limited and critical resource. There is only a finite amount of time in which to accomplish a long shopping list of educational goals and objectives. Historically, there has been little change in the length of the school day. However, the number of curricular requirements which must be incorporated into the daily schedule has increased over the years. The net result is less time for each of a greater number of course requirements. And yet, increased content demands are but one source of competition for time in the classroom. A combination of academic and nonacademic factors vie with the teacher for the limited time available during the school day and over the course of the school year.

Teachers know that time is a critical factor in student achievement. If this author did not believe that teachers have significant control over their classrooms and the use of time within their instructional day, there would be no justification for the writing of this book. What teachers lack is an understanding of the dynamic relationship between instructional time and learning outcomes, and an appreciation for their own critical role in the management of time resources. This author concurs with the sentiments of McKenzie who, in describing the thrust of current research on teaching and school improvement, stated that "the master variable of pedagogy is the amount and intensity of student engagement in appropriate learning tasks, ... that effective learning time depends heavily on the atmosphere of the classroom and on the teacher's leadership skills in managing the instructional task" (1983, p. 9). The statement underscores the importance of instructional time, appropriate learning tasks and the managerial and instructional skills of the teacher. We shall see that the teacher's mastery of this trilogy is the key to use of instructional time toward maximum student achievement.

Chapter 2

Learning Time in Theory and Practice

The resurgence of interest in the variable of time, specifically the linkage between the use of school time and student achievement, is generally credited to John Carroll's publication in 1963 of "A Model of School Learning." Other theorists, notably B. Bloom (1976), D. Wiley, and A. Harnischfeger (1974) expanded upon Carroll's work with their own theoretical conceptualizations. Collectively these theorists introduced and refined the concept of learning time and delineated its importance for the learning process. Their work forms the theoretical foundation for current empirical and applied research efforts. This chapter, therefore, begins with a brief review of each of their models of learning.

Carroll's Model of School Learning

In 1963 Carroll proposed "A Model of School Learning" (MSL) to foster an understanding of school success and failure through a better understanding of the factors that effect students' school performance. Carroll proposed that learning was a function of the amount of time a student spent learning in relation to the amount of time he or she needed for learning. Learning, or in Carroll's terms, the degree of learning, is a ratio between the time needed to learn and the time spent learning. The conceptualization can be displayed in equation form as follows:

$$\text{Degree of Learning} = f\left(\frac{\text{time actually spent}}{\text{time needed}}\right)$$

There are five factors in the MSL:

1. Aptitude—the amount of time an individual needs to learn a given task under optimal instruction conditions
2. Ability—to understand instruction which is closely tied to general intelligence

3. Perseverance—the amount of time the individual is willing to engage actively in learning
4. Opportunity to learn—the time allowed for learning
5. Quality of instruction—the degree to which instruction is presented so as not to require additional time for mastery beyond that required by the aptitude of the learner

Time actually spent in learning is a function of the time allocated for learning and the student's willingness to persevere at the task. Time needed is the result of aptitude (general intellectual ability), ability to understand instruction, and the quality of instruction. Of the five factors, opportunity to learn and quality of instruction are extrinsic to the learner. These factors offer the greatest possibility of experimental modification (Borg, 1980). The equation representing learning can now be restated to reflect the five factors of the MSL:

$$\text{Degree of Learning} = f \left(\begin{array}{ll} \text{1. Time Allowed} & \text{2. Perseverance} \\ \text{3. Aptitude} & \text{4. Quality of Instruction} \\ \text{5. Ability to Understand Instruction} \end{array} \right)$$

The time factor is a pivotal element in the model. Borg (1980) notes that Carroll's model of school learning was one of the first to fit engaged time into a model of cognitive learning in a school setting. No less important is Carroll's conceptualization of time as a varying, rather than fixed, factor. At the time of the model's initial publication, educational practice dictated that children were generally given equal amounts of time to accomplish learning tasks. Under such "fixed time conditions" (Anderson, 1984) achievement variability among children will be great. Carroll's model embodies the principle that the amount of time needed to learn varies among students. Given enough time and proper instruction most students can learn up to high levels. Carroll believed that performance outcomes should be held constant and each student should be given adequate time to reach performance criteria. Under such "fixed achievement conditions" (Anderson, 1984) variability in performance among students is sharply reduced. The reduction in achievement variability under "fixed achievement conditions" has been documented in the research of Bloom (1974) and others under the instructional rubric of mastery learning. Mastery learning approaches which embody "fixed achievement conditions" have produced the intriguing finding that students become more efficient learners; that is, the amount of time that students need to accomplish designated learning tasks to criterion level decreases as students progress through a series of learning units under fixed achievement conditions. Anderson

(1984) reports that the amount of learning time needed by students to attain the desired performance levels decreased from 7 to 1, to 4 to 1 in a study by Arlin (1973) and from 4 to 1, to 2 to 1 in 2 studies by Block (1970) and Anderson (1976) respectively. These findings suggest that optimal instructional practices do contribute to more effective learning or, as Bloom (1980) puts it, students are "learning how to learn."

Carroll had hoped that his MSL would encourage research on each of the factors that it contained. In a recent retrospective of the model and its impact Carroll (1984) expressed his gratification that the MSL has indeed been the catalyst for a vast amount of research effort. In 1963 Carroll had viewed "quality of learning" as the most elusive of the model's five variables and he believes it remains so even today. Researchers have by no means revealed the full nature of quality instruction. But current work on time and learning is adding significantly to our knowledge and understanding of the learning process and of quality in instruction.

Bloom's Theory of School Learning

Bloom's theory of school learning embodies his belief that the educational system, not solely the innate characteristics of children and their environments, foster significant degrees of variation in achievement among learners. His perspective is at odds with those professionals and lay persons who readily accepted as a "given" achievement variability among learners. Concern for the vast and, Bloom believes, unnecessary differences in learning outcomes among students was the impetus for development of his model. He hoped to show how the educational system and current instructional practices, if altered, could foster high levels of achievement for most students.

Bloom's model which builds upon and extends Carroll's theory is composed of three major variables: student characteristics, instruction, and learning outcomes. Student characteristics refer to: (1) cognitive entry behaviors; and (2) affective entry characteristics. The cognitive entry characteristics allude to mastery of the prerequisite learning necessary for the learning tasks to come. Affective entry characteristics refer to the student's motivation for learning. Historical, familial, and social factors outside the control of the school are not included. Their exclusion is not meant to suggest that these factors do not affect the learner; rather, Bloom focuses attention on "alterable variables" with empirically established relationships to learning outcomes. "These two measures of the individual represent an economical current summary of the individual's history with respect to the learning yet to be accomplished" (Bloom, 1976, p. 14).

Figure 2.1. Blooms Theory of School Learning

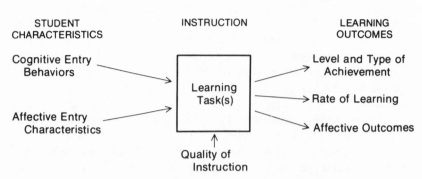

From *Human Characteristics and School Learning* by B.S. Bloom, 1976, NY: McGraw-Hill, Copyright 1976 by McGraw- Hill Publishing Co. Reprinted by permission.

     The instructional variable deals specifically with the quality of instruction which, in turn, is determined by the appropriateness of instruction for the individual's needs. Bloom stresses the importance of cues, participation, reinforcement, feedback and correction as major characteristics of quality in instruction. "The one quality that appears to be the strongest symptom of the entire quality of instruction is the level of participation" (Bloom, 1976, p. 134). Bloom believes that the equality of instruction can account for at least one-fourth of the variance in student achievement on cognitive achievement measures. The demonstrated causal relationship of quality of instruction to achievement underscores the importance of this factor in the learning process.

     Quality of instruction, cognitive entry behaviors, and affective entry characteristics, in concert, exert a powerful effect on learning outcomes. Where conditions for learning are favorable, *e.g.*, students have the prerequisite skills for the tasks to come, are motivated to participate, and instruction is effective, etc., levels of learning are high and variation in learning outcomes among students are reduced. When less than optimal instructional conditions exist, learning outcomes are lower and variation among students is greater. Given optimal conditions, Bloom believes that the vast majority of students, up to 90 or 95 percent, can be helped to achieve the high levels previously attained by only a minority of students.

Within Bloom's model, learning outcomes are presented in terms of:)(1) level and type of achievement; (2) rate of learning; and (3) affective outcomes. The beneficial effects which occur in the level and rate of learning when instruction adheres to Bloom's model have been documented in numerous studies of mastery learning (Block, 1974; Bloom, 1976). Student subjects in many mastery learning investigations have demonstrated improvement in academic, cognitive, and affective outcomes. There is evidence of decreased achievement variability within the mastery learning group and an increased efficiency in learning, *i.e.,* students' rate of learning. It appears that rate, or time needed to reach criterion, is alterable through optimal instruction methods. A more extensive discussion of the research pertaining to mastery learning is contained in chapter ten.

Bloom has built upon the ideas of Carroll to develop a more complete and specific model (Borg, 1980). Bloom has also accomplished the important feat of translating a theoretical conceptualization into a working model (Block, 1970) which has spawned extensive and important research on time and learning, instructional variables, and student learning.

Wiley and Harnischfeger's Model of Instructional Exposure and Achievement

Wiley and Harnischfeger (1974) share Carroll's appreciation for the central importance of the time factor in school achievement. However, they saw a need for further refinement of Carroll's model to adequately express the complexity of the time for learning concept. Although the interaction of time needed and time spent are factors of the school and classroom which determine, in large measure, the time available for learning, Wiley and Harnischfeger (1974) stress that the "wide variations in quantity of schooling also implies large differences in educational opportunity" (p. 10). Variations in the length of the school day result in significant differences in the total school exposure which in turn has a significant impact on school achievement (Wiley, 1973). The authors point out that the maximal quantity of schooling (determined by the length of the school year and the length of the school day) is subsequently reduced by numerous intervening factors (pupil attendance, nature of the instructional program, allocation decisions, etc.) to the actual exposure level of pupils to instruction.

Figure 2.2. Individual Instructional Exposure and Achievement

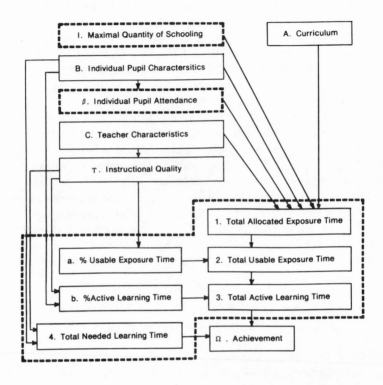

From "Explosion of a Myth: Quality of schooling and exposure to instruction, major educational vehicles," D.E. Wiley and A. Harnischfeger, 1974, *Educational Researcher, 3*, p. 10. Copyright 1974 by the American Educational Research Association. Reprinted by permission.

Within the Wiley and Harnischfeger model, achievement is determined by 4 main concepts: exposure time, percent active learning time, percent usable exposure time, and total needed learning time. They stress that the bedrock of their conceptual model is the total time for a given instructional task and the time that the student is actively engaged.

Their conceptualization of learning expressed in equation form follows:

$$\text{Achievement} = f\left(\frac{WXY}{Z}\right)$$

W is the total Allocated Exposure Time
X is the percent Active Learning Time
Y is the percent of Usable Exposure Time
Z is the total Needed Learning Time

Their conceptualization of school achievement introduces administrative and policy considerations into the time and learning equation and reveals that exposure time is open to manipulation. Data on achievement differences resulting from variations in time allocated for learning underscore the administrative implications of this view of learning and achievement. The introduction of administrative and policy considerations (by implication if not directly) as independent variables which carry the potential for significant impact on student learning, is an important extension of Carroll's model which further expands our understanding of the relationship between school time and student learning outcomes.

In summary, the importance of the contributions of Carroll, Bloom, and Wiley and Harnischfeger cannot be overemphasized. Carroll's theory, expressed in his "A Model of School Learning," projected the variable of time into the center of the learning process by defining learning in temporal terms. The development of the time concept, first introduced as a primary factor by Carroll, has been translated into a working model for classroom instruction by Bloom. Within Bloom's model, time is both an intervening and an outcome variable; that is to say that time contributes to the quality of instruction and is also a measure of instructional effectiveness. The degree of student participation in learning intervenes between instruction and learning outcomes and the rate of learning is viewed as an indicator of learning efficiency. Optimal learning conditions, including sufficient time for learning, will increase student achievement and reduce the amount of time needed to achieve mastery. Bloom explained how student characteristics and instructional variables interacted with time to produce learning. Wiley and Harnischfeger expanded upon both Carroll's and Bloom's work to develop a model of learning that cast learning time within an organizational and administrative framework. By doing so they sensitized educators to the administrative and policy issues which impinge upon students' exposure to schooling and hence their opportunity to learn.

Instructional Time: Definitions and Classroom Applications

It should come as no surprise that a select vocabulary has emerged which is used to discuss and describe the relationship between time and learning. Therefore, an understanding of some essential terms and concepts is necessary for further progress through the text. These terms and concepts are listed below in alphabetical order and defined. In addition, the literature contains various terms which are used interchangeably and are essentially synonymous in meaning. These terms are listed under the relevant term or concept to which they apply.

Academic Learning Time (ALT) is "the amount of time a student spends engaged in an academic task that she/he can perform with high success: (Fisher, Berliner, Filby, Marliave, Cahen, and Dishaw, 1980, p. 8).

Active Academic Responding "involves opportunities for pupils to practice the academic task" (Hall, Delquadri, Greenwood, and Thurston, 1982, p. 8).

— active academic learning

—opportunity to respond

—opportunity to learn

—active responding time

Allocated Time is "the amount of time that teachers allocate to instruction in a particular content area" (Borg, 1980, p. 49).

—scheduled time

Engaged Rate is "the percentage of the class actively working, or engaged, in a subject area" (Caldwell, Huitt, and Graeber, 1982, p. 474).

—student engaged rate

—engagement rate

Engaged Time is "that part of allocated time during which the student is paying attention" (Fisher *et al.*, 1980, p. 9).

—on-task

—on-task behavior

—attention to task

—at-task behavior

A hypothetical example will serve to further explain and illustrate the differences among these terms and concepts. A second grade classroom of average children in a public school setting will serve as our "hypothetical classroom". The school board of this particular district, in keeping with state regulations and consistent with educational practice of the day, has designated a school year of 180 days and an elementary school instructional day of 5 hours. In effect, the board has established the outer limits on the amount of schooling available to all elementary school pupils. Furthermore, reading and language arts are viewed as the critical disciplines for the primary grades and teachers are expected to provide sufficient time for adequate instruction in these essential subject areas. Special subjects, *e.g.*, art, music and physical education must be provided as well as other subject areas mandated by State regulations.

To this point, our second grade teacher has had no input into these time related decisions, *e.g.*, the number of school days per year and the number of hours per school day, which will determine the amount of available school time for all students. Very likely she has had minimal, if any, direct input into the specification of the district's instructional priorities (though reading and language arts are probably deemed priority subjects by all elementary school teachers) nor any say about the state's educational regulations. Within these parameters, our teacher will construct her daily schedule.

Allocated Time

Our teacher has determined that the range of abilities and functional levels among her children warrants three instructional reading groups. She allocates 1/2 hour per day for reading instruction for each group, thus allocating a total of 1.5 hours per day for direct reading instruction. Allocated time reflects the teacher's plan for the use of daily instructional time. It is our teacher's intention to provide each of her three reading groups with 1/2 hour of direct reading instruction per day. But, the best intentions sometimes fall short of total fulfillment.

As we know, our teacher has separated her pupils into 3 instructional groups for reading. Grouping necessitates transitioning between instructional groups, and invariably some instructional time will be lost as children change places (teachers typically have a reading area and children move to and from this designated instructional area), gather their materials, settle down to assigned tasks, etc. In addition, we anticipate that all children, those at their seats working independently and those involved in teacher-led activities, will let their attention wander away from the teacher or task for some portion of the lesson. One does not expect 100 percent on-task behavior at all times. Whenever children are off task, instructional time is lost. In addition, teachers and children may be distracted from their work by a variety of disruptions and/or interruptions, *e.g.*, a disruptive student in the classroom, announcements over the intercom, visitors to the classroom, playground noise, etc. Instructional time is also lost whenever other activities, curricular or extracurricular, supersede the normal daily schedule. Activities such as assembly programs, book fairs, and parent conferences to name just a few, disrupt the daily schedule in many schools. Indeed, such activities are important, but we must bear in mind that they intrude upon allocated instructional time and cause a loss of instructional time. There are also essential and unforeseeable events, *e.g.*, fire drills, snowstorms, etc., that disrupt the school day and cause a loss of learning time.

It is apparent that allocated time, the amount of time designated for daily instruction, is not the same as the actual amount of time during which children receive or attend to instruction. The difference between allocated instructional time and actual instructional time can be substantial.

Engaged Time and Engaged Rate

For our second grade teacher the most important consideration is engaged time, that is, the portion of allocated time during which the students are paying attention to and are involved in appropriate academic tasks. The reader will recall from Chapter 1 that both allocated and engaged time are related to achievement. But engaged time, being the more specific measure of the actual time that children are on task, has the stronger relationship to achievement.

Given that engaged time will be less than allocated time, we need to be concerned about the amount of time lost between the planning and execution of instruction. In our hypothetical second grade classroom, each reading group has been allocated thirty minutes of instructional time, but each group will not receive a full 30 minutes of teacher-led instruction. Ideally, interruptions will be kept to a minimum, the children will be attentive, and the amount of time lost will be negligible. The research available to us at this time highlights the variability that is found in both allocated and engaged time. We have evidence of significant variability across school districts, within school buildings, from class to class, and among children within the same classroom. The degree of variability in engaged on-task behavior can be startling. Undoubtedly the reader can recall her own classroom experience and call to mind a child who was a diligent worker and another child, perhaps in the same class, who was off task with equal frequency. If the amount of engaged time were calculated for each of these children, the differences in the degree of attentiveness would be revealed in stark detail.

When comparing children or groups of children, it is often more accurate to speak in terms of percentage of engaged time (engaged rate) rather than absolute amounts of engaged time. For instance, if one child in our hypothetical class was engaged in reading activities for 20 minutes and another child was engaged for 10 minutes, comparison of their absolute engaged time could lead to the conclusion that the first child is more attentive than her peer. And yet, this conclusion may be erroneous. While it is true that the former child participated in instruction for a longer period of time—in terms of absolute minutes—the 20 engaged minutes may have been part of a 35 minute lesson. The latter child may have been engaged for 10 minutes of a 15 minute lesson. If we convert engaged time to engagement rates, we can see that the first child's engagement rate was 57 percent and the second child's engagement rate was 67 percent. In fact, the latter child was the more attentive. If the engagement rates are characteristic of these 2 students, given lessons of equal length, it is the second child who would very likely be on-task for the longer period of time. Engagement rate, therefore, is the percentage of time during the day or lesson that a child or group of children is actively involved in academic tasks. For comparison purposes, engagement rates (percentage figures) are often more useful than absolute numbers.

Academic Learning Time

Our second grade teacher is well aware of the importance of maintaining high levels of engagement during instructional activities. She also understands that an important aspect of engagement concerns the difficulty level of the tasks to which children must attend. Research on effective instructional practices and the most effective use of instructional time reveals that student engagement is affected by task difficult (Fisher et al., 1978; Gickling and Armstrong, 1978; Gickling and Thompson, 1985; Krupski, 1985). Tasks at an inappropriate level of difficulty—either too hard or too easy—have a negative impact on attentiveness. Children will quickly turn away from a task that is too difficult and that offers few opportunities for success. On the other hand, tasks which are too quickly accomplished leave children with excessive amounts of free time which represents lost instructional opportunity and which may precipitate classroom management problems (Gickling and Thompson, 1985). Ideally, academic tasks should be of an appropriate level of difficulty; that is, children should enjoy a high level of success—though not total success—to make the best use of instructional time.

The dual dimensions of time on task and task difficulty have been merged into the concept of Academic Learning Time (ALT). ALT is the time spent by a student engaged on relevant academic tasks that she can perform with high success (Fisher et al., 1980). Appropriate task difficulty is quantified differently by various authorities. Rosenshine (1981) suggests that children should experience at least an 80 percent success rate. Gickling and Armstrong (1978) and Gickling and Thompson (1985) define task difficulty in terms of the ratio of known to unknown elements within a given assignment. In the former study appropriate task difficulty was set at 70 percent to 85 percent known elements for seatwork and 93 percent to 97 percent known elements for reading assignments; in the latter study an 80 percent success rate was applied.

Active Academic Responding

Another important aspect of engagement for our teacher involves the nature of children's participation during instruction. Not only must we provide sufficient time for academic instruction, but we must also provide children with sufficient opportunities for active academic responding (Delquadri, Greenwood, Stretton and Hall, 1983; Greenwood, Delquadri and Hall, 1984; Hall, Delquadri, Greenwood and Thurston, 1982). Children's participation during instruction—that is during engaged time—may be characterized as "passive" or "active" (Hall, et al., 1982). These 2 types of participatory behavior are not equally beneficial for students nor equally related to achievement gains. According to Hall et al. (1982), active responding involves the child practicing the academic task, e.g., answering a question, doing a problem, reading the text, etc. Examples of passive responding include general attending behavior such as listening to another child read, watching another child do a problem, etc. Research indicates that achievement gains are more highly related to active academic responding (Becker, 1977; Delquadri, Greenwood, Stretton and Hall, 1983; Fisher, et al., 1980; Rosenshine, 1981; Stallings, 1975). The research on classroom practices also reveals that the level of responding and opportunities for active academic responding are limited for the disadvantaged and low achieving (Allington, 1980, 1977; Fox, 1974; Greenwood, Delquadri, Stanley, Terry and Hall, 1981) and the handicapped (Greenwood, Delquadri, and Hall, 1984; Thurlow, Ysseldyke, Graden, and Algozzine, 1984).

Children need sufficient opportunities to respond—that is, to practice academic tasks in order to learn efficiently up to their ability levels. The problem may well be that "in many classrooms the instructional arrangement may fail to generate the necessary level of opportunity to respond required for mastery of key academic skills" (Delquadri, et al., 1983, p. 227). In addition, active responding on the part of the children affords the teacher numerous opportunities to monitor student progress and provide corrective feedback as needed. Sufficient instructional time, high levels of student engagement and active responding, teacher monitoring of student progress, and corrective feedback are basic elements of effective instruction in any elementary classroom.

Fortunately, our hypothetical second grade teacher is sensitive to the relationship between time use and effective instruction. Although the basic framework of the instructional day is outside of her control, the elements which may well be the keys to effective instruction are clearly under her control. In the chapters which follow we will delve deeper into the effective use of instructional time in order to help teachers understand how to make the best use of the time resources at their disposal.

Engaged Time versus Time On-Task

The terms "engaged" and "on-task" appear repeatedly and are used interchangeably throughout the text. However, the terms are not, strictly speaking, synonymous. There is a difference in meaning which requires some explanation.

Engaged time (and all of its derivations) is a widely recognized and accepted concept in regular education. The term is part of the professional vocabulary and its meaning is understood by practitioners. References to engaged time or engaged rate have only recently begun to appear in the special education literature (Bickel and Bickel, 1986; Goodman, 1985; Zigmond, Sansone, Miller, Donahue, and Kohnke, 1986). On-task or off-task behavior has been the common terminology used in the special education literature to designate attending behavior.

Engaged time and on-task behavior both deal with students' attending behavior. The difference in the terms stems from the nature of the student's response and involvement during instructional activities. The concept of engaged time goes beyond merely attending to what students actually are doing during instruction. In the definition of academic learning time, the concept of engagement has been extended to include students attending to tasks of appropriate difficulty and in which they meet with a high level of success. A further refinement of the concept of engaged time, active academic responding distinguishes between active and passive responding. Active responding involves the actual practicing of the academic task, *e.g.*, doing math problems, answering questions, reading textual material, etc. In passive responding a student could be attending to the task but would not be actively involved or responding. Engaged time then is concerned with the nature of student responding during instructional activities as well as the maintenance of overt attending behavior.

The extensive use, for many years, of the term "on-task" by special educators attests to their long-standing concern for the attending behavior of handicapped students. Problems of attention are recognized as a major deficit area for handicapped students (Bryan and Wheeler, 1972; Deshler, 1978; Forness and Esveldt, 1975; Keogh and Margolis, 1976; Ross, 1976). Efforts to define and describe children with attention problems and to develop effective interventions go back to the seminal work of Strauss and Lehtinen (1947) who pioneered in educational interventions for children characterized as hyperactive and distractable. Efforts to understand and to deal effectively with the educational manifestations of attending problems have continued through the years. Most recently, attention deficit disorder with or without hyperactivity has captured the interest of the educational community (Douglas and Peters, 1979; Kuehne, Kehle and McMahon, 1987; O'Brien and Obrzut, 1986-1987).[1]

In special educational settings and applied research studies, on-task behavior is frequently designated as the target behavior. On-task behavior is operationally defined in terms of the student being physically and visually oriented toward the source of instruction, be it the teacher, a book, a teaching machine, etc. For example, Lloyd, Hallahan, Kosiewicz, and Kneedler (1982) defined on-task as "sitting in his seat, looking at his assigned work" (p. 221). And Krupski (1985) used the following to define on-task behavior: "if the child exhibited physical orientation toward the task, eye contact with the task, or meaningful manipulation of the task materials" (p. 54).

Definitions of on-task behavior define attending behavior, but do not generally delve any deeper into the nature of the student responding, the instructional conditions, or the interaction between instructional conditions and student responses (Greenwood, Delquadri, and Hall, 1984). And increases in attending behavior alone do not necessarily generate increases in learning or achievement gains (Snider, 1987). The critical difference between merely attending and actively responding has been demonstrated. For example, Harris and Hall (cited in Greenwood, Delquadri, et al., 1984) in a study of reinforcement techniques with inner city youth found that monetary reinforcement for attending behavior alone did not lead to improved academic performance. Reinforcement proved unsuccessful despite the fact that daily observations revealed that the students were neither disruptive nor off- task. Under the existing instructional conditions in which students sat passively listening to teacher lectures mean academic performance never surpassed a minimal grade level of "D." However, instructional alterations which increased students' opportunity to respond and receive feedback boosted student grades from a "D" to "C" level.

The studies of Hall and Harris and others which have demonstrated that a high level of student responding is linked to higher achievement lend support to the concept of student responding as a mediating variable between instructional conditions and student achievement gains (Greenwood, Delquadri, *et al.*, 1984). It appears that qualitatively different student responses will yield different achievement outcomes. Increasing attention to the phenomenon of engagement and active academic responding in special education topical journals (Bickel and Bickel, 1986; Goodman, 1985; Zigmond, Sansone, Miller, Donahue, and Kohnke, 1986) are a sign that special educators are beginning to better understand and appreciate the difference between on-task behavior and engaged behavior. Special educators and regular educators are beginning to use a common vocabulary to address problems in learning irrespective of whether or not the child bears an exceptional label. This avenue of research in special education is by no means of flood proportions, but it is gaining a foothold and greater visibility through the professional communications media, *i.e.* journals and conferences.

Although studies of engagement in regular education and past studies of on-task behavior in special education represent compatible but not identical avenues of investigation, special education and regular education concerns are coming closer together within the crucible of classroom instruction and instructional processes. The terms "engaged" and "on-task" are used interchangeably within this text as an indication of the shared concern emerging among regular and special educators for the most effective use of instructional time.

In Summary

Collectively the contributions of Carroll, Bloom, and Wiley and Harnischfeger form the theoretical underpinnings for current research on time and learning. Carroll's "A Model of School Learning" moved the time variable from the background to center state in the instructional drama. Bloom, Wiley, and Harnischfeger fleshed out Carroll's original conceptualization with the addition of instructional and student variables and organizational and administrative variables respectively.

A complex set of student, instructional, and situational variables interact to facilitate, and in some instances to hinder, learning outcomes. The conceptual and applied models focus attention on the components under the control of teachers and administrators— "alterable variables"—which impact directly on the provision of and exposure to instructional time, appropriateness and quality of instruction, and ultimately student learning outcomes. Additionally, the translation of Carroll's theoretical model into a working applicable model for the classroom is a major contribution to the field and teachers in general.

These research and development efforts of the past quarter century were greatly aided by the parallel interest in and development of the methodology for process-product research which provided the empirical framework for the study of cause and effect relationships within the instructional setting. "By this approach we search for 'processes' (teacher behaviors and characteristics, in the form of teaching styles, methods, models, strategies) that predict and preferably cause 'products' (that is, educational outcomes in the form of student achievement and attitude)" (Gage, 1978, p. 69). The process-product paradigm, focuses attention upon instructional dynamics at the school, classroom, or student level and highlights the role of the teacher in the delivery of effective instruction.

A specialized vocabulary has emerged which reflects key time concepts at the applied level. Major terms include allocated time, engaged time and rate, academic learning time, and active academic responding. The terminology highlights the importance of the efficient and effective use of instructional time in the classroom and the participatory behavior of students during instruction. Teachers must understand that the critical time for learning is the time during which students are actively attending and engaged in appropriate academic tasks. That these terms are becoming familiar to both regular and special education is a promising sign that educators of the handicapped and non handicapped share a common concern for the importance of the time and learning relationship in the learning process for all children.

Chapter 3

Patterns of Time Use

The amount of schooling children receive in any academic year is determined by the number of days in the school year and the number of hours within the instructional day. The product of these two factors (days per year X the hours per day) sets the outside limits on the maximum amount of schooling available. It is interesting that the length of the school year and the length of the school day have varied so little over the years and across districts. Kemmerer (1979) determined that the average school year nationwide was 179 days. Wiley and Harnsichfeger (1974) reported that the difference between the longest and the shortest year across the nation for the 1969/70 school term was 10 school days. The average school day is 5 hours (Brady, Clinton, Sweeney, Peterson, and Poyner cited in Caldwell *et al.*, 1982). The reader can contrast her experience or knowledge of school systems to these figures; most will confirm that current school calendars and schedules do not deviate markedly from the figures cited.

In determining children's "exposure to schooling", Wiley and Harnsichfeger (1974) stress that average daily attendance (ADA) must be taken into consideration. They have demonstrated that the maximum amount of available school time (days per years x hours per day) multiplied by the additional factor of ADA reveals marked variability in students' exposure to schooling over the course of the school year.

Beyond the bare bones outlines of an academic year created by the designated number of days per year and number of hours per day, federal and state regulations and local school district policies further impose restrictions and priorities which determine how the finite amount of available school time shall be used. The classroom teacher has no direct control or input at this decision making level. But this author's concern, and the focus of this book, is the use of instructional time by the individual teacher in her classroom. Within the confines of the classroom, teachers exercise considerable control over the manner in which class time, particularly instructional time, is used (Brown and Sax, 1979). How do teachers use their instructional time? The current research literature provides at least a partial answer to this important question.

Time Use in Elementary Classrooms

There is a body of literature, by no means complete, which provides at least an initial perspective on how time is used in elementary schools. One research study in particular far exceeds most other studies in its scope and comprehensiveness. The Beginning Teacher Evaluation Study (BTES) (Fisher, Filby, Marliave, Cahen, Dishaw, Moore, and Berliner, 1978) has been extensively reviewed and referenced and has been used as a "baseline" or "benchmark" for comparison purposes (Rosenshine, 1981). In this text the BTES findings will also serve as a benchwork for discussion of relevant research on patterns of time usage in both regular and special education classroom.

Beginning Teacher Evaluation Study

The Beginning Teacher Evaluation Study encompassed a six year research program conducted by the California Commission for Teacher Preparation and Licensing. The purpose of the research effort was to "identify teaching activities and classroom conditions that foster learning in elementary schools" (Fisher, Berliner, Filby, Marliave, Cahen, and Dishaw, 1980, p. 7). Initial research objectives were: (1) the identification of generic teaching competencies for beginning teachers; and (2) evaluation of teacher education programs.

Over a six year period and three distinct research phases the study was altered by shifts in project goals, the addition of new objectives, and the inclusion of exploratory research on instructional processes (Powell, 1980). Although the original concern for teaching competencies was retained, the emphasis on the beginning teacher was not, and teacher training program evaluation was set aside altogether. The primary focus on math and reading instruction in grades 2 and 5 were retained throughout. An unforeseen but auspicious occurrence was the emergence of instructional time as a concept deserving far greater study (Powell, 1980). Over the life of the project, instructional time evolved as a measure of both teaching effectiveness and student learning.

The BTES study singled out two measures of student learning: (1) achievement test scores; and (2) student classroom behavior (Fisher *et al.*, 1980). Achievement tests were viewed as indirect and inferential measures of student learning. Student classroom behavior—specific behaviors indicative of academic engagement—were viewed as immediate and direct measures of student learning. Thus student classroom behavior reflective of engagement and learning was termed academic learning time (ALT), and ALT was specifically defined as "the amount of time a student spends engaged in an academic task that she can perform with high success" (Fisher *et al.*, 1980, p. 8). The BTES findings demonstrated that ALT was consistently and positively related to achievement (Fisher *et al.*, 1980). Presumably, the more ALT was observed the more children were learning. ALT was also used as an index of teaching effectiveness with high levels of observed ALT cited as evidence of teaching effectiveness and low levels of ALT taken as an indication of less effective teaching. ALT as defined in the BTES has been widely used in other investigations; the reader should expect to encounter this measure of engaged time in other studies of time and learning.

The BTES project encompassed both instructional processes and teacher effectiveness. These topics, and related BTES outcomes and findings, will be discussed in greater depth in later chapters. At this juncture, BTES findings which reveal patterns of time use in elementary classrooms are of primary concern.

BTES Findings on Allocated and Engaged Time

BTES findings on the allocation of school time across academic subjects has been summarized by Rosenshine (1981).

Allocated time by subject area. At grade level 2, the average time allocated for reading and language arts was 1.5 hours per day; the time allocated for math instruction was 35 minutes per day. The average amount of time allocated to other academic subjects and activities averaged 8 minutes per day. For fifth graders, the average time allocation per day for reading and language arts was 1 hour and 50 minutes per day and the time allocation for math instruction was 45 minutes per day; other academic activities averaged 17 minutes per day. On average 73 percent of all allocated time was devoted to reading, language arts, and math instruction (Rosenshine, 1981).

Allocated time for academic and non academic activities. BTES findings on allocated time were also aggregated under the headings of academic activities (reading, math, science, etc.), nonacademic activities (art, music, story time, sharing, etc.), and noninstructional activities (transitions, waiting time between activities, class business, etc.). At the second grade level the portion of the school day devoted to each category was 57 percent (2'15") for academic activities, 24 percent (55") for nonacademic activities, and 19 percent (44") for noninstructional activities respectively. For fifth graders the distribution of class time was 60 percent (2'50") for academic activities, 23 percent (1'05") for nonacademic activities, and 17 percent (45") for noninstructional activities.

Rosenshine (1981) draws attention to the fact that there was considerable variance across teachers with regard to academic activities but little variance across teachers in the amount of time devoted to noninstructional activities. Almost 20 percent of in class time was taken up by noninstructional demands, and the largest portion of time was devoted to transitions (35 of 45 minutes, 15 percent). Rieth and Frick (1982) found proportionally somewhat less time per day devoted to transitions in special classrooms (average 45 mpd, 12 to 13 percent of class time) but also found the amount of time taken up by transitions to be consistent across 6 different delivery systems. And Thurlow, Ysseldyke, Graden, and Algozzine (1984) reported that the amount of time devoted to nonacademic activities did not differ significantly across five special education classroom settings (approximately 14 to 21 mpd, 8 to 11 percent of class time). In the only study at the secondary school level available to us at this time, Rieth, Polsgrove, Okolo, Bahr, and Eckert (1987) reported that students were involved in nonacademic activities 7.2 percent of the time and that teachers were coded as pursuing noninstructional activities for 6 percent of the time.

The apparent consistency in the amount of time needed for noninstructional class management suggested to Rosenshine (1981) that the time used for "management" might not be an easily accessible source for added instructional time as has been suggested by some researchers. The data from special education suggest that management needs also preempt a fairly consistent amount of class time within and across special education classrooms. A certain degree of time loss for "management" needs is inevitable. It remains to be seen if instructional time can indeed be recouped from this source. The issues of time loss and enhancement of learning time are discussed at length in chapters 4 and 5.

Engaged Time. It bears repeating that engaged time differs from allocated time. Allocated time is scheduled time and represents the teacher's planned and intended use of instructional time. Engaged time is the actual time in which children are actively attending to appropriate, relevant academic tasks. Engaged time will, in all likelihood, fall short of allocated time. The difference between allocated and engaged time represents a loss of instructional time. How much time is typically lost in the elementary classroom? We turn once more to the BTES findings.

The average amount of engaged time for second graders for both reading and mathematics was on average 1.5 hours; the corresponding engagement rate was 71 percent. For fifth graders the average amount of engaged time for reading and mathematics was 1 hour and 55 minutes; the corresponding engagement rate was 70 percent. The amount of academic time lost was 36 and 30 minutes per day respectively for second and fifth grade students. The data indicate that both second and fifth graders were engaged in academic activities for approximately 40 percent of in class time (Rosenshine, 1981).

The BTES data reveal that only a moderate amount of the time (less than half) available for instruction actually involves children in meaningful academic pursuits. This may come as a surprise to some readers. Undeniably, there is competition between instructional and noninstructional activities within the classroom. The challenge is to achieve an optimal balance between competing instructional and noninstructional demands.

Other Research Findings on Allocated and Engaged Time

How do the findings on allocated and engaged time from other research studies compare to those of the BTES? The BTES findings and data on allocated and engaged time from other studies representing both regular and special education are presented in Table 3.1. The reader should bear in mind that no 2 studies were exactly alike in either design or execution.The data in Table 3.1 must be interpreted with restraint and comparisons between studies made with caution. Data was entered in Table 3.1 under the headings of Subjects, Observations, Allocated Time, Engaged Time, and Engaged Rate. Data was entered under the respective headings for each study only if the information corresponding to the specific heading could be found in the research report. The reader will readily see that the elementary grades are well represented but that only one study employed secondary age students. Observations varied; some were carried out over the course of the entire school day (nonacademic and noninstructional activities were sometimes excluded) and others were focused on a particular curricular area, most often reading. It is important that the data on allocated and engaged time be interpreted in the context of the observation sessions. The findings resulting from observations reported for the entire day will differ from the findings of observations reported for only a portion of the school day. For example, Thurlow, Ysseldyke, Graden, and Algozzine (1983) conducted observations of reading instruction for the same group of learning disabled youngsters in both the resource rooms and in regular education classrooms. The amount of time allocated for reading instruction in the resource room was 10 times greater than the amount of time allocated for reading instruction in the regular education setting (75 percent versus 6 percent). Yet in absolute terms, there was no significant difference in the amount of time (minutes per day) of reading instruction between the resource rooms and regular education classrooms (29 mpd versus 19 mpd).

Time and Learning

Table 3.1.
Allocated and Engaged Time in Regular and Special Education Classrooms

Source	Subjects	Observations	Allocated Time		Engaged Time	Engaged Rate
Rosenshine (1981)	2nd graders N = 139[a]	Full day	Reading & Lang. Arts	1'30" (38%)	1'04"	73%
			Math	35" (16%)	26"	71%
			Other Academic	8" (3%)		
	5th graders N = 122[a]	Full day	Reading & Lang. Arts	1'50" (39%)	1'20"	74%
			Math	45" (16%)	35"	74%
			Other Academic	17" (6%)		
	2nd graders	Full day	Academics	2'15" (57%)		
			Nonacademics	55" (24%)		
			Non-instructional	44" (19%)		
	5th graders	Full day	Academics	2'50" (60%)		
			Nonacademics	1'50" (23%)		
			Non-instructional	45" (17%)		
Good Beckerman (1978)	6th graders high achievers mid achievers low achievers 6 classrooms	Full day				75% 73% 67%
Hall Delquadri Greenwood Thurston (1982)	2,3,4,5th graders N = 12	Full day	Academics	75%		25%[b]
			Reading Spelling Handwriting Math	41.8% 25.8%		
			Nonacademic	25%		
Thurlow Ysseldyke Graden Algozzine (1984)	3,4th graders Learning Disabled N = 26	Full day	Academics	134"-190" 39%-49%	43"[b]	
			Non Academic	8"-11" 14%-21%		
Thurlow Graden Ysseldyke Algozzine (1984)	2nd graders N = 35	Reading Instruction		81"	21"[b]	
Thurlow Graden Greener Ysseldyke (1983)	3,4th graders Learning Disabled N = 17 Non Learning Disabled N = 17	Full day	Academic LD	180" (85%)	47"[b]	
			Reading	61" (29%)		
			Language	30" (14%)		
			Math	42" (20%)		
			Academic Non LD	185" (85%)	47"[b]	
			Reading	66" (30%)		
			Language	26" (12%)		
			Math	50" (21%)		
			Non Academic LD	32" (15%)		
			Non Academic Non LD	33" (15%)		
Thurlow Ysseldyke Graden Algozzine (1983)	3,4th graders Learning Disabled N = 8	Full day Res. Rm. Reg. Ed.	75% Res. Rm. time for reading instruction 6% Reg. Ed. time for reading instruction		29"[b] Res. Rm. 19"[b] Reg. Ed.	
Haynes Jenkins (1986)	4,5,6th graders Mild Hand N = 18	Reading Instruction Res. Rm. Reg Ed.			30.52" (59%) Res. Rm. 25.11" (15%) Reg. Ed.	92% Res. Rm. 87% Reg. Ed.
	4,5,6th graders Mild Hand N = 117	Reading Instruction Res. Rm.			19" (44%)	

Table 3.1. Continued

Source	Subjects	Observations	Allocated Time		Engaged Time	Engaged Rate
Leinhardt Zigmond Cooley (1981)	6-12 yrs. old Learning Disabled N = 105	Reading Instruction	60% of day		27" (12%)	85%
Quirk Trisman Weinberg Nalin (1976)	2,4,6th graders	Compsentory Reading Instruction				42-61%
Rieth Frick (1982)	1,2,3,4,5th graders Mild Hand N = 43	Fullday (1st yr) Read & Math Instruction (2nd yr)				73%
Rieth Polsgrove Okolo Bahr Eckert (1987)	Secondary Mildly Mentally Handicapped 52 classrooms	Res. Rm.	Academic Math Reading & Lang. Arts } Nonacademic		74.7% 30.0% 25.0% 7.2%	76% 36.7%[b]
Roehler Schmidt Buchman (1979)	2,3,4,5th graders 6 classrooms	Full day	Instructional Reading Lang. Arts } Math Non-instructional	58%-73% 80"-126" 38%-53% 23"-63" 12%-24% 97"-105" 27%-42%		
Sindelar Smith Harriman Hale Wilson (1986)	Learning Disabled N = 69 Educable Mentally Retarded N = 53	Reading Instruction				90.3% LD 91.5% EMR
Ysseldyke Thurlow Christenson Weiss (1987)	2,3,4,5th graders Mild Hand N = 29 Nonhandicapped N = 30	Full day	Academic Mild Hand Reading Math Academic Non Hand Reading Math Non Academic Mild Hand Non Academic Non Hand	143"-170" 63"-66" 28"-45" 168" 66" 39" 44"-62" 38"		

[a] source Fisher et al (1980)
[b] active academic responding
Res. Rm. — resource room
Reg. Ed. — regular education
LD — learning disabled
EMR — educable mentally retarded
NonLD — non learning disabled
Mild Hand — mildly handicapped

The research studies sited in Table 3.1 differ also in their working definitions of academic, nonacademic, instructional, and noninstructional time. For example, the BTES study did not include music and physical education as academic activities; rather, these subjects are categorized as nonacademic activities. In Hall, Delquadri, Greenwood, and Thurston (1982) academic activities included reading, math, spelling, handwriting, science, and social studies. And Roehler, Schmidt, and Buchman (1979) coded activities in language arts, reading, mathematics, science, social studies, music, art, physical education and seatwork involving a mixture of such subjects as instructional (in contrast to noninstructional) activities. On first appearance "academic" and "instructional" would appear to be roughly equivalent terms, but even the relatively limited number of studies cited indicate that operational definitions do differ and may, in part, account for differences in study findings. Finally engaged time and engaged rate were not uniformly provided across all of the research reports. Furthermore, some authors distinguished between passively engaged and actively engaged (or responding), *e.g.* the secondary students observed by Rieth *et al.* (1987) were engaged 76 percent of the time but engaged *and* actively responding only 36.7 % of the time. The distinction between active and passive engagement lies in the nature of the responding and attending behavior of the student. When actively engaged, the student is practicing the academic task. Passively engaged refers to listening and/or attending responses which do not require the student to produce a response. Engagement rates based upon active academic responding will differ (generally will be lower) from engagement rate derived from less stringent definitions of student attending behavior. The distinction between active and passive engagement is explored more fully in chapter 4.

The incomplete state of the data in Table 3.1 reflects the present state of our knowledge about patterns of time use in the classroom. Table 3.1 is not presented as an indictment of the research literature; rather, the uneven presentation of research findings in Table 3.1 reflects the fact that the field is in an early stage of inquiry in this research area. The reader should not be dismayed by the lack of definitive answers. On the basis of the collected findings to date, some observations and generalizations, if not final and firm conclusions, are possible.

The accumulated research on allocated and engaged time is decidedly biased toward the elementary grades; only one of fifteen studies provides data for a secondary school setting. Investigations of instructional time and processes in reading are more numerous (Haynes and Jenkins (1986); Leinhardt, Zigmond, and Cooley (1981);

Thurlow, Graden, Ysseldyke, and Algozzine (1984); Thurlow, Ysseldyke, Graden, and Algozzine (1983, 1984); Thurlow, Graden, Greener, and Ysseldyke (1983). Roughly speaking the time allocations for primary reading and for language arts instruction combined varied from 1 to 2 hours per day (range 61 to 126 mpd). The time allocation for instruction in mathematics was roughly 1/2 to 1 hour per day (range 35 minutes to 72 minutes per day). The greater time allocation for reading and language arts instruction attests to the primary importance of instruction in communication skills in the early grades. It is not at all clear how time is distributed between reading *per se* and language arts instruction which may include activities appropriate for language arts but only tangentially related to reading instruction. Roehler, Schmidt, and Buchman (1979) investigated teachers' differential use of instructional time, but this study is the only one of its kind.

The daily time allocations for reading, math, etc. noted in Table 3.1 represent total daily allocations for instruction for a given subject area. If small group instruction is provided, the amount of allocated time will be divided across all instructional groups with each group receiving only a portion of the daily time allocation. The range in time allocations within subject areas is substantial. This variability is one indication that teachers exercise considerable control over time use at the classroom level. The reported time differences within academic subjects represent significant differences in children's exposure to instruction. The data we have, limited as it is, suggests that some children may be receiving twice as much reading instruction as other children of comparable grade and age. Bearing in mind that allocated time represents only the intent to provide instruction and that the actual amount of instruction will be less than planned (the degree of time loss may be great or small), the data indicate that some children embark upon their instructional day with a decided disadvantage. This observation is borne out by studies which documented vast differences in instructional time among students—even students in the same class.

In the study of patterns of time use, engagement times and/or engagement rates are most important as they represent the extent of students' actual involvement in academic activities. Without student attention and active participation, learning will not occur. Attention is the *"sine qua non"* of learning (Samuels and Turnure, 1974). The student who withholds her attention, for whatever reason, effectively negates the learning process. The special education teacher is all too familiar with this phenomenon. The terms "passive learner" (Torgeson, 1982) and "learned helplessness" (Luchow, Crowl and Kahn, 1985) are recent additions to the vocabulary of special education which describe passive, unmotivated, uninvolved students who lack an essential commitment to learning. Unfortunately such students are all too common in special education programs.

Engagement times and rates are the most specific of the terms used to define and quantify instructional time. In any group activity individual children will vary in their level of attentiveness. Interestingly, the level of involvement of the teacher and student are not necessarily the same even during the same instructional episode (Quirk, Trismen, Weinberg, and Nalin, 1976). Of all the indices of time, student engaged time and engaged rate represent the actual behavior of students; engaged time and engaged rate determine the degree of student academic involvement. In addition, these time indices yield the strongest statistical relationship to achievement.

On the high end of the scale, engagement rates in the low 90 percentile range have been reported for handicapped students by Haynes and Jenkins (1986) and Sindelar et al. (1986). The lowest engagement rate of 42 percent was reported by Quirk, Trismen, Weinberg, and Nalin (1976) for elementary level students during compensatory reading instruction. The engagement rates for active academic responding reported in two studies are markedly lower than the engagement rates for general engaged behavior (Hall, Delquadri, Greenwood, and Thurston, 1982; Rieth, Polsgrove, et al. 1987). The contrast between engagement and active academic responding is most evident in the Rieth, Polsgrove, et al. (1987) study in which the percentile figures for general academic engagement and active academic responding were 76 percent and 36.7 percent respectively for the same group of students.

How shall we judge the adequacy of reported engagement times and engagement rates? Is an engagement rate during reading instruction of 75 percent adequate or inadequate? Is a daily ratio of engagement in academics versus nonacademics of 75 percent to 25 percent (3 to 1) adequate? Should the teacher strive for a higher rate of student attentiveness? Will reading achievement increase if a group of children maintains an 80 percent level of engagement during reading instruction and related tasks? There are no definitive answers to these questions at this time. We do not know the optimal engagement rates for children to achieve desirable levels of achievement in basic skill subjects. The descriptive data on childrens' current levels of on-task behavior are extremely helpful but by no means conclusive. Studies which distinguish between the high and low achiever and report their respective engagement rates provide some useful guidelines. For example. Good and Beckerman (1978) reported engagement rates of 74 percent, 73 percent, and 67 percent for high, middle, and low achievers respectively. Dervensky, Hart, and Farrell (1983) report an engagement rate during math and reading instruction of 85 percent for high achieving students and an engagement rate of 75 percent for low achieving students. The fact that the reported engagement rate for the high achievers in one study (Good and Beckerman, 1978) approximates the engagement rate for the low achievers in the second study (Dervensky *et al.*, 1983) only complicates the issue. In the BTES findings, the engagement rate for second graders ranged from a low of 72 percent to a high of 82 percent; for fifth graders the low was 69 percent and the high was 82 percent. Based upon the studies of Good and Beckerman (1978) and Dervensky *et al.* (1983) in which the higher engagement rates were associated with higher achieving students, one could speculate that a similar pattern might apply for the BTES findings on engagement rate. The range in engagement rate across all of these studies extends only 16 percentage points. The magnitude of the difference does not appear great but, once again, the cumulative impact of relatively small daily differences in engaged time needs to be appreciated. As to guidelines for desirable engagement levels, it appears that engagement rates from the mid 70 to mid 80 percentile range are associated with adequate academic performance while lower engagement rates are often associated with the slower or underachieving student.

Instructional Time and the Low Achiever

Many authors emphasize the need to provide more instructional time for the slow learner or underachieving student (Karweit and Slavin, 1981; Stallings, 1980; Stallings and Kaskowitz, 1974; Evertson, 1982; Caldwell, Huitt and Graeber, 1982). In addition it appears that the low achiever profits most from additional learning time. For example, Stallings (1975) found that low achieving third graders in Follow-Through programs prospered more from an increase in time spent in reading and math than did the higher achieving students. Kiesling (1978) found that allocation of additional classroom time was consistently of greatest benefit to elementary students below grade in reading. The evidence indicating that increased instructional time is particularly beneficial for low achievers is consistent with Carroll's model of school learning which posits that students of lesser ability or lower achievement levels will need more instructional time to attain acceptable levels of performance. Moving from theory to practice, proponents of mastery learning have repeatedly demonstrated that most students can achieve to high standards if given sufficient time and adequate instruction (Bloom, 1976). Furthermore, there is research evidence that under mastery learning conditions learning efficiency improves, *i.e.*, the initially slower students require less time to achieve mastery on subsequent units of instruction (Anderson, 1976; Arlin, 1979; Block, 1970), and the difference in rate of learning between the slow and fast learner is significantly reduced.

Slow learners, underachievers, and low functioning students, by whatever label, constitute the population pool from which the mildly handicapped are drawn. Recognition that such students need extra help is not new. The growing and nagging awareness that the source of their achievement problems may lie, in part, in insufficient time provided for instruction and/or students' inadequate engagement rates during instruction is a new perspective on an old problem (Allington, 1983; Berliner, 1981). The question of whether or not special education programs are providing sufficient instructional time for mildly handicapped students is emerging as a serious issue in special education.

Haynes and Jenkins' (1986) investigation of time use in resource rooms led them to question whether special education programs "supplement" or "supplant" regular education. Meyen and Lehr (1980) and Gallagher (1984) have questioned the instructional intensity of special education programs and asked if programs for the handicapped provided enough time for disabled students to overcome their academic handicaps. Time becomes an issue when: (1) there is an insufficient amount of instructional time; and (2) when instructional time is utilized poorly or inefficiently. The research findings on patterns of time use reveal that handicapped and non-handicapped students seem to be the recipients of equal amounts of instructional time. The "specialness" of special education certainly does not lie in added time for instruction. This issue will be discussed in the context of comparative studies of time use involving handicapped and nonhandicapped students.

The current research literature on patterns of time usage provide only a bare bones picture of how teachers use their time resources; many of the fine and critical details are still missing. As research efforts continue, and there is no doubt that they will, our knowledge and understanding will increase. But even at this early stage, it is clear that a unitary answer to the question, what is the desirable level of student engagement? is highly unlikely, nor is it desirable. There will be differences related to subject matter content and situational factors. Student characteristics are of paramount importance and must certainly be taken into consideration. It is very likely that the optimal level of engagement for a given student or group of students will vary in response to a combination of instructional variables and student characteristics.

Teacher-led versus Independent Seatwork

Table 3.1 does not address differences in engagement rates during teacher-led versus independent seatwork activities. Differences in engagement under different instructional conditions is an important issue as yet only rarely discussed in the research literature. The BTES findings do shed some light on this question; the data revealed a difference of approximately 15 percent in student engagement rates during teacher-led and independent seatwork (85 percent versus 70 percent respectively). Other researchers have also noted a marked difference in engagement during teacher-led versus independent work with engagement dropping in the absence of teacher or adult supervision (Good and Beckerman, 1978; Soar, 1973; Rieth and Frick, 1982; Stallings and Kaskowitz, 1974).

The importance of the difference in engagement rates under alternate grouping conditions becomes apparent when we realize that children typically spend the greater portion of their instructional school day in independent seatwork rather than in teacher-led group activities. Rosenshine (1981), drawing from the BTES findings once again, reported that children spend 70 percent of their day in independent activities and only 30 percent of their day in teacher-led group activities. At the elementary level, Haynes and Jenkins (1986) report that mildly handicapped students spent 52 percent (25.12 mpd) of their daily resource room time in individualized seatwork activities. Rieth and Frick (1982) reported that target students in 6 different instructional settings spent the majority of their academic time (60 percent) under non-direct instruction, *i.e.*, seatwork. And at the secondary level Rieth, Polsgrove, Okolo, Bahr, and Eckert (1987) found that instruction in resource rooms was about evenly divided between teacher-led activities (43.9 percent) and independent (seatwork) paper and pencil activities (40.7 percent). Thus, children in both regular and special education spend a major portion of the school day in the instructional setting in which their engagement rate is at its lowest level. For the classroom teacher the situation is problematic. The management of large groups of children of varying ability and achievement levels necessitates some sort of grouping and accompanying independent seatwork activities. Good management skills and some innovative approaches to lesson planning and delivery can go a long way toward reducing time lost to student disengagement during independent seatwork activities.

Research specifically concerned with the content and nature of seatwork activities is very sparse. In a study of first grade reading instruction Anderson, Brubaker, Alleman-Brooks, and Duffy (1985) found that seatwork accounted for fully 60 percent of reading instructional time and that teachers relied heavily upon the use of commercial materials, *e.g.* workbooks, readers, and ditto sheets. Anderson *et al.* also found that seatwork activities were poorly integrated with the content of the reading lesson *per se* and that teachers' interactions with students engaged in seatwork activities was, for the most part, devoted to behavior management, and not to assessing or monitoring student progress or understanding of the seatwork assignments. This heavy reliance upon commercial materials and lack of meaningful interaction between teachers and students involved in independent seatwork was also observed by Durkin (1978) in an investigation of Reading instruction among upper elementary school students. Such findings strongly suggest that seatwork is too often employed as "busywork" to keep some students engaged while the teacher provides instruction to other classmates.

Do special education classrooms experience a similar drop in student attentiveness during independent seatwork? Undoubtedly the emphasis on individualization and the heterogeneity typical of most special education classrooms create an environment in which children frequently work alone. Is unsupervised independent seatwork more prevalent in special education or do the reduced numbers of students allow the teacher (and aides) to provide more attention to all children regardless of the grouping structure? Sindelar, Smith, Harriman, Hale, and Wilson (1986) reported the percentage of on-task behavior for learning disabled and educable mentally retarded under teacher directed instruction (TDI) and independent work condition (IND). The mean time on task under TDI was 96.2 percent and under IND was 89.3 percent for EMR students. For the learning disabled students, engagement level under TDI was 94.6 percent and 85.1 percent under IND. In another study of mildly handicapped, Rieth and Frick (1982) found an overall engagement rate of 73 percent and an engagement rate of only 34 percent under nondirect instructional conditions. The impact of the lower engagement rate under nondirect instructional conditions is augmented by the fact that the authors found that students spent 60 percent of their instructional time under nondirect instructional activities. The results of these 2 studies are quite divergent regarding the level of observed engaged behavior."Nondirect instructional activities" (Rieth and Frick, 1982) and "independent work conditions" (Sindelar *et al.*, 1986) connote comparable instructional conditions—students working independently without direct or significant adult supervision. The exceedingly high level of on-task behavior under both TDI and IND conditions reported by Sindelar and his colleagues is out of step with the levels of on-task behavior reported by other researchers for both handicapped and nonhandicapped students. The degree of variance in the reported engagement figures points out the need for additional investigations into patterns of student engagement to resolve or explain the discrepancies among different research findings and to provide a more complete picture of student engagement under different instructional conditions.

The "Average" Student

The data on allocated and engaged time presented in Table 3.1 represents aggregated figures for "average" students. Whenever large amounts of data are summarized into "average" numbers there is a loss of information. For instance, the figures in Table 3.1 mask the degree of variability in patterns of time use that exist from school to school, teacher to teacher, and child to child. Almost without exception every author cited in Table 3.1 addressed the issue of variability, yet the data as presented do not shed any light on this issue.

For the individual student, variance in instructional time can have a marked daily and cumulative effect. For example, the BTES findings revealed an average engagement time of 104 minutes per day for second grade students. But the amount of engaged time varied from a low of 43 minutes per day to a high of 1 hour and 25 minutes per day among the second graders observed (Rosenshine, 1981). Engaged time for the highest student was almost 3 times greater than that of the student with the lowest engaged time. Thurlow, Graden, *et al.* (1984) found considerable interstudent variability in a study of reading instruction for second graders. Silent reading time ranged from 36 seconds to 26 minutes per day; oral reading time ranged from 0 minutes to 8 minutes per day. The authors state that "if the daily differences continued at the same rate, the student who read 26 minutes in one day would read for 68 more hours over the course of the school year than the student who read for 36 seconds" (Thurlow, Graden, *et al.*, 1984, p. 271). There are numerous other examples, but the point is clear. The "average" figures mask the cumulative impact of daily differences in allocated and engaged time. Enormous disparity can, and indeed does, exist from school to school, class to class, and student to student in the same grade level and even within the same class. In light of the relationship between academic engagement and learning, one must be particularly concerned about those children whose engagement rates consistently fall markedly below the "average."

Increasing Instructional Time

Several authors have predicted the magnitude of achievement gains which would result from daily increases in instructional time and/or engagement. We are told that "one minute per day of additional silent reading time increases posttest performance by one point" (Leinhardt, Zigmond, and Cooley, 1981, p. 355). Another prediction states that "an increase of five minutes per day would be equivalent to about one month (on a grade equivalent scale) of additional reading achievement" (Haynes and Jenkins, 1986, p. 335). And finally, Wiley (1973) predicts that a 24 percent increase in quantity of schooling (brought about by increases in attendance, length of the school year and school day) would produce achievement gains in verbal ability (34 percent), mathematics (34 percent), and reading comprehension (66 percent). The predictions are striking, tantalizing, and encouraging. But it remains to be seen whether instructional time can be increased and whether the predicted achievement gains do follow.

Comparing Levels of Engagement for Handicapped and Nonhandicapped Students

Six descriptive studies involving comparison of special education populations and nonhandicapped populations are available to us at this time. The studies are entered in Table 3.2 under the headings of Group Comparison, Observation, and Findings. Once again, differences in definitions, methodology, and instrumentation as well as the small number of studies limit the utility and generalizability of the study findings. Bearing these limitations in mind, some insights can nevertheless be gleaned from these research reports. In discussing the studies' results, the BTES findings for handicapped students will again be used as a point of reference.

Three studies, those of Thurlow, Graden, Greener, and Ysseldyke (1983), Haynes and Jenkins (1986), and Ysseldyke, Thurlow, Christenson, and Weiss (1988), involved full day observations. Thurlow, Graden, *et al.* (1983) focused upon academic instruction, specifically reading and mathematics instruction, throughout the school day. Haynes and Jenkins (1986) limited coding to reading instruction whenever it occurred during the school day. Ysseldyke *et al.* (1987) gathered data on both academic versus nonacademic activities as well as specific subject disciplines throughout the school day.

The remaining two studies (Dervensky, Hart, and Ferrell, 1983; Knowles, Aufderheide, and McKenzie, 1982) restricted observations to specific instructional sessions. The reader is reminded that comparison of findings across studies without regard for the context in which those findings were derived, *e.g.*, full day observations compared to part day observations, can lead to erroneous conclusions.

Table 3.2. Comparison of Time Usage Across Handicapped and Nonhandicapped Learners

Source	Group Comparison	Observation	Findings
Chow (1981)	Mainstreamed LD vs Nonhandicapped (N= 222; 1st yr, N= 228, 2nd yr)	Math Instruction	Significant differences in allowed time, engaged time, ALT, favoring nonhandicapped in yr 1 Significant difference on ALT, favoring nonhandicapped in yr 2
Dervensky, Hart, Farrell, (1983)	High Achievers vs Low Achievers (N = 136)	Reading and Math Lessons	Significantly more engaged time for high achievers
Haynes, Jenkins, (1986)	Mildly Handicapped vs Nonhandicapped (N = 36)	Full day	Significant group differences on 2 of 29 reading instructional variables
Knowles, Aufderheid, McKenzie, (1982)	Emotionally Disturbed Learning Disabled Educable Mentally Retarded vs Nonhandicapped (N = 120)	Physical Education Classes	N.S.D.*
Thurlow, Graden, Greener, Ysseldyke, (1983)	Learning Disabled vs Non Learning Disabled (N = 34)	Full day	N.S.D.*
Ysseldyke, Thurlow, Christenson, Weiss, (1988)	Emotionally Behaviorally Disturbed vs Learning Disabled vs Educable Mentally Retarded vs Nonhandicapped (N = 122)	Full day	Significantly less academic instructional time for EMRs Significantly more free time for EMRs Significantly more math instruction for LD than EMR Significantly more science instruction for nonhandicapped

*N.S.D. = No Significant Difference

In discussing the findings of the Thurlow, Graden, *et al.* (1983) there is no need to distinguish between the learning disabled and non-learning disabled subjects as no significant between group differences were found for either allocated or engaged time. The results reveal a consistent pattern of time usage for both groups. The authors found that approximately 45 percent of the school day was allocated for academic instruction (63 minutes per day for reading and 43 minutes per day for mathematics). The 45 percent figure for allocated time contrasts with the 54 percent (at the second grade level) and 55 percent (at the fifth grade level) allocated time for academic activities in the regular education classrooms observed in the BTES investigation (Rosenshine, 1981). Thurlow *et al.* underscore the fact that on average children were involved in active academic responding (as opposed to passive responding) for only 47 minutes per day. The consistency of results for both handicapped and nonhandicapped raises concern about the low level of active participation found for all children.

In a multifaceted study of reading instruction, Haynes and Jenkins (1986) conducted specific comparisons between handicapped and nonhandicapped upper elementary aged students. One comparison involved a subsample of 18 mildly handicapped students in resource rooms and matched nonhandicapped peers in regular education classrooms. Some group differences were found; the most important revealed that considerably more time (proportion of total time) is devoted to reading in the resource room than in the regular classroom. But in absolute numbers, special education students receive as much or more reading instruction in the regular classroom than they did in the resource rooms. In addition the special education students received more than twice as much teacher directed reading instruction in the regular classrooms than in the resource room settings. Many authorities believe, and much research evidence indicates, that direct and active teaching is important for student achievement (Rieth, Polsgrove, and Semmel, 1981; Zigmond, Sansone, Miller, Donahue, and Kohnke, 1986; Stalling, 1975; Stallings, Needels, and Stayrook, 1979). Haynes and Jenkins' results bring into question: (1) the distribution of instructional responsibility between regular and special education teachers (reading instruction which may be more equally divided than generally thought); and (2) the amount and intensity of instruction provided in special education resource rooms.

To this author, there mere fact of an approximately equal distribution of reading instructional time received in regular and special education does not indicate that teachers knowingly or equally share responsibility for the instruction of handicapped children. Do these respective teachers know how much reading instruction is being provided in each of their classrooms? Are the teachers equally involved in the development and delivery of the students' instructional program? Does each teacher know how much and what type of instruction is being provided in the other classrooms by her teaching colleagues?

Are the instructional programs coordinated toward the same set of instructional objectives and learner outcomes? The reporting of data on instructional time—as important as that is—does not provide a complete and detailed account of the context of instruction and tells us little or nothing about the teachers' perceptions of their roles and responsibilities. Hopefully, exposure to data on how instructional time is used and how children spend their instructional sessions will sensitize teachers to important questions of instructional responsibility and efficient use of instructional time.

The second group comparison in the Haynes and Jenkins study involved the comparison of handicapped and nonhandicapped students' performance on 29 reading process measures. The results of a multiple regression analysis indicated that there were significant between-group differences on only 2 of 29 classroom process variables. Handicapped students spent more time than their nonhandicapped peers reading letters or single words and they spent more time working individually with a teacher. Haynes and Jenkins stress the "remarkable consistency" across performance variables for the handicapped and nonhandicapped as well as the amount of time spent in reading instruction. They conclude that the handicapped are getting essentially the same type and no less, but also no more, reading instruction than their nonhandicapped classmates.

The third study in which full day observations of academic instruction were carried out was reported by Ysseldyke et al. (1987). In this study the authors distinguished among the 3 categories of mildly handicapped—ED (emotionally disturbed), LD (learning disabled), and EMR (educable mentally retarded)—as well as between the handicapped and nonhandicapped. Time allocation data were gathered for academic versus nonacademic instruction for specific subject areas. The authors found that approximately 143 to 170 minutes per day were allocated to academic activities and that the average amount of time allocated to nonacademic activities ranged form 44 to 62 minutes per day. These figures are substantially lower than the allocated time for academic activities documented in the BTES project data for the second and fifth graders (BTES data indicate that 2'15" at the second grade level and 2'50" at the fifth grade level were allocated for academic instruction). The differences in amount of time allocated for nonacademic activities between the Ysseldyke et al. (1987) and the BTES findings were negligible. If we contrast the Ysseldyke et al. (1987) findings for reading instruction with the findings on reading instructional time reported by Haynes and Jenkins (1986), we find little difference. Haynes and Jenkins reported approximately 70 minutes per day for reading instruction for learning disabled students; Ysseldyke *et al.* (1987) reported approximately 64 minutes per day for the learning disabled and a range of 63 to 66 minutes per day across all the mildly handicapped and nonhandicapped students observed. It seems time allocations for handicapped populations establish the lower end of the range on allocated time for handicapped and non-handicapped overall. As to the contrast between the handicapped and the nonhandicapped, Ysseldyke *et al.* (1987) concluded that there were few differences between the groups in the amount of time allocated to various activities. The proportion of the school day devoted to reading and mathematics instruction was greater in the special classrooms, but not significantly so. They concluded that the handicapped were not allocated more time for reading and mathematics instruction than their nonhandicapped peers. In this study, as in the report of Haynes and Jenkins, the data reveal "remarkable consistency" between the handicapped and nonhandicapped.

The inter-categorical comparisons among the mildly handi-capped students in the Ysseldyke *et al.* (1987) study yielded some unexpected results. The data revealed that EMR students had more free time than nonhandicapped students and less time for academic instruction than the nonhandicapped or other categories of exception-ality. In a related study also involving inter-categorical comparisons, Sindelar *et al.* (1986) found that EMR and LD students received compa-rable amounts of instruction and exhibited equally high levels of engagement (proportion of allocated time used for instruction was 83.8 percent for LD and 79.5 percent for EMR). However, differences were found in the distribution of instructional time across teacher directed (TDI) and independent (IND) instructional activities. LD stu-dents received 40 percent of their instruction under TDI and 60 per-cent under IND conditions while EMR students received the reverse, 60 percent under TDI and 40 percent under IND conditions. The data are important for two reasons: (1) the evidence of categorically based difference; and (2) teacher-directed reading instruction was found to be the single best predictor of reading achievement gains. The contra-dictions and inconsistencies within these 2 studies raise questions about the nature and extent of instructional differences that may exist among different types of handicapped populations. The fact that Sindelar *et al.* (1986) found that the EMR and LD students responded differently to certain types of instructional activities heightens the need to explore categorical differences in patterns of time use and the long term implications of differences which are found to exist.

In the study of Dervensky, Hart, and Farrell (1983), engagement rates for low and high achievers were contrasted. An engagement rate of 85 percent for high achievers and 75 percent for low achievers was reported during reading and math lessons. The difference was statistically significant. These engagement rates, which are higher than those reported by any other researchers, represent student engagement rates during reading and math lessons. Engagement rates very likely would have been lower if observations have been conducted over the full day and the results interpreted in terms of a full day of instruction. However, it should be noted that these engagement rates are equal to or higher than the engagement rates reported by other researchers for students in subject specific areas.

In discussing their findings, Dervensky *et al.* discount the impact of the observed difference in engagement rates of 6 minutes per day. Despite statistical significance, the authors discount the time-on-task difference as a plausible explanation of the achievement differences between high and low achievers (other authors attach far greater importance to daily time differences). They believe that time alone is an insufficient explanation for the achievement differential and suggest that the explanation of the performance difference lies not in the time factor alone, but in task appropriateness as well. Accordingly, they favor the ALT model which incorporates the dimension of task appropriateness to the engagement model which reflects only the time dimension. They stress that the better use of instructional time must involve both more time and appropriate tasks.

The strongest evidence of group differences were found and reported by Chow (1981) in a study of ALT among mainstreamed fifth and sixth grade LD students and their regular education peers. Observations were confined to math instruction in the regular education setting. First year results yielded significant between group differences in the amount of allocated time, engaged time, and ALT. Handicapped students received less allocated time and were observed to be less engaged in math instruction. More importantly, LD students were engaged in high success tasks for only 15.7 percent of the time as compared to 36.7 percent engagement in high success tasks for their non-handicapped classmates. The second year's results did not reveal significant differences in either allocated or engaged time. Regarding task difficulty, all students spent most of their engaged time on tasks of medium difficulty, and the amount of time spent on high success tasks once again favored the nonhandicapped students. LD students spent significantly less time on high success tasks and significantly more time on low success tasks than their regular education peers. This finding is

disconcerting because ALT, by definition, hinges upon the dual components of engagement and task difficulty, the optimal instructional situation involving high levels of engagement in tasks in which the students
experience high rates of success. Such findings cast doubt on the task
appropriateness of work assigned to the learning disabled students.
Chow also found that ALT difference between mainstreamed and regular education students were not strongly related to student background
variables, e.g. sex, age, achievement level. Differences in student
engaged time were strongly related to teachers' instructional behaviors,
e.g. teacher explanation, academic feedback and questioning, structuring and directing instruction, teacher as a source of instruction, and
group based instruction. Significant negative correlations resulted for
negative feedback and student as the source of instruction. These findings underscore the importance of teachers' classroom and instructional
behaviors as a precursor to high and desirable levels of student engagement. The impact of teachers' classroom behaviors on student engagement will be discussed more fully in chapters to follow.

The study of Knowles, Aufderheide, and McKenzie (1982) was the
only research effort not concerned with an academic subject area. The
authors conducted observations of mildly handicapped and nonhandicapped in physical education classes to determine the level of ALT for
both groups. The application of the ALT concept to physical education
is somewhat problematic in that physical education is not generally
viewed as an academic subject and is usually excluded when observations of academic instruction are conducted (Rosenshine, 1981).
However, some other researchers do justify the use of the ALT construct
for the area of physical education (Sidentop, Burdell, and Metzler, cited
in Knowles et al. 1982). The authors report no significant difference in
the level of ALT for the two groups when the groups are constituted on
the presence or absence of a handicapping condition, i.e., mildly handicapped versus nonhandicapped. However, comparison of teachers who
do and do not individualize did yield a significant difference in student
level of ALT in favor of teachers who individualized to a greater extent.

In summary, the research studies to date involving the quantification and comparison of instructional time for special and regular education students offer little evidence of important between group differences (handicapped versus nonhandicapped or among the various
exceptionalities). Ironically, in the only study to yield clear group differences, the authors dispute their own findings. The provocative results
for EMR students reported by Ysseldyke et al. (1987) and Sindelar et al.
(1986) are important in light of numerous efficacy studies of special edu-

cation programs which reveal that EMR students who remain in regular education do as well as or better than EMR students who are placed in special classes (Carlberg and Kevale 1980; Cegelka and Tyler, 1970; Sindelar and Deno, 1978). Clearly there is a pressing need to study and evaluate current programming for this particular population of mildly handicapped students. Wherever group differences are found, the instructional implications of such differences must be fully explored. An investigatory perspective which includes instructional time use, teachers' instructional behaviors, student and task variables, and student performance outcomes may yield directions for future programs to better meet the needs of all mildly handicapped students.

Equal Opportunity Model

Though the number of studies which contrast instructional time between the handicapped and nonhandicapped is very limited at this time, as a group they convey an implicit (if not explicit) concern for the equitable treatment of handicapped students in both mainstreamed and segregated instructional environments. Equitable treatment connotes equal treatment, that is, equal amounts of time for instructional activities and/or equal emphasis across subject areas for both the handicapped and nonhandicapped. In this context, the finding of no significant difference between handicapped and nonhandicapped students in the amount of allocated time or the level of academic engagement would appear to be a "good" or "positive" outcome. However, let us not accept "educational equality" of this kind too hastily. Allington (1983) and Haynes and Jenkins (1986) point to the very equality of engaged time across handicapped and nonhandicapped students as a possible explanation for the inability of many handicapped students to overcome their academic performance deficits. Equal amounts of instructional time for the handicapped—that is, equal in amount of time provided to the nonhandicapped—may fall far short of the level and intensity of instruction needed by the slow learning or underachieving child. Many authors stress the point that the slow and underachieving student requires more, not equal, and certainly not less instructional time if she is to have any hope of "catching-up." Evidence that the low functioning child benefits more from added instruction than her more able peers bolsters this point of view. Ysseldyke, Thurlow, Christenson, and Weiss (1987) pinpoint the essential flaw in the equal opportunity model; that is, given the current level of academic programming, the relative standing of the mildly handicapped will not change. The "equal educational opportunity model" should not be the goal for the mildly handicapped.

Therefore, as we study patterns of time use among the handicapped and nonhandicapped, the critical question is not the presence or
absence of significant differences in the absolute amount of time provided for instruction for the 2 student groups. Rather the question must be
whether or not instruction sufficient in amount and intensity is being
provided to handicapped students in order to bring about significant
improvement in the academic deficiencies which separate them from
their nonhandicapped peers. This is the standard by which programs
for the mildly handicapped must be judged; anything less will not do.

Beyond Time On Task

A basic assumption underlying the provision of special education services and programs to handicapped learners is that special
education is different from the regimen of regular education
(Ysseldyke *et al.*, 1987). Early investigations focused upon time allocations and levels of student engagement, important issues to be sure.
But equally important is the nature of the instruction to which student
time and attention are devoted. Dervensky *et al.* (1983) touched upon
this fundamental concern in their call for attention to task appropriateness as well as more time on task. Although there are many questions
about patterns of time use still to be answered, research which
inquires beyond the mere measurement of time (allocated or engaged)
to the nature of the task itself is well underway. There are examples in
the studies already cited above.

For example, in the 4 studies authored by Thurlow and her colleagues (Thurlow, Graden, Ysseldyke, and Algozzine, 1984; Thurlow,
Ysseldyke, Graden, and Algozzine, 1984, 1983; Ysseldyke, Thurlow,
Christenson, and Weiss, 1988) the *Code for Instructional Structure and
Student Academic Response* (CISSAR) was used as the observation instrument (Greenwood, Delquadri, and Hall, 1978). The instrument codes
student and teacher behavior in 6 observation categories each of which
contains multiple coding options. The 6 categories address (a) activity,
e.g., time allocated to academics; (b) task, *e.g.*, student use of reading,
worksheets, etc.; (c) teaching structure, *e.g.*, whole group, small group or
individual; (d) teacher location, *e.g.*, behind desk, behind student, etc.;
(e) teacher activity, *e.g.*, approval, disapproval, etc.; and (f) student
response, *e.g.*, writing, reading silently, disruption, etc. Clearly, CISSAR
directs observations beyond the time dimension to what the teacher and
students are actually doing during the instructional process. In other
studies only the reading instructional process is targeted for in depth
investigation. The studies of Leinhardt, Zigmond, and Cooley (1981)
and Haynes and Jenkins (1986) share a common focus on reading

instruction and the use of the same observation instrument, the *Student Level Observation of Reading Behavior* (SORB) developed at the University of Pittsburgh (Leinhardt and Seewald, 1980). Among other dimensions of reading instruction, the SORB enables the researcher to distinguish between direct and indirect reading activities. Leinhardt, Zigmond, and Cooley (1981) found that direct reading activity—*i.e.*, oral and silent reading of words, sentences and paragraphs, but not indirect reading activity (*i.e.*, reading related but not involving the decoding of print)—is significantly related to posttest reading achievement.

Haynes and Jenkins (1986) in a partial replication of Leinhardt *et al.* failed to replicate the results regarding the relationship between direct reading activity and reading achievement. Haynes and Jenkins attributed the variance between their findings and those of Leinhardt *et al.* to methodological differences and limitations in their research design. More recently, Wilkinson, Wardrop, and Anderson (1988) reanalyzed the data of Leinhardt *et al.* and produced conflicting results. Silent reading time (a direct reading activity according to the SORB) was not shown to have a significant effect on posttest reading performance; rather, oral reading time emerged as the more important variable for posttest reading performance. Their analyses culled out ability level of students, difficulty of reading materials, and nature of teacher feedback as important variables for effective reading instruction. Sindelar *et al.* (1986) found neither oral or silent reading to be significantly related to reading performance in a study of LD and EMR elementary school children. And Stallings (1980) found that oral reading was positively related to reading gains among secondary remedial students. The oral reading versus silent reading question is far from resolved; resolution of the contradictory results must await the results of further research efforts. The salient point for our discussion is the emerging interest in systematic in depth investigation of instructional time variables *and* instructional process variables.

There are other examples of research which goes beyond time on-task to the nature of the task itself and the relationship of different tasks to achievement. Stallings, Needles, and Staybrook (1979) in a study of reading instruction in secondary schools found that reading activity variables differed in their relationship to reading achievement. Reading activities which they labeled "Interactive On-Task Instruction" were positively associated with student reading gains. Reading activities which they labeled "Noninteractive On-Task Instruction" were negatively related to reading gains. Examples of the former include discussion/review, reading aloud, drill, and practice. Examples of the latter include class management, silent reading, and written assignments.

The important implication for the classroom teacher is that all instructional activities do not have equal instructional value. It follows then that the use of instructional time should reflect (but not exclusively) instructional activities with the strongest relationship to achievement.

Carroll (1963) cautioned us long ago that time was necessary but not sufficient for learning. Since then educators have been repeatedly criticized for their preoccupation with the time dimension and their neglect of the finer points of instructional process and task variables (Doyle, 1979; Frymier, 1981; Stallings, 1980). The literature offers ample evidence that researchers are rapidly moving beyond a one dimensional view of the time and learning relationship. The research clearly points to the conclusion that time and task are inseparable dimensions of the instructional process. The efficient use of time in the classroom occurs only when sufficient instructional time is focused on appropriate instructional tasks.

In Summary

Research findings reveal that the pattern of time use in regular education and special classrooms are more alike than different. Roughly speaking, a significant portion of the scheduled school day is devoted to nonacademic and noninstructional activities. The remainder of the day is devoted to instruction. Reading and language arts instruction is preeminent in the primary grades and accounts for a major portion of instructional time. The amount of time taken by noninstructional management activities, primarily transitions between activities (about 45 minutes per day), is surprisingly similar across teachers, grades and instructional settings.

The dimension of time use of greatest importance is student engaged time, that portion of instructional time when students are attending to and actively responding to appropriate academic tasks. The BTES results show that the average engaged rate for second graders was 71 percent and that the average engaged rate for fifth graders was 78 percent. The data also show a distinct decline in student engagement during independent or seatwork activities—approximately 15 percent. Data on student engagement for handicapped learners reveals considerable variability with reported engagement levels ranging from the low 40 to mid 90 percentile range. Most figures cluster in the 70-80 percent range. The available data is very limited, however, and should be regarded as tentative at this time.

In special education, some researchers distinguish between engagement and active academic responding. Engagement levels associated with active responding are far lower than those reported for general engagement. The distinction emphasizes the importance of students' participatory behavior during the learning process. Studies which have compared patterns of time use across handicapped and nonhandicapped have found few differences in either allocated time, engaged time or the content of the instruction provided. Apparently an equal education model for handicapped students prevails at the current time. This finding is disconcerting in light of evidence that the slow or problem learners very likely require more instructional time than their nonhandicapped peers if academic deficiencies are ever to be overcome.

The literature overflows with recommendations for the teachers and administrators on how to enhance learning time and engagement. This information is valuable and useful, but the reader must bear in mind that time alone is insufficient for maximal learning to occur. The goal is not merely to increase learning time; the goal must be increased instructional time on appropriate academic tasks.

Chapter 4

Conserving Instructional Time

Every school day is a composite of instructional and noninstructional activities. It is unrealistic to expect that every moment of the school day will be devoted to academic pursuits. The management, supervision, and care of large numbers of children necessitate a host of activities which can be characterized as "procedural" or "housekeeping" in nature and generally have no direct relevance to educational objectives or goals. But such housekeeping and procedural tasks, *e.g.*, taking attendance, collecting lunch money, fire drills, moving children within the building, etc., are essential to the smooth and safe operation of the overall school program.

How much time is devoted to noninstructional activities? According to Rosenshine (1981) 17 percent and 19 percent (approximately 45 minutes per day) for second and fifth graders respectively is devoted to noninstructional activities. Rossmiller (1983) concluded that 40 percent of the school day is taken up with noninstructional activity. Although the estimates vary, there is general agreement that the amount of time devoted to noninstructional activities is significant. The consistency of time used for noninstructional activity across both the more effective and less effective teachers (Rosenshine, 1981) and across various special education settings (Rieth and Frick, 1982) indicates that some degree of time loss to noninstructional activity is inevitable.

The far larger portion of the school day is devoted to instructional activities. Some professionals assign instructional status to both academic (*e.g.*, Reading, Math, Science, etc.), and nonacademic (*e.g.*, Art, Music, and Physical Education) activities. The current literature contains time figures for strictly academic activities and also for the composite of all instructional activities. Referring back to the BTES study once again, we are told that second grade level academic activity accounts for 57 percent of the school day (2 hours and 15 minutes) and that at the fifth grade level academic activities account for 60 percent of the school day (2 hours and 50 minutes). Educators readily accept the inevitability of some time loss due to noninstructional activities. There is far less awareness of the time loss within instructional activities.

The first step in the conservation of school time for learning involves understanding how time is allocated across the instructional and noninstructional demands of the school day and the pattern of time usage in regular and special education classrooms; these important topics were discussed at length in chapter 3. The next step entails an awareness of how and where instructional time is lost during the school day and identification of ways to conserve time for learning. These topics are the focus of chapter 4.

Administrator's Role and Responsibility

Although administrators and teachers are united by shared educational goals, they have separate roles and responsibilities. With regard to time for schooling and learning, the administrator's role is to provide teachers with the resources needed for instruction, including adequate time, and to protect classroom time from encroachment and erosion.

Administrators have a vital role to play in helping teachers to make the best use of learning time. From the onset, it is important for administrators to distinguish between school time and learning time (Reck, 1984). The research literature clearly distinguishes time in school (school time) from student engaged time (learning time). Both time dimensions relate to overall school progress and achievement, but the most important factor for student achievement is the degree of actual student involvement in academic activities. One plausible administrative response to the call for more learning time would be an increase in school time achieved by lengthening the school day and/or year. But such a response does not guarantee improved student performance (Reck, 1984)—and that must be the goal. Further, it represents little more than a reflexive reaction and a "naive misuse" (Shulman, 1986, p. 11) of research information.

Curricular Priorities

To begin, Railsback (1985) suggests that administrators examine time allocations in terms of curricular priorities. Do they match? Is the allocation of school time to specific curricular areas commensurate with the importance of those disciplines and sufficient for the attainment of the instructional objectives they contain? For example, is there adequate time provided for instruction at the elementary level in the fundamental subjects of reading, mathematics and language arts? If continuation of basic reading instruction is a priority for the junior or senior high school, is time provided for reading instruction as a separate discipline or is it submerged in content subjects? In the latter instance, it will be important to determine if the subject matter teachers acknowledge and accept their responsibility for basic reading instruction and development. Educational priorities must be matched with realistic time commitments which, in turn, make the attainment of designated educational goals a real possibility. Inbalances, when found, should be addressed and corrected.

An educational priority acknowledged by most, if not all, school districts is the provision of appropriate educational programs for the slower learning and educationally needy child. Slow learners and duly identified exceptional students present a special challenge for every school district. With regard to time for learning the research data shows that the achievement of these students is tied to more, not less, learning time (Stallings, 1975; Tobias and Ingber, 1976). Unfortunately, the research data also reveals that such learners are frequently getting less learning time than their more able peers (Allington, 1980). The research literature reveals that at present the "equal opportunity model" (Haynes and Jenkins, 1986) prevails to the detriment of these students. Administrators, in collaboration with their teaching staffs, should explore avenues to increase instructional time and intensity for the slow learner and the handicapped. It will be time well spent.

Noninstructional Activities

Administrators must be sensitive to the amount of time devoted to noninstructional activities and thus lost for learning (Railsback, 1985). A variety of noninstructional and extracurricular activities intrude upon the school day and erode instructional time. Teacher involvement in such activities is often at the expense of teaching time. An administrative survey to assess the impact of noninstructional and extracurricular activities on school time and learning time is long overdue in many school districts. Administrators, with concrete data in hand, should take the lead role in controlling the erosion of school time. Teachers will applaud the effort.

Lists of potential "time wasters" are readily found in the research and popular literature (Railsback, 1985; Reck, 1984). Some of the specific items are: lunch related activities; breaks; opening and closing activities; assemblies; special programs; announcements; soliciting; fund raisers; and unscheduled class visitors. Many more items could be added to the list. There is no intent to suggest that noninstructional and extracurricular activities be eliminated; rather it is suggested that essential activities be conducted efficiently and that nonessential activities be controlled in order to minimize the loss of instructional time. In addition, teachers must be freed from organizational and procedural tasks to the greatest extent possible. Computerized systems should be explored as a means of reducing teachers' paperwork, as well as improving the overall information flow within the schools and their districts (Williams and Highsmith, 1983). Volunteers and paraprofessionals, for example, can take over many noninstructional and extracurricular tasks.

Management Skills

Reducing intrusions upon the school day is one means of increasing learning time. Another means to accomplish this same goal involves the upgrading of teachers' managerial skills. There is ample evidence of the interrelationship between managerial skills and teaching effectiveness (Anderson, Evertson, and Brophy, 1979; Evertson, Anderson, Anderson, and Brophy, 1980; Evertson, Emmer, Clements, Sanford, and Worsham, 1984; Hawley and Rosenholtz, 1984; Medley, 1979). Management skills, teaching effectiveness, and student engagement are interrelated. With increasing frequency, student engagement is cited as an indicator of teaching effectiveness and is being used as a dependent outcome variable in classroom based research (Rosenshine and Stevens, 1984). It is time to consider the use of observational measures of student engagement (as well as other specific behaviors) in the clinical supervisory process for teachers in training and teachers on the job. Objective, nonjudgmental, data-based feedback to teachers on the level of student on-task behavior has been shown to be effective in improving the level of students' on-task behavior, presumably as a result of altered teacher behavior (Leach and Dolan, 1985). Of course, any decision to incorporate specific student outcome measures in the supervisory process carries with it an obligation to provide meaningful pre-service and in-service training to upgrade the managerial skills of teachers, particularly those skills which impact on the use of time in the classroom.

Administrators need to be sensitive to two other integral components of the school program which significantly influence school time, particularly for youngsters "at risk" for academic failure, e.g., slow learners, problem learners, and special education students. These two programmatic components are transportation and pull-out programs.

Transportation

Transportation is an essential service for many students who would not be able to attend school in its absence. Transportation is a legislated related service for special education students and many special youngsters have school provided transportation specified in their individual education programs (IEP). Unfortunately, situations exist where the length of the school day for some students is reduced in order to comply with the exigencies of the transportation schedule. Special education students seem to be especially hard hit in this regard—"the last to arrive and the first to leave". The issues involved have been subject to both legal and administrative review with far-reaching consequences, e.g., required adjustments in transportation schedules, length of the school day, and provision of compensatory education for lost school time (Education of the Handicapped Law Report, 1987). In light of the relationship between learning time and learning outcomes, the preeminence of transportation schedules needs to be carefully reconsidered. Situations in which particular groups of children bear the burden of lost school time cannot be countenanced.

Pull-Out Programs

Pull-out programs, many of which are federally funded, are commonplace in today's schools. Many of these programs are specifically targeted to the "at risk" student (Madden and Slavin, 1989). It is ironic that programs intended to provide extra assistance for educationally needy or handicapped learners often deprive these very same children of crucial school time (Hill and Kimbrough, 1981; Reck, 1984). Pull-out programs not only cause the removal of the targeted students during regular instruction, but the coming and going of these children is disruptive to the class as a whole (Evertson and Emmer, et al., 1984: Conroy, 1988). A number of questions are being raised regarding pull-out programs—questions for which administrators will need to find adequate answers. Do the benefits of pull-out programs justify the costs in time? Can such programs be organized and administered so as to eliminate the forced choice between time in class and participation in special programs? The issue of program supplementation versus program supplantation, raised in chapter 3, is critical to the education of handicapped learners and is relevant to the debate surrounding pull-out programs and the growing concern about the provision of sufficient instructional time for adequate learning progress.

It might be very helpful for administrators to assess teachers' perceptions of and feelings about pull-out programs. A recently published poll (Conroy, 1988) reveals marked differences among teacher groups in their attitudes and assessments of pull-out programs, which by no means enjoy the whole hearted support of teachers. Evertson and Emmer, et al., (1984) offer some suggestions for the administration and coordination of pull-out programs which can help to minimize disruption and time loss for both teachers and students; (1) coordinate the schedule for pull-out programs among all sending and receiving teachers; (2) stay on schedule; (3) have alternative activities for students who must wait for instruction to begin; (4) plan procedures and activities to reengage returning students; and (5) have supplementary activities planned for those occasions when special classes are not held.

Teacher's Role and Responsibility

It is the teacher's responsibility to plan and implement the instructional program within the parameters of the school year and school day. The teacher must create and maintain a classroom environment conducive to learning (Anderson *et al.*, 1979). Good management is a key factor for success or failure in this endeavor. Emmer *et al.* (1984) emphasize that good management results from the deliberate actions of the effective teacher who works very hard to produce classroom conditions and student behaviors essential for a good learning environment.

The relationship between managerial skills and teaching effectiveness is buttressed by an ample body of research evidence. Paradoxically, the research evidence also reveals that the amount of time devoted to classroom management is negatively related to school achievement (Anderson *et al.*, 1979; Coker, Lorentz, and Coker, 1976; Stallings, Needles, and Staybrook, 1979). The paradox stems from the fact that management needs diminish instructional time and that good management skills involve as little class time as possible. Effective management, therefore, requires a minimum of instructional time.

In the current literature, good management is defined in terms of specific teaching skills and/or key instructional variables (Anderson *et al.*, 1979; Goss, 1984; Rieth, Polsgrove, and Semmel, 1981; Rosenshine and Stevens, 1984). Even though authorities do not agree *in toto*, the published "lists" of instructional variables or teaching skills overlap to a considerable degree and readily reveal a core of essential management skills. Two elements stand out due to their immediate relevance for the conservation of instructional time: maintaining student engagement, and managing transitions. The maintenance of student engagement concerns the sustaining of student on-task behavior during instructional activities. Managing transitions deals with minimizing the loss of instructional time as children move (physically or attentionally) from one planned activity to another throughout the school day. Discussion of the two management skills necessarily touches upon a number of managerial and instructional topics. All of the discussion of managerial and instructional variables to follow is generic in nature; that is, the managerial and instructional variables discussed have wide applicability across subject areas. The specific teaching skills discussed are especially relevant for the child experiencing learning or behavioral difficulties.

Maintaining Student Engagement

The importance of maintaining student engagement during instructional activities lies in the well documented relationship between student engaged time and achievement (Berliner, 1979; Fisher et al., 1978; Good and Beckerman, 1978). Of the different measures of school time, engaged time, which denotes the amount of time that students are actively attending to and involved in appropriate academic tasks, is the most important. Maintaining high levels of engagement must be a priority for every classroom; the adept teacher will have a range of strategies for maintaining students' attention to task.

Sequencing activities. To better understand and manage engagement and time on task, it is useful to view the school day as a series of activities or activity segments (Ross, 1984), rather than lessons. Researchers have found that "activity" is a useful unit of analysis in studying the structure of the school day (Burns, 1984); this concept is useful for the teacher as well.

An activity is an "organized behavior" that the teacher and students engage in for a common purpose (Emmer et al., 1984, p. 112). Every activity has a central focus or purpose (Ross, 1984). In addition, an activity is defined by an activity pattern which prescribes the nature of the teacher and student participation, a grouping pattern, interrelationships among students, student behaviors, and pacing. Finally Ross (1980) points out that activities have physical and temporal boundaries; that is to say, an activity occurs in a designated location, has a discernible beginning and ending, and intended outcomes. Some activities are nonacademic or procedural in nature, *e.g.*, opening exercises and recess. Other activities are instructional in nature, *e.g.*, group discussion and seat work. The concept of activities is important for instructional planning. As teachers plan the day or specific lesson they are planning activities which will hopefully "lead to attaining the objectives within the allotted period of time" (Emmer *et al.*, 1984, p. 112).

Activities are not only important for planning instruction; it has been shown that activities impact on the behavior of both the teacher and students (Gump, 1974) and that the activity pattern of a lesson can influence the level of student involvement (Ross, 1984). It is well established that the level of student engagement is generally higher under teacher led discussion than during independent seatwork. In planning instruction, the teacher needs to consider the number, nature, and sequence of activities, as well as strive to maintain student engagement through activities that are integral to academic lessons and to maintain work momentum across the transitions which separate activities. Two activity sequences for basic skill instruction at the elementary level are presented by Evertson, Emmer, *et al.* (1984, p. 117-118).

Activity Sequence A	*Activity Sequence B*
Checking or recitation	Checking or recitation
Content development	Content development
Classwork	Classwork or seatwork, usually
Seatwork	with checking
	Content development
	Classwork, usually brief seatwork

Emmer *et al* (1984, p. 116) offer sample activity sequences for the academic instruction at the secondary level:

Activity Sequence C	*Activity Sequence D*
Opening routine	Opening
Checking	Checking
Content development	First content development
Seatwork	activity
Closing	First seatwork activity
	Checking
	Second content development
	activity
	Second seatwork activity
	Closing

The activity sequences at both levels are very much alike; the rationale is the same for the alternate activity sequence at each level. The inclusion of 2 content development activity segments enhances the effectiveness of the content presentations by providing more opportunities for student practice and teacher monitoring prior to independent seatwork activities. The varied sequence also demands less sustained attention from the students, *i.e.*, 2 relatively short versus 1 long presentation session, thus helping to maintain engagement through the activity sequence.

Of the many types of activities that could be used in classroom instruction, recitation and seatwork dominate class time (Gump, cited in Ross, 1984). This observation is buttressed by the BTES findings which revealed that elementary students spend 2 thirds of their academic time in seatwork activities and most of the remaining time in recitation (Rosenshine, 1981). Based upon observational data from many sources we can state unequivocally that student engagement is higher during recitation rather than seatwork activities (Fisher *et al.*, 1978; Good and Beckerman, 1978; Soar, 1973; Stallings and Kaskowitz, 1974). Ross (1984) attributes the difference in student behavior to the difference in activity patterns. She describes recitation as whole group, teacher-led and paced, and constantly under teacher supervision. Feedback is provided and participation is expected. In contrast, she describes the activity pattern of seatwork as students working on their own, with much less monitoring and feedback and accountable for the completion of their work at some later point. The implication for instruction of the slow or problem learner is quite evident—it will be difficult to sustain student attention and involvement through long periods of seatwork. Some suggestions to help maintain student engagement during seatwork activities are: (1) change the nature of tasks during seatwork (Ross, 1984); (2) control the pace of the activity (to avoid self-paced activity) through the use of audiovisual media or the assistance of peer tutors (Ross, 1984); (3) monitor seatwork (Brophy and Evertson, 1976); and (4) teacher-student contacts during seat work should be short, not sustained, and academically related (Scott and Bushell, 1984; Rosenshine and Stevens, 1984).

It will be apparent that the managerial requirements increase as the number and/or complexity of the activity structure increases. At the very least additional activities create more transitions which must be managed. The activity structure can become very complex if the teacher introduces overlapping activities, each of which may require teacher attention. "It is important for teachers to realize when scheduling simultaneous activity segments that if the programme of one segment utilized the teacher as a continuous source of input for students, then the programme of the second segment cannot permit children to seek attention from the teacher but must still assure that students are able to complete their assignments successfully" (Ross, 1984, p. 81). Conceptualizing the school day in terms of activities and the demands that various activities place upon both the teacher and the student can help teachers to structure the school day so the demands upon the teacher for direct supervision and instruction and the demands upon the student for sustained attention and independent work are in harmony rather than in conflict.

Pacing. "Pacing refers to how quickly pupils proceed through their instructional materials; that is, how much material they cover daily" (Barr, 1975, p. 483). Student engagement and achievement is affected by the pace of instruction imposed by the teacher (Anderson et al., 1979; Good and Beckerman, 1975; Good, Grouws, and Beckerman, 1978). Sustained attention and higher levels of achievement are associated with briskly paced lessons and greater content coverage (Carnine, 19676; Carnine and Silbert, 1979; Berliner, 1984).

Though the pace of instruction is controlled by the teacher, Barr (1975), in a study of grouping and pacing practices in first grade reading, found that not only did teachers have great difficulty explaining why and how they make pacing decisions, but they did not realize the degree to which they manipulated the pace of reading instruction. "It appears that, while grouping is a planned decision, pacing is a function of reactive considerations during instruction" (Barr, 1975, p. 492). Some other findings reported by Barr were: (1) that many, though not all, teachers group students early in the year on the basis of their perception of children's readiness for instruction; (2) that groups tend to remain stable over the course of the school year; and (3) that teachers adjust the pace of instruction intuitively on the basis of their expectations for student performance.

The scenario which emerges from the findings of Barr and others is not particularly auspicious for the slow learner or problem learner. If problem learners are placed early in the school year in instructional groupings according to teachers' perceptions of their ability or readiness for instruction, there is every probability that these children will be locked into a cycle of lower paced instruction, less content coverage, and lower achievement.

How, then, should teachers pace instruction for the slow learner, problem learner, or the learning disabled student? Emmer et al. suggest that pacing in content development activities refers to the "fit between the rate of presentation of information and student's ability to comprehend it" (1984, p. 117). The sentiment of this statement is consistent with a basic tenent of special education practice—namely, the importance of matching task demands to the level of students' knowledge and ability (Zigmond, Vellacorsa, and Silverman, 1983). The rate of presentation of content materials for special learners cannot exceed the rate at which students achieve mastery of the knowledge, concepts, and skills presented. Content coverage and content mastery must go hand and hand for children with learning problems. Thus we come to a second basic tenent of special education—namely, that the learner must achieve proficiency at one level before proceeding to the next level of skill development. To allow children to progress with faulty or only partially learned skills merely compounds the problem and sets the stage for learning difficulties in the future. This is not to say that teachers should allow children with a history of learning difficulty to progress at a slow, leisurely pace. On the contrary, the pace of instruction and the level of mastery to be attained should be based upon the actual performance of the disabled student under good, even ideal, instructional conditions. The student's past rate of performance, dismal in many cases, should not be the standard by which we set projections for future achievement. We must strive not only for progress, but for sufficient progress to bridge the academic gap and reach both short and long range goals. Teachers must find ways to intensify instruction for such students. Increasing student learning and engagement is one means of achieving this goal; an "experimental approach" to instructional planning in which teachers explore student capabilities and instructional approaches to identify optimal instructional interventions is another (Zigmond *et al.*, 1983).

Success Rate. The ratio between the number of correct responses and the number of incorrect responses in a student's performance of a designated assignment constitutes the success rate for the student's performance. Research on student engagement reveals that success rate contributes to student attentiveness and achievement (Gickling and Thompson, 1985). Appropriate success rate, i.e., appropriate difficulty level of tasks or materials, appears repeatedly on lists of instructional variables cited as important for effective teaching.

Success rate or task difficulty is quantified differently by various authors. Rosenshine (1981) suggests that children should experience at least an 80 percent success rate. Gickling and Armstrong (1978) and Gickling and Thompson (1985) define task difficulty in terms of the ratio of known to unknown elements within a given assignment. In the 1978 study appropriate task difficulty was set at 70 percent to 85 percent known elements for seatwork assignments and 93 percent to 97 percent known elements for reading assignments; in the 1985 study a flat 80 percent success rate was applied. Brophy and Evertson (1974) suggest that task difficulty levels should reflect students' ability and SES level. A somewhat higher success rate should be required of lower ability, lower SES students (80 percent) than the success rate required of high SES students (70 percent). Emmer *et al.* (1984) suggest a success rate of 90 percent at the elementary level. The common concern implicit in all of these success rate guidelines, and numerous others that could be cited, is that students should encounter a preponderance of success in their daily assignments, and that the ratio between known and unknown should favor success by at least a 4 to 1 margin.

The concept of success rate should not be jarring to special education teachers. There are many examples in special education practice of similar performance guidelines (which imply a success and failure ratio) used to judge the appropriateness of curricular materials and task assignments. The most obvious example entails the widespread use of individual reading inventories with which teachers identify reading materials according to instructional, frustrational, or independent readability. The difficulty of specific reading materials is determined by comparing a student's performance to preset performance standards for word recognition and comprehension. Reading fluency (words read per minute) is emerging as a third performance criterion. Materials which a child reads slowly, with many errors and limited comprehension, is deemed too difficult and is thought to be at the frustration reading level. Reading materials which are read with relative ease, few errors, and at a good pace are considered appropriate for instruction. Reading materials in which the child displays almost error free reading with a high level of comprehension would be selected for independent, or leisure reading activities.

Task difficulty can positively or negatively impact upon student engagement. The research literature shows that students spend more time engaged in tasks that match their current level of knowledge and skill (Anderson, 1981). And clearly, task difficulty is an instructional variable under the teacher's control. Guidelines for appropriate levels of task difficulty and student success rate are becoming available and should be eagerly sought out and applied by all teachers.

Transitions

As previously described, the school day is a series of activities which fill the time between the opening and closing of school. A transition is an "interval between any two activities" (Emmer et al., 1984, p. 117), and generally involves a teacher initiated directive to students to end one activity and to start another (Arlin, 1979). Transitions, and the management of transitions, are important for many reasons. First, a major portion of noninstructional time in the classroom is taken up by transitional activities (Rosenshine, 1981; Rieth and Frick, 1982). Second, transitions are an intrusion upon instructional time, and if mismanaged or mishandled transitions can take up far too much instructional time (Berliner and Pinero, 1984). Third, off-task behavior increases markedly during transitions as does the potential for disruptive behavior (Arlin, 1979). Fourth, transition time is negatively correlated with student achievement (Arlin, 1979; Rosenshine and Stevens, 1984). And finally, the teachers' ability to manage transitions is, for many, an indicator of the general level of her managerial skills (Arlin, 1979; Doyle, 1979).

Transitions are the separations between classroom activities; they can occur both between and within lessons. An example of a transition between lessons would be the teacher concluding academic instruction in one subject area and preparing the children to commence instruction in another subject area, *e.g.*, reading activity giving way to a science lesson. An example of a transition within a lesson would be the teacher regrouping children from a whole class activity to small group or individual seatwork activities within the same subject area, *i.e.*, precisely what elementary teachers do routinely as they conclude a whole group activity to commence small group or individual follow-up activities. Some transitions are clearly noninstructional while others are embedded within instructional or academic activities. It is important that transitions be smooth and well coordinated and move children quickly from one activity to another if student engagement, which typically plummets during transitions (Arlin, 1979; Brophy and Evertson, 1976; Kounin, 1970), is to be maintained.

The best management strategy for noninstructional transitions is to instill within the students rules and procedures for such activities. Teachers whose classrooms are examples of good management invest considerable time and effort, particularly early in the year, to train students in the rules and procedures necessary for smooth classroom operations (Good and Beckerman, 1978; Doyle, 1979). Arlin (1979) also offers some suggestions for smoothly coordinated transitions that are particularly applicable to instructional transitions which occur between instructional activities or within an academic activity. Among these suggestions are to "wrap up" a previous lesson before going on to the next one, giving students a clear indication that one activity has (or shortly will be) stopped and another is to begin. Also, cue students that the end of an activity is approaching; *e.g.*, "in two minutes we will . . ." In addition, wait for full attentiveness from all students before a new activity is begun or new instructions are given; *e.g.*, "all pencils down and all eyes on me." And finally, break the momentum of one activity but not the overall work momentum.

The application of some basic management strategies can greatly enhance smooth transitions while reducing overall disruption to the classroom program. Transitions in the classroom are most noticeable when they are handled poorly. Arlin (1979) observes that teachers spend a great deal of time planning activity A and activity B, but the transition from A to B is too often left to chance. The knowledgeable teacher who gives thought and planning to transitions as well as other activities increases her chance of enhancing the overall classroom program.

In Summary

The amount of time in the school day and cumulatively over the course of the school year is finite. These limited time resources must satisfy instructional and competing noninstructional demands. Administrators and teachers share responsibility for the conservation of instructional time and should proactively seek to reduce time loss.

Administrators, by virtue of their role within the school organization, are in position to assess the congruence between educational priorities and time allocations. Imbalances require attention and correction. Administrators also need to be sensitive to the impact of school operations and services such as transportation and pull-out programs on the availability of instructional time for disabled learners. Participation in pull-out programs often creates a conflict between participation in the on-going class program, i.e., the special programs for some children, and the special services. Transportation schedules frequently impinge upon the school schedule of handicapped learners. These "forced choices" in many instances are the result of administrative or organizational decisions. Legal issues arise when handicapped learners are forced to forego classroom instruction or accept a significant reduction in the length of their school day as a condition for their attendance in school or participation in special services. In such instances, handicapped children are doubly handicapped, once by their disability and then by conflicts and constraints inherent in the educational system.

The degree of time loss in the classroom will be closely tied to the teacher's management skills. Some time loss to managerial needs is inevitable in every classroom, but the goal should be to keep lost time to a minimum. The best antidote for time loss is good classroom management. The teacher should strive to maintain a high level of student engagement through appropriate pacing, sequencing of activities, and assignment of tasks and materials which are at an appropriate difficulty level for the students. Students should encounter a relatively small proportion of unknowns in their assignments as students learn best when they are attending to materials or tasks in which they encounter a high level of success. Transitions pose a special challenge for every teacher. As the complexity of the class program increases, so does the number of transitions to be managed. Every transition has the potential for student disengagement and/or class disruption. The management of transitions deserves the teacher's attention; transitions that are managed well will do much to enhance the overall classroom program.

Chapter 5

Enhancing Learning Time and
Student Engagement

In this chapter, discussion is continued of classroom and instructional variables empirically linked to student engagement and achievement. The research literature indicates that classrooms in which instructional time is used effectively and in which teachers employ good management strategies have higher levels of student achievement and lower levels of disruption and misbehavior. The central role of the teacher in the classroom and the instructional process is emphasized. Attention is focused upon what teachers can do to create and maintain a learning environment which encourages success among students prone to academic failure. The previous chapter dealt with preventing the loss of instructional time; this chapter goes beyond prevention to identify ways to increase learning time and student involvement. The combined contents of chapters 4 and 5 provide an orientation to classroom management and many proactive strategies for optimizing learning time and student engagement.

Discussion of the enhancement of learning time and engagement is relevant for students with a wide variety of learning and behavior problems. In regular education, the students of concern are those who wear a variety of labels: *e.g.*, slow learners, low ability, low achievers, problem learners, etc. It is this student population that supplies the seemingly endless stream of candidates for special education. Once the process of referral, assessment, and placement is completed in accordance with federal and state regulations, many of these students merely trade one set of labels for another and become the mildly handicapped, learning disabled, emotionally/socially maladjusted, behaviorally disordered, educable mentally retarded, and so forth in special education. MacMillan, Keogh, and Jones (1986) use the encompassing term "inefficient school learners" to designate "learners whose deviations in school achievement, and possibly social adjustment, are so marked as to necessitate specialized intervention. At the same time, these are usually ablebodied, normal-appearing children whose learning problems are not compounded by physical stigmata or physical disabilities" (p. 686). These "inefficient school learners" are the students we must keep uppermost in our minds as the discussion of enhanced learning time and engagement unfolds.

The effective schools literature and process-product research consulted in the preparation of this textbook are decidedly biased toward regular elementary school education but important research in remedial and special education can be cited. Stallings and her colleagues (1974, 1975, 1979) have made significant contributions to the research literature regarding instructional processes in remedial and compensatory education. Rieth, Polsgrove, Okolo, Eckert, and Bahr (1987) investigated instruction provided to handicapped students in secondary school resource rooms. Despite the literature's bias toward regular elementary school education, the collective body of research contains much that is relevant for teachers who deal with problem students in both regular and special education. Many of the instructional and classroom variables discussed apply to basic skills instruction for most students in any educational settings.

The literature is vast; consequently, a degree of selectivity was essential. Strategies for increasing learning time, student engagement, and the quality of instruction were considered most important and are highlighted in this chapter. The chapter begins with a topic of major importance, the differential treatment of problem learners. There is a need to make teachers aware that the same classroom may not provide the same learning experience for all students. Though the "typical" classroom may provide a positive learning environment for the average or above average student, it may be far less appropriate or supportive for the less able or lower achieving youngster. A heightening of teachers' sensitivity to the differential treatment given to some children is the first step in correcting a situation which is, at best, inappropriate and, at worst, harmful for many of our students. The chapter continues with discussion of 2 instructional variables closely associated with effective instruction and student achievement: academic focus and interactive teaching. Exploration of these topics leads to many practical suggestions for the classroom.

Differential Treatment of the Low Achieving Low Ability Student

There is ample research evidence which shows that the teacher's behavior toward children in her charge can differ markedly from one child or group of children to another (Allington, 1980a, 1980b; Eder, 1981, 1982; Evertson, 1982; Evertson and Emmer, 1982; Thurlow,

Graden, Greener, and Ysseldyke, 1982; Hall, Delquadri, Greenwood, and Thurston, 1982). Although a particular classroom may be well suited to the majority of "average" students, youngsters at the extremes—those most and least able—may not be receiving appropriate instruction. Youngsters at the low end of the achievement scale who are in serious academic difficulty and who are "at risk" for academic failure and/or special education referral are our primary concern. These students are frequently the recipients of instruction which is not only different from that accorded their "average" peers but also detrimental to their optimum learning and success.

A teacher's behavior will reflect her personal expectations for student performance. The research on teacher expectancy and student performance, which demonstrates a consistent relationship between expectations and performance, also reveals that student achievement is greater when teachers hold and communicate high expectations for performance (Amer, 1983; Eder, 1982; Purkey and Smith, 1983; Hawley and Rosenholtz, 1984). Teachers tend to take credit for the achievement of good learners but blame the failure of the poor learners on lack of ability, the home environment, or other factors beyond the purview of the classroom and school (Hawley and Rosenholtz, 1984). A similar phenomenon—taking credit for learning success but eschewing blame for learning failure—has been observed among special education teachers (Zigmond, Levin, and Laurie, 1985). Hawley and Rosenholtz (1984) believe that this "transfer of responsibility" impacts on teacher behavior such that "ineffective teachers, believing that there is little that can be done to improve the performance of low achievers act in ways to confirm their initial beliefs, while effective teachers take firm responsibility for student learning at all levels of achievement, behaving in accord with the belief that all students can in fact learn" (p. 34). Hawley and Rosenholtz (1984) have summarized some of the ways in which teachers communicate low performance expectations to low achieving students:

1. Some teachers tolerate more behavioral interruptions when working with low than high ability groups. Disruption in turn results in lower student engagement and ultimately lower student learning.
2. Some teachers require more seatwork of low than high achievers, while devoting more interactive teaching time to high as opposed to low achievers. As we noted in the section on interactive teaching methods, seatwork generally results in lower academic learning time than interactive teaching.
3. Low achievers sometimes receive fewer opportunities to perform academically than high achievers and are, therefore, given less opportunity for corrective feedback.

4. When called upon to perform, some teachers give low achievers less time to answer questions than high achievers and fail to give corrective feedback.

5. When given incorrect answers, some teachers prompt high achieving students, more than low achieving students, in the proper direction. The guiding of an incorrect response to the appropriate answer is a strategy used by effective teachers.

6. Low achieving students are sometimes praised more often for marginal and inadequate answers than high achievers and criticized more often than high achievers for failure.

7. Some teachers are more enthusiastic teaching high rather than low achievers. Low achievers receive fewer teacher smiles, less teacher eye contact, and less teacher responsiveness than high achievers. Enthusiasm appears to capture sufficient student attention to ensure their task engagement and learning.

8. The amount of corrective feedback given to low versus high achievers also can vary. Briefer and less informative feedback is sometimes given to lower achievers (p. 33).[*]

Restricted involvement for low functioning students in the instruction processes as evidenced by lower engagement rates and fewer directive and supportive teacher-student interactions is the ultimate outcome of all of the teacher behaviors stated above. A persistent pattern of such behavior imposed upon particular students—in this instance those most in need of greater involvement and more direction and support—can and will take its toll on student performance. There is no intent to suggest that teachers deliberately or maliciously alter their behavior toward the low ability or low achieving student; rather, the purpose is to make teachers aware of how their behavior can impact on student performance. With greater awareness teachers can avoid deleterious behavior patterns and knowingly adopt teaching strategies which are instructionally effective with students experiencing learning problems.

Reading problems are pervasive among low achievers and have received the most attention from researchers and teachers alike. Research by Allington (1977, 1980a, 1983) reveals that differential instructional treatment for reading is given to children of lower ability.

---

[*]From "Effective Education" by W.D. Hawley and S.J. Rosenholtz, 1984, *Peabody Journal of Education, 61*, pp. 15-52. Copyright 1984, Peabody College. Adapted by permission.

The academic consequences of differential treatment have been discussed in general terms, and its potential impact on reading performance must be of greatest concern. Allington (1983) concurs with Hawley and Rosenholtz's premise that teachers shift responsibility for academic failure to the student by attributing failure to such characteristics of the learner as "unmotivated, immature, distractible, and hyperactive" (p. 549). For his part, Allington (1983) attributes reading failure (and off-task behavior) to deficiencies in the instructional environment and differential teacher behavior toward low and high achieving students. His research findings indicate that low and high achievers in reading are generally allocated equal amounts of instructional time but that engagement rates are lower for the poor readers and that the content of reading instruction differs in important ways. Specifically Allington (1980b, 1977) reports that good and poor readers differ in the amounts of contextual reading (words read per day) with good readers enjoying a 3 to 1 ratio over poor readers. Poor readers read orally while good readers are more often engaged in silent reading (Allington 1980a). Teachers interrupt poor readers more frequently than good readers and by so doing create an obstacle to the development of reading fluency and student self monitoring (Allington, 1980a). In addition, teachers tolerate a higher level of "call-out" behavior from poor readers than good readers. By so doing teachers very likely hope to encourage participation but may be reinforcing a pattern of student behavior which can become a problem at a later time or in other instructional settings. For good readers, teachers emphasize reading for meaning and comprehension; for poor readers, teachers emphasize reading as decoding (Allington, 1983). Allington concludes that, at present, equality in reading instruction for good and poor readers does not extend beyond allocated time and that the instructional process differs in may important respects. He believes that "good and poor readers differ in their reading ability as much because of differences in instruction as variations in individual learning styles or aptitudes" (Allington, 1983, p. 548).

If poor readers are to overcome their reading deficiencies they will need "unequal treatment" which provides them with more instructional time and more appropriate instruction. Others share this point of view (Bloom, 1976; Haynes and Jenkins, 1986). To this end Allington (1983) offers some suggestions for improving the instructional environment for poor readers which are paraphrased as follows: (1) assess the current instructional environment with particular attention to specific teaching behaviors (i.e., employ direct observation techniques to secure baseline data on teacher behaviors), and student success rate as reflected in the number of students returning to regular ability reading groups (not simply achievement gain scores); (2) add a second reading session for the poor reading group; (3) increase the amount of silent reading time for poor readers and teach effective silent reading behavior, *e.g.*, pre-reading purpose setting, strategies for decoding unknown words, and reading for meaning; (4) provide daily opportunity to read easy material that will enhance reading fluency; (5) develop and encourage self monitoring behavior; and (6) decrease assignments of worksheets and workbooks, for such activities do not involve the best use of instructional time nor provide maximum opportunity for direct student-teacher interaction.

Interactive Teaching

Clearly teacher behavior impacts on student behavior and performance. The immediate effects can be seen in the level of student engagement and compliance; the long term effects will be seen in the level of student attainment and affective development. Viewed in this light, teaching style becomes an important issue. There are many proponents, as well as a substantial research literature, that support a directive and interactive teaching style. The literature contains a number of different terms for the same concept, *e.g.*, "active teaching" (Stallings and Kaskowitz, 1974; Stallings, Cory, Fairweather, and Needles, 1977), "teacher directed instruction" (Rosenshine and Stevens, 1984), "interactive instruction" (Zigmond, Sansone, and Miller; Donahue and Kohnke, 1986), and "direct teaching" (Hawley and Rosenholtz, 1984). All of these terms refer to a teaching style in which the teacher is the primary instructional agent and is very actively and directly involved with students in academic and instructional activities. Interactive teaching encompasses a constellation of specific teaching behaviors repeatedly shown to be related to high levels of engagement and achievement gains. We now turn our attention to the most important of these teaching skills.

Academic Focus

Teachers' expectations for student performance can have a positive or negative influence on student achievement. Teacher expectations have a self fulfilling capacity in that low expectations can become a factor contributing to the inadequate performance of many students. Unfortunately, teachers' expectations for students with learning problems and poor academic records are frequently low. An antidote for low expectations in both regular and special education is awareness of the importance of high expectations expressed through a strong and pervasive academic focus in the classroom. Academic focus is reflected in the amount of time devoted to academic versus nonacademic activities and to the type of instructional interaction and activities which prevail in the classroom. In classrooms with a strong academic focus much time is devoted to academic pursuits and far less time to nonacademic activities. Research findings indicate that classes in which more time is devoted to academic pursuits produce greater student achievement gains than comparative classrooms in which academic activities receive less emphasis and less instructional time (Fisher et al., 1978; Stallings and Kaskowitz, 1974; Stallings, Needles, and Stayrook, 1979; Stallings, Cory, and Fairweather, and Needless, 1977; Zigmond, Leinhardt, and Cooley, 1981).

Rosenshine and Stevens (1984, p. 757) have described classrooms with strong academic focus (their term is "academic emphasis") as "task oriented" and "business like", and delineate specific teaching behaviors which contribute to the academic focus of the classroom:

- Systematic, goal-related activities;
- Lessons and content related to attaining specific goals;
- Rapid pacing of lessons;
- Few vacillating, and/or aimless comments, questions, or discussions;
- Ready availability of materials;
- Student participation in answering and responding;
- Efficient use of time;
- Emphasis on assigning regular homework;
- Weekly and monthly tests;
- Student accountability for homework;
- Emphasis on marking and grading student work; and
- Positive encouragement of good work habits.

There is some concern that a strong academic focus is gained at the expense of affective outcomes. However, the evidence reveals that classrooms characterized by a strong academic focus are not necessarily cold or harsh environments detrimental to the well being of children. Quite the contrary, academically focused teachers need not sacrifice warmth and humor and the children in such classrooms do well academically and have positive attitudes about themselves (Rosenshine and Stevens, 1984).

Interactive versus Noninteractive Activities

The nature of children's involvement during academic activities has also been studied. Research results suggest that all academic activities are not of equal instructional value. While some types of tasks and activities are strongly related to achievement, others contribute far less to students' academic progress. Stallings, Needles, and Stayrook (1979) in a study of remedial reading in secondary schools distinguished between "interactive on-task instruction" and "noninteractive on-task instruction." Interactive on-task instruction, *e.g.*, discussion, review, reading aloud, drill and practice, praise and support, and supportive corrective feedback, was positively related to reading gains. Noninteractive on-task instruction, *e.g.*, classroom management, silent reading, sustained silent reading, and written assignments were negatively related to reading gains. As one might expect, nonacademic off-task activities such as organizing, social interaction, and negative interactions were consistently negatively related to achievement. The Stallings *et al.* study involved 4 student groups which varied as to initial achievement level and subsequent achievement gains: low pretest and high gains, moderate pretest and moderate gains, high pretests and high gains, and no gains. The student group characterized as low pretest and high gains is of most interest. This group, which very likely contained the inefficient learners, demonstrated strong reading gains over the course of the investigation. Stallings *et al.* (1979), in seeking some explanations for this result, found that the teachers of these classes allocated more time to interactive activities, directly instructing and interacting with students with little time spent interacting with individual students or in noninteractive activities.

The research endeavors of Stallings and her colleagues have significantly contributed to our understanding of academic activities and achievement. Rosenshine and Stevens (1984) have extracted the important activity-achievement relationships from this series of research studies, and summarized them in tabular form.

Table 5.1 presents data on various instructional activities and their correlational relationship to reading achievement. The research findings indicate that activities which stress directive teaching, students' engagement in academic work, and involve student use of primary instructional materials, *e.g.*, textbooks, workbooks, etc., yielded positive achievement results. The reader should take note of the fact that nonacademic activity was consistently negatively associated with reading achievement. This series of studies revealed no evidence of indirect enhancement of reading performance through nonacademic activity (Rosenshine and Stevens, 1984).

Table 5.1. Correlation Between Academic Activities and Achievement Gain

STUDY	VARIABLE	CORRELATIONS WITH READING ACHIEVEMENT GAIN
	POSITIVE CORRELATIONS	
Stallings & Kaskowitz (1974) 1st grade	Adult instruction, academic	.11
	Approximate number of students involved in reading	.40**
	Reading, alphabet, language development	.40**
	Time spent using texts, workbooks	.24**
	Numbers, math, arithmetic	.29**
	Approximate number of students involved in math	.35**
	Total academic verbal interactions	.41**
Stallings & Kaskowitz (1974) 3rd grade	Adult instruction, academic	.29*
	Approximate number of students involved in reading	.18
	Numbers, math, arithmetic	.52**
	Approximate number of students involved in math	.53**
	Total academic verbal interactions	.34**
Stallings et al. (1977) 3rd grade	Adult instruction, academic	.30*
	Time spent by teacher (and other adults) on academic instruction	.25
	Average occurrence of reading per child	.31*
	Percent of activities on academics	.41**
	Total academic interactions	.43**
Solomon & Kendall (1979) 4th grade	Businesslike and task-oriented, e.g., orderly sequence of activities, calm and quiet classrooms	.54**
	NEGATIVE CORRELATIONS	
Stallings & Kaskowitz (1974) 1st grade	Activities involving arts and crafts	−26*
	Activities involving games and puzzles	−10
	Activities involving group time	−22*
	Active play	−23*
	Use of games, toys, or play equipment	−20*
	Story, music, dancing	−15
Stallings & Kaskowitz (1974) 3rd grade	Activities involving arts and crafts	−18
	Activities involving games and puzzles	−17
	Activities involving group time	−20
	Use of games, toys, or play equipment	−32*
	Story, music, dancing	−22
Stallings et al. (1977) 3rd grade	Group sharing time	−42**
	Use of games, play equipment	−43**
	Number of social interactions	−43**
Stallings et al. (1979) secondary	Social interactions	−30*

* $p < .05$
** $p < .01$

Active Academic Responding

Another important aspect of instruction and engagement involves the nature of children's participation. Teachers must not only provide sufficient time for academic instruction, they must also provide children with sufficient opportunities for active academic responding (Greenwood, Delquadri, and Hall, 1984; Hall, Delquadri, Greenwood, and Thurston (1982). Children's participation during instruction can be characterized as "passive" or "active" (Hall *et al.*, 1982). These 2 types of participatory behavior are not equally beneficial for students nor equally related to achievement gains. According to Hall *et al.* (1981), active responding involves the child practicing the academic task, *e.g.*, answering a question, performing a problem, reading the text, etc. Examples of passive responding include general attending behavior such as listening to another child read or watching another child do a problem, etc. Research indicates that achievement gains are more highly related to active academic responding (Delquadri, Greenwood, Stretton, and Hall, 1983; Stallings, 1975; Becker, 1977).

The research on classroom practices also reveals that the level of responding and opportunities for active academic responding are limited for the disadvantaged and low achieving (Fox, 1974; Allington, 1977, 1980b; Hall Delquadri, Greenwood, and Thurston, 1982; Greenwood, Delquadri, Stanley, Terry, and Hall, 1981) and the handicapped (Thurlow, Ysseldyke, Graden, and Algozzine, 1984; Greenwood, Delquadri, and Hall, 1978).

Children need sufficient opportunities to respond—that is, to practice academic tasks—in order to learn efficiently up to their ability levels. The problems may well be that "in many classrooms the instructional arrangement may fail to generate the necessary level of opportunity to respond required for mastery of key academic skills" (Delquadri, Greenwood, Stretton, and Hall, 1983, p. 227). In addition, active responding on the part of the children affords the teacher the numerous opportunities to monitor student progress and provide corrective feedback as needed.

Student-Teacher Interactions

In accordance with the interactive teaching approach, classroom and instructional activities are selected by the teacher. The research has consistently found that students learn more when the teacher, not the students, select and direct learning activities. This outcome has been reported for low and middle SES students (Good and Brophy, 1987; Good and Beckerman, 1978; Soar, 1973; Stallings and Kaskowitz, 1974; Stallings, Cory, Fairweather, and Needles, 1977), regular education students (Solomon and Kendall, 1979), and secondary level remedial reading students (Stallings, Needles, and Stayrook, 1979). The findings that students perform better when the selection of instructional activities is made by the teacher is consistent with the often reported findings that student engagement is higher during teacher-led instructional activities rather than independent seatwork activities. The explanation for higher achievement under teacher selected activities may be due to the higher engagement rates which occur under teacher directed activities (Rosenshine and Stevens, 1984).

Interactive teaching, as the name implies, involves a high level of interaction between teacher and student. Frequent teacher student interactions are especially important for low achieving pupils (Stallings, 1980). Yet we have data which clearly shows that teachers are less interactive with less able students (Stallings, Cory, Fairweather, and Needles, 1978; Brophy and Good, 1987). Interaction must be frequent and academically focused. According to Zigmond, Sansone, Miller, Donahue, and Kohnke, (1986) interactions between teacher and student occur through direct talk, questioning, and feedback. Direct talk involves the "giving of information, lecturing, demonstrating verbally" (Zigmond *et al.* 1986, p. 111), as opposed to eliciting or probing, actions intended to draw out information or a response from the student. Interactions in which the teacher seeks to draw out information of an altered or expanded response from the student will occur, but they should not dominate student-teacher interaction. Questioning should focus upon initial concept development, drill, and review. Questioning activity provides numerous opportunities for active student participation and responding, and opportunities for the teacher to monitor student progress. The number of questions asked during instruction has been shown to be related to achievement; a higher level of teacher questioning aids achievement (Evertson, Anderson, Anderson, and Brophy, 1980; Stallings and Kaskowitz, 1974).

As the teacher interacts and directs questions to students, it is important that all children are given an opportunity to participate, not just those who are eager to respond. The common practice of selecting a respondent from among those children whose hands are raised is not a recommended practice as participation will fall to the more able and outspoken youngsters. A better questioning technique for basic skill instruction involves the teacher directing questions to students randomly or in "ordered turns"—moving in sequence among all children in the group or class. The teacher must be careful to include all children and distribute opportunities to respond in an equitable manner. These latter questioning techniques enhance both participation and attention.

Children perform better when they are given frequent feedback as to how they are doing (Stallings and Kaskowitz, 1974; Anderson, 1981; Hawley and Rosenholtz, 1984). Interactive teaching provides numerous opportunities for the teacher to assess student progress and provide appropriate feedback. Feedback in the context of group instruction helps both the individual student and all members of the group (Zigmond, Sansone, *et al.*, 1986). Frequent and regular feedback is more beneficial than sporadic or intermittent feedback because it reduces the amount of time students spend making—in effect practicing—incorrect responses (Evertson, Emmer, Clements, Sanford, and Worsham, 1984). Feedback from the teacher to student can either terminate or continue the interaction (Rosenshine and Stevens, 1984). A correct answer is generally acknowledged as such and the teacher moves on to the next student. An incorrect or inadequate response requires a decision on the teacher's part. The teacher can give terminal feedback, *e.g.*, indicate the correct answer and move on, or sustaining feedback, *e.g.*, assist the student by asking a different question or giving clues to the correct answer. The teacher may choose to remind the student of the process by which one can arrive at the correct answer, *i.e.*, process feedback. The teacher must balance students' needs for feedback about their work with the need to maintain the pace and momentum of the lesson. An understanding of how feedback fits into and supports the structure of the instructional lesson can help teachers to carry out interactions in a manner most beneficial to students and most effective in the use of instructional time.

Praise versus Feedback

A cautionary note about praise in the classroom is relevant at this junction. Praise and feedback are not synonymous nor do praise and feedback serve the same purpose in the classroom. Feedback is merely affirmation of the correctiveness of a response while praise, and criticism, are defined as "teacher actions that go beyond simple feedback about the appropriateness or correctness of behavior" (Brophy, 1981, p. 6). Brophy reports that teachers use praise infrequently and often ineffectively. In addition, the power of praise to reinforce behavior and enhance achievement varies depending upon age, grade, student background, and ability level, to name only a few intervening variables. Praise seems to have a positive reinforcing effect on student learning for the younger, lower SES, low ability student (Brophy, 1981). It is recommended that praise be used sparingly with the older students (Zigmond, Sansone, *et al.*, 1986). Stallings (1975) suggests that only 5 to 10 percent of student responses should be praised. Regarding achievement, correlations between time spent in certain types of instructional activities and achievement tend to be stronger than correlations between praise rates and achievement (Brophy, 1981). Brophy suggests, therefore, that eliciting good responses in the first place is more important than praising responses after they occur. To be most effective, praise should be specific and sincere, and linked directly to a specific behavior or performance that the teacher wishes to reinforce (O'Leary and O'Leary, 1977). On the other hand, criticism in the classroom is best prevented or avoided as the frequency of occurrence of criticism has a negative impact on student achievement (Dunkin and Biddle, 1974; Medley, 1979; Rosenshine, 1976; Stallings and Kaskowitz, 1974).

Delivery of Instruction

The effective school and process-product research literature of the 1970s and 1980s has been reviewed by many authorities in an effort to identify the characteristics which distinguish between effective and ineffective teaching (Edmonds, 1979; Medley, 1979; Purkey and Smith, 1983; Hawley and Rosenholtz, 1984).

A number of desirable, *i.e.*, effective, teaching behaviors are related to the teachers' method of delivery of instruction. Rosenshine (1983) has identified 6 "teaching functions" which he believes are essential if effective instruction is to occur. They include: (1) Daily review, checking previous day's work, and reteaching if necessary; (2) Presenting new content skills; (3) Initial student practice; (4) Feedback and correctives (and recycling of instruction if necessary); (5) Independent practice so that students are firm and automatic; and (6) Weekly and monthly reviews (p. 338).

Rosenshine's teaching functions stress monitoring, delivery of instruction, feedback, and corrective activities. An initial reaction on the part of the reader may well be that the list is both "common sense" and commonly found in most classrooms. Unfortunately, research findings do not support this point of view. The available research indicates that basic teaching functions are frequently not part of teachers' instructional formats, not accorded sufficient time or emphasis, or not carried out in an optimal or effective manner. For example, in one study of math instruction classroom observations revealed that only 80 percent of the trained teachers routinely included daily review in their lessons. Of the comparison teachers who had not been trained in effective teaching methods, only 50 percent incorporated review of the previous day's work into daily instructional sessions (Good and Grouws, 1979). Another example is provided by Evertson *et al.*, (1980) who reported that effective math teachers spent 23 minutes per day in lecture, demonstration, and discussion in contrast to ineffective math teachers who spent only eleven minutes per day on these essential activities.

The classroom examples cited above underscore the importance of the essential teaching functions and the amount of time devoted to these critical instructional activities. Stallings (1981), in a study of more effective and less effective teachers, found that the amount of instructional time available was generally the same for all teachers but that student learning was related to how that time was used. Effective teachers used more of the available time for instruction and explanation, reviewing, discussion, drilling, practice, and oral reading. These teachers spent their time actively directing instruction and interacting with their students. The less effective teachers, on the other hand, "provided less instruction, discussion, review, and drill/practice" (Stallings, 1981) In some classes observed, workbook assignments were preeminent and instruction from the teacher was noticeably absent. The distribution of instructional time across activities in the classrooms of effective teachers who helped secondary level students who read between first and fourth grade levels gain up to 2 grade levels in reading in one school year was as follows:

Instruction—giving examples, explanations, linking to student experience:	16%
Review, discussion of seatwork, and story content:	12%
Drill and practice to help memorization:	4%
Oral reading in small groups:	21%
Silent reading:	9%
Written assignments:	4%

In the realm of mathematics, Good and Grouws (1979) have identified key instructional behaviors (and the time allotted to them) related to significant achievement gains among fourth grade students. The progress of the students taught by teachers who had received training in effective instructional techniques was impressive in two respects: (1) the experimental students outperformed the control students; and (2) the experimental students made impressive gains (27 percent to 51 percent) on national norms of math achievement. The key instructional behaviors and daily time elaborations related to math achievement were:

Daily review (8 minutes daily excluding Monday);
Development activities (approximately 20 minutes);
Seatwork (approximately 15 minutes);
Homework (about 15 minutes at home):
Special Reviews, *i.e.*, weekly review for maintenance every
    Monday (approximately 20 minutes); and
Monthly reviews every fourth Monday

The studies of Stallings *et al.* (1981) and Good and Grouws (1979) which identify key instructional activities and provide the distributions of time across instructional activities should prove useful to teachers in assessing their own instructional programs in the basic skills of reading and mathematics.

Zigmond, Sansone, *et al.* (1986) discuss 3 additional aspects of instructional delivery that impact upon instructional effectiveness: clarity, order, and structure. Clarity is the "absence of vagueness, uncertainty, and irrelevant information in presentations." Lack of clarity in instruction interferes with learning and performance (Lana and Smith, 1979). Oder, as an organizing concept for instruction, deals with the sequence of content presentation and the emphasis placed upon key concepts. Teachers need to adopt instructional strategies that will assist students to master content materials. A "rule-example-rule" presentation sequence in which the teacher states the concept, elaborates or provides examples, and restates concepts will help many students. Emphasis and repetition of key concepts throughout a lesson is another helpful strategy. Order strategies have been shown to aid student achievement (Rosenshine, 1976; Smith and Sanders, 1981). Finally Zigmond, Sansone, *et al.* (1986) stress the importance of communicating directions and the intent of the lesson to students at the very beginning of instruction. When lesson structure was shared with some students but not disclosed to others, the students who had knowledge of lesson structure performed better than their uninformed peers (Kallison, 1980).

In summary, interactive teaching occurs when the classroom teacher assumes a central, active, and direct role in the instructional process. The teacher will select the academic activities and lead students through academic tasks in order to accomplish specific instructional objectives. There will be a high, even intense, level of teacher-student interaction, most of which will be initiated by the teacher. Much time will be devoted to lecture, explanation, and demonstrations. Drill, practice, and review of activities will figure prominently in daily lessons as will teacher questioning. The teacher will monitor student progress closely and provide ample feedback, particularly corrective feedback, to the students. The ambiance of the classroom will be comfortable and supportive for students but clearly focused on academic work. The teacher will hold and convey high expectations for student performance. Student engagement will be generally high and students will spend more time in teacher-led than independent seatwork activities.

At this junction it must be stated that interactive teaching is not appropriate for all teaching situations or all students; it "is effective in producing basic skills mastery but does not necessarily generalize to other higher order learning goals" (Hawley and Rosenholtz, 1984). Yet, for the students labeled low achievers, slow learners, disabled, etc., success in basic skills would be a significant accomplishment. Interactive teaching has been shown to be effective with this population of students. Therefore, the specific teaching behaviors (or functions *à la* Rosenshine) that contribute to the interactive teaching style should be part of the instructional repertoire of every teacher who teaches children with academic problems.

Table 5.2. Strategies for Enhancing Student Engagement

Increasing Time-On-Task

Choose tasks at appropriate level of difficulty (Anderson, 1981)

Teach more and test less (Wilson & Wesson, 1986)

Increase teacher questioning (Wilson & Wesson, 1986)

Ensure that all students participate (Wilson & Wesson)

Use signals effectively, to hold and/or direct student attention (Wilson & Wesson, 1986)

Be enthusiastic (Wilson & Wesson, 1986)

Communicate clearly so students know what to do and how to do it (Anderson, 1981)

Maintain a high degree of continuity through behavior settings and learning activities (Anderson, 1981)

Provide feedback to students on attainment of specific tasks (Anderson, 1981)

Correct errors quickly (Anderson, 1981)

Exhibit behaviors such as "with-it-ness", smoothness, momentum, and group alerting (Anderson, 1981)

Reward correct student responses (Wilson & Wesson, 1986)

Use a reinforcing error-correction procedure, i.e., count the number correct instead of the number wrong (Wilson & Wesson, 1986)

Table 5.2. Continued

Increasing Instructional Time

Give concise instructions (Wilson & Wesson, 1986)

Organize seatwork inactivity time (Wilson & Wesson, 1986)
  – activities to do when accepted seatwork is done
  – procedures for getting help which are minimally disruptive and don't
  lead to off-task behavior

Use novel, innovative seatwork activities (Wilson & Wesson, 1986)
  – avoid the "purple plague", i.e. over reliance on ditto worksheets
  – make study corals available for those students who need them

Allocate more time for instruction (Wilson & Wesson, 1986)
  – schedule a second instructional session for academically needy
  students

Manage learning time efficiently (Hawley & Rosenholtz, 1984)
  – begin lessons on time (even if some students are tardy)
  – minimize down time when students have nothing to do or don't know
  what to do
  – delegate organizational/management tasks to noninstructional time
  slots and/or enlist the aid of volunteers, aides, etc.

Plan and organize activities in advance (Halasz, 1984)

Reduce transition time (Wilson & Wesson, 1986)
  – arrange physical space (equipment, supplies, etc.) to minimize
  disruption and enhance a smooth flow of activity.

Maintain student attention and engagement (Hawley & Rosenholtz, 1984)
  – require student attention during instruction
  – monitor students behavior for signs of inattentiveness and off-task
  behavior
  – refocus student attention quickly

Establish and maintain standards for student behavior (Hawley & Rosenholtz,
1984)
  – post classroom rules and procedures
  – set high expectations for student behavior and hold students
  accountable
  – intervene quickly to halt disruption

Maximizing Student Engagement

The importance of student engagement has been discussed at length. The rationale for deliberate efforts to maximize the level of student engagement rests upon a body of research evidence which ties learning time, specifically student engagement, to learning outcomes. The literature contains much relevant information and many suggestions for the practitioner. Lists of strategies and methods for enhancing student engagement—what the teacher can or should do—are readily available. While some authors have focused upon increasing time-on-task (Anderson, 1981), others are focused upon maximizing ALT (Hawley and Rosenholtz, 1984; Wilson and Wesson, 1986). Inspection of the various lists reveals considerable overlap among them. A composite listing of strategies for enhancing student engagement is presented in Table 5.2.

In Summary

The well documented relationship between student engagement and learning outcomes highlights the importance of maintaining student attention and involvement during instruction and argues for the enhancement of engagement of students with learning deficiencies. The handicapped, slow learners, and low achieving students need more learning time; research has shown that these students respond positively to added instructional time. Unfortunately, research findings also reveal that such students often receive less instructional time and that teachers may display a differential pattern of behavior toward low ability, low achieving students which can discourage their engagement and limit their active participation in instructional activities.

Many strategies for enhancing student engagement are discussed in the research literature. The major themes involve interactive teaching and academic focus. In interactive teaching the teacher is dominant in the instructional process. The teacher, not the student, selects learning activities and sets the pace of instruction. The teacher, not teaching aids or teaching machines, delivers primary instruction to the students. Instructional sessions are group based, i.e., whole group or small group, rather than individualized, and entail a high level of questioning, responding, monitoring, and feedback from the teacher. The major portion of instructional time is devoted to academic activities. Time devoted to nonacademic or managerial tasks is kept to a minimum. Overall, the teacher, through her deliberate actions, conveys a strong commitment to academic work and accomplishment for all students. Classrooms run in this manner are characterized by high levels of student involvement and achievement.

Chapter 6

Grouping for Instruction

Every teacher must address the issue of group structure within the classroom. The decisions made about grouping for instruction are important because of their management implications and instructional impact. Group structure within the classroom will impact on academic performance as well as affective and social outcomes. The handicapped, low achieving, or low ability student benefits more from certain group structures than from others. Negative, even harmful effects for such students are associated with particular grouping patterns. In addition, the level of student engagement differs under alternate group structures. Therefore, decisions about how to best group children for instruction, particularly those children who are experiencing academic difficulty, should reflect our knowledge of engagement patterns and how to make the best use of instructional time.

On the surface, the most obvious options for grouping involve numbers and ability levels. The former involves whole group, small group, or individual instruction. The latter responds to the heterogeneity in ability levels among students by designating smaller, more homogeneous instructional groups. Another option for grouping, perhaps less obvious than those based upon numbers and ability levels, involves the interactive patterns among students; the options here are competitive, cooperative, and individualistic learning.

As we continue to explore the topic of grouping for instruction, discussion will focus on grouping for size, *i.e.*, the numbers of students in the instructional group, and grouping to achieve desirable student to student interaction. The topic of ability grouping, *i.e.*, tracking as a district imposed policy, will not be discussed in any great detail. Adequate treatment of this vast and complex topic goes far beyond the scope of this text, has been extensively discussed and reviewed in numerous publications and textbooks, and would needlessly divert attention from our primary foci of time usage and instructional processes for problem learners at the classroom level. Suffice it to say that ability grouping has not been found to be of benefit for the low ability, low achieving student (Espisito, 1973; Good and Brophy, 1987; Hawley and Rosenholtz, 1984; Leinhardt and Palley, 1982; Rosenbaum, 1980). Overall, the results of research on ability grouping have been weak and mixed (Slavin, cited in Good and Brophy, 1987). A study by Kulik and Kulik (1982) which did report a positive impact on achievement as a result of homogeneous grouping at the secondary school level is inconsistent with the general trend of research findings. Despite the positive findings, however, even this study found no positive achievement effect for low achieving students. Consequently these results further confirm the general finding of a negative impact of ability grouping for the slow or low achieving student. Other criticisms, in addition to the lack of positive achievement gains, have been leveled at ability grouping. These include undesirable peer structures, low teacher expectations, permanency of low track placements, inadequate instruction for low achievers, and a fundamental, ethical conflict between ability grouping and national commitments to desegregation in order to achieve racial diversity and mainstreaming so as to achieve maximum integration of the handicapped in our public schools (Good and Brophy, 1987). It is clear that a tracking system based upon student ability is a grouping option which is not in the best interests of the low functioning, low ability students or the special education students who are drawn from this very student population.

Whole Group versus Small Group Instruction

From a management perspective, whole group instruction is less complex and less demanding than small group instruction. In whole group instruction, all students in the class are taught the same material at the same time. During follow-up seatwork or practice activities, the teacher is free to circulate among the students supervising, monitoring, and providing individual assistance. However, the variance in student ability and readiness for instruction in the "typical" class may make it impossible or impractical to teach effectively within a whole group structure. Student characteristics and/or the subject matter itself may indicate a need for small group instruction. For example, Brophy and Good (1984) point out that beginning reading which requires intensity of instruction and monitoring, attention to pacing, and individual oral reading demands small instructional groups within highly heterogeneous classes. Small instructional groups allow the teacher to reduce the degree of variance in skill and functional levels, and intensify and individualize instruction within the small group setting. But small group instruction is more difficult to manage. The teacher must divide her time and attention across the groups and prepare multiple lessons and activities for independent seatwork. The class must be organized and the children trained for independent seatwork, often without direct adult supervision or assistance. Maintaining engagement during independent seatwork is an immediate management concern as engagement rates drop during seatwork activities. Multi-group and small group instruction also increase the number of transitions which must be managed effectively. Ineffective management of transitions can result in increased down time, loss of student attention, and increased student misbehavior and disruption. Brophy and Good (1984) accurately and succinctly describe the dilemma facing the teacher when they state that whole group versus small group instruction ultimately involves a trade-off between instructional and managerial needs.

If a teacher decides to create small instructional groupings based upon student ability, she should bear in mind the negative aspects of ability grouping in general and strive to avoid or minimize them within the small group structure. Small group instruction need not be based upon ability differences, but when it is, care must be taken to avoid the negative consequences identified in research on district-wide or school-wide tracking systems. Good and Brophy (1987) offer some suggestions to help teachers avoid the undesirable effects of ability based instructional grouping.

1.	Group composition should reflect achievement level and instructional need, not an arbitrary division of children into equal sized groups. Groups should be relatively homogeneous; "equal numbers" across groups should raise questions.
2.	Grouping should enable the teacher to meet individual needs more effectively, and not merely alter the pace of instruction across the student groups.
3.	Student assignments to particular instructional groups should be flexible, reviewed regularly, and altered in response to student needs.
4.	Group scheduling and instructional practices should be flexible. There is no need for all groups to receive equal instructional time.
5.	Group membership should not carry over into other school activities and experiences, e.g., the composition of instructional reading groups should not automatically be repeated for math instruction.
6.	Low achievers should receive much needed extra instruction, e.g., fewer students in the lower level functioning group, and more time scheduled for instruction for the low functioning group.

Managing Seatwork

The success of small group instruction depends nearly as much on what is going on outside of the instructional group as that which is on-going within the group, namely, seatwork or other independent activities for the students working without direct teacher supervision. The flip side of small group instruction entails appropriate activities for the other students—those not being instructed by the teacher, or those otherwise meaningfully occupied. Descriptive research on patterns of time usage, discussed at length in chapter 3, clearly documents the considerable amount of time, indeed, the greater portion of instructional time, that students spend in independent activities. The research also documents a definite decline in the level of engagement under independent activities as compared to teacher-led activities. One recent study probed more deeply into the issue of independent seatwork. Anderson, Brubaker, Alleman-Brooks, and Duffy (1985) attempted to find out what students actually do during seatwork activities. Data were gathered on 32 first graders during the time allocated for reading instruction. Seatwork activities accounted for 30 percent to 60 percent of all the time allocated for reading instruction. On average, during 50 percent of the time students worked with commercial materials, *e.g.*, workbooks, dittos, reading books, etc. The format of seatwork assignments tended to be repetitive from one day to the next. Teacher interactions or instructions to students doing seatwork seldom dealt with what was to be learned or the relevance of the activity to previously learned material; rather, teacher-student interactions dealt with the monitoring of behavior, not the understanding of the assignment.

The Anderson *et al.* (1985) study provides invaluable insight into the nature of seatwork in the regular education classroom. Parallel research in special education (and further research in both regular and special education) needs to be done. In light of the portion of instructional time that students devote to seatwork activities and the contribution of seatwork to effective small group instruction, there is a pressing need for the development of strategies to maximize the effectiveness of such classroom activities. Teachers need to be concerned about the effectiveness of seatwork activities in terms of both the use of instructional time and the attainment of instructional objectives.

Small Group Instruction

Special education class enrollments are usually lower than those found in regular education. But the actual number of students whom the special education teacher will instruct varies according to the service delivery options within the continuum of special education services, *e.g.*, self-contained classroom, resource room, etc., and the regulations for program operation imposed by the individual states. Age and severity of handicap are factors which tend to limit teacher case loads; program guidelines for the younger, more severely or multiply impaired generally stipulate lower teacher-student ratios than those for the mildly handicapped. In many instances, the heterogeneity in special education classes for the mildly handicapped will preclude whole group instruction in the basic skill subjects. The realistic choices for the special education teacher, therefore, are small group or individual instruction.

The logistics and mechanics of small group instruction have received far more attention in regular education than special education where individualization is greatly valued. The special education emphasis on individualization tends to divert attention away from group processes. At the same time, recent trends in special education toward noncategorical and mixed categorical classes call for the group instruction of students with dissimilar labels but similar instructional needs (Hallahan and Kauffman, 1977). Group instruction has an important role in special education as well as regular education, though the topic of instructional processes within a group context has received scant attention from special educators. And small group instruction, albeit with very small numbers, may be much more common in special education than suspected. Group based instruction need not inhibit individualization. Insight into instructional processes and in particular instructional variables which contribute to the effectiveness of small group instruction is important for all teachers.

A study of small group instruction in reading by Anderson, Evertson, and Brophy (1979) provides information that is relevant for all teachers who conduct small group instruction in basic skills. The study attempted to assess the effectiveness of a set of principles for small group instruction in reading. The authors view the principles as a model of reading instruction; they describe the model and the rationale for its implementation as follows:

> The model was presented to the first grade teachers as a set of guidelines for teacher management of reading group instruction. The model was curricular free. It did not focus on the content or the materials used in teaching reading, but only on teachers' behaviors involved in managing the group as a whole or managing responses of individual students. The major rationale for the model was that it made it possible for the child to receive as much individual attention as possible in the group setting. A major objective of the model was to help teachers achieve an ideal balance between attention to the group and attention to individuals (Anderson, Evertson, and Brophy, 1979, p. 195).

The set of instructional principles (22 in all) were shared with a group of first grade teachers at the beginning of the school year. Results from beginning and end of year testing revealed that students in the experimental classes significantly outperformed students in the control classes on tests of reading achievement. Classroom observational data indicated behavioral differences between the experimental and control teachers consistent with the instructional model. Classroom observational data was also analyzed for evidence of specific teaching behaviors consistent with the instructional principles. The authors found that many, though not all, of the instructional principles were implemented. Those that were utilized "suggested individual opportunities for practice, minimal choral responses, ordered turns, sustaining feedback and moderate use of praise" (Anderson, Evertson, and Brophy, 1979, p. 220). These were the principles that were most clearly related to achievement. The results of the study which further substantiate the fact that teaching behavior and student performance are related should be an inducement for further research and for the practitioner to seriously consider the potential benefits of small group instruction.

The findings of the 1979 study were the basis for revision of the 22 instructional principles (Anderson, Evertson, and Brophy, 1982). Six general principles for small group instruction in reading were highlighted; they are presented in Table 6.1. The extended list of instructional principles for small group instruction is presented in Appendix 6-A. Anderson and his colleagues suggest that these principles, with some modifications, could be applied to other subject areas. The principles do, in fact, reiterate generic instructional themes discussed earlier: active student involvement, brisk pacing, monitoring and feedback, attention to individual needs, etc. The instructional principles, both the short and expanded listing, can assist the teacher in carrying out more effective small group instruction. Many of the points may be common practice while others may help to add 1 or 2 new skills to the teacher's repertoire. The principles do underscore the need for teachers to reflect upon the mechanics and nuances of small group instruction and the importance of conducting small group instruction in the most efficacious manner possible.

Table 6.1. Anderson, Evertson, and Brophy's (1982) Revised Principles for
Small-Group Instruction in Beginning Reading

1. Reading groups should be organized to for efficient, sustained focus on content.

Table 6.1. (Continued)
Anderson, Evertson, and Brophy's (1982) Revised Principles for Small-Group
Instruction in Beginning Reading

2. All students should be not merely attentive but actively involved in
    the lesson.

3. The difficulty level of questions and tasks should be easy enough to
    allow the lesson to move along at a brisk pace and the students to
    experience consistent success.

4. Students should receive frequent opportunities to read and respond
    to questions, and should get clear feedback about the correctness of
    their performance.

5. Skills should be mastered to overlearning, with new ones gradually
    phased in while old ones are being mastered.

6. Although instruction takes place in the group setting, each individual
    should be monitored and provided with whatever instruction, feed-
    back, or opportunities to practice what he or she requires.

Individualization within Small Group Instruction

Small group instruction is undertaken in response to excessive
group heterogeneity; it is a means to reduce the student numbers and
the degree of variance within instructional groups to more manage-
able proportions. But even within relatively small groups, students
will vary in their level of understanding and rate of progress; attention
to individual needs will still be required.

Individualization and student participation can be addressed
during group lessons. Anderson *et al.* (1979) suggest that a strategy of
ordered turns—that is, calling upon all students within the group in
sequence rather than selecting from among volunteers—enables the
teacher to ensure equal and generally more frequent opportunities to
respond for all members of the group. Ordered turns was one of the
instructional principles in Anderson's *et al.* (1979) study of small group
instruction in reading which yielded a positive relationship to reading
achievement. Every student response gives the teacher an opportunity
to gauge the individual student's mastery or nonmastery of the skill or
concept being taught and an opportunity to provide appropriate feedback. Anderson *et al.* (1979) point out that the teacher's feedback
response following a student's response can either terminate or prolong the interaction. Terminal feedback, that is, a brief acknowledg-
ment and indication as to whether the response was right or wrong,

will end the interaction, allowing the teacher to turn her attention to the next question and to another child. If an initial answer is found wanting the teacher may wait for the child to offer another response, or may try to draw out additional information or a better quality answer form the student through further questioning; this type of feedback is called sustaining feedback. When the teacher explains to the students how to arrive at the answer and waits for a second response, process feedback has occurred. Both process and sustaining feedback will prolong the interaction between the teacher and student and may also slow the pace of the lesson. Terminal feedback will keep up the pace of the lesson; sustaining and process feedback will help to improve the quality of responses from individual students. If the teacher is sensitive to the different types of feedback and the effect on the pacing of group lessons, the teacher will be in a better position to control lesson pacing according to the overall objectives of the lessons, as well as individual student skills and capabilities.

Small group instruction is a complex undertaking that poses many managerial and instructional demands for the teacher. The very brief discussion of ordered turns and feedback response underscores the complexity of small group instruction. It must also be stressed that small group instruction does not negate individualization of instruction. Additional strategies for enhancing attention to individual student needs include the following: (1) group instruction supplemented with extra instruction for individuals; (2) group instruction followed by differentiated seatwork assignments; (3) engagement of peer tutors and use of cooperative learning strategies to increase academic guidance and assistance for individual students; (4) differentiation of patterns of teacher-student interactions, *e.g.*, type of feedback provided after a student response that avoids falling into a pattern which communicates low expectations for particular students; (5) employment of technology aides, *e.g.*, computer assisted instruction mindful that low functioning, low ability students benefit more from direct and active instructional interaction with the teacher, and that mechanical devices or technical devices should supplement, not supplant, direct instruction; and (6) employment of curricular programs which emphasize and provide for individualization within group instruction, *e.g.*, *New Primary Grades Reading Program* (Glasser, 1977) and ALEM (Adaptive Learning Environments Model) (Wang, Gennari, and Waxman 1985). The potential benefits of small group instruction should be an inducement for special education teachers to seriously and thoughtfully consider the possibility of shifting the balance in instruction from individual to small group structures as one means of enhancing instructional effectiveness.

Individualization in Special Education

Meeting the needs of the individual student is the corner stone of special education philosophy and practice. According to Reynolds and Birch (1977, p. 107),

> Individualized or personalized instruction places the emphasis of the instructional process on each individual pupil's skills, interests, abilities, learning styles, motivation, goals, rate of learning, self discipline, problem solving ability, and prognosis for moving ahead in various skill and content aspects of curriculum. To put instruction on that basis is a tall order, to be sure. Yet pupils can differ on all of those dimensions and more.

Whether or not special educators can fully meet the challenge contained in these words remains to be seen, but there is no doubt that we are committed to try. As the quotation implies, special educators proceed on a one-by-one basis with every child. The commitment to individualized instruction is reaffirmed in the *Education of All Handicapped Children Act* (PL94-142) in the form of the *Individual Education Program* (IEP). An IEP, developed jointly by the school and family, must be prepared for each child and contain 6 required components: (1) the present educational levels; (2) annual goals, including short-term objectives; (3) special or related services, if needed; (4) programs to be followed; (5) date of program initiation and expected duration; and (6) evaluation procedures. The IEP specifies the type and level of special education service to be provided, the degree of access to regular education and nonhandicapped peers, and the specific direction and content of the instructional program. But to understand how individualization is achieved in the classroom one must look beyond the IEP document, especially for the mildly handicapped student.

Individualized instruction in special education meets the needs of individual students by accommodating, adjusting, or modifying instruction. Any and all aspects of the individual student's program, *e.g.*, materials, methods of instruction, setting, grading and testing practices, etc., may be modified. Accommodations are made because the student is experiencing academic and/or behavioral difficulties and, without accommodations, is likely to fail in her academic endeavors. Special education students need more, not less, teacher attention and support—at least for a time. It is on this point that the concept of individualization for regular and special education diverge. The distinction is an important one.

Good and Brophy (1987) hold that individualized instruction adheres to 3 general formats: (1) same content and methods but the student proceeds at her own pace; (2) different materials or methods but the required demonstration of mastery is not altered; and (3) demonstration of mastery in different ways. "Thus individualized instruction implies some degree of planned differentiation in the treatment of students in the same class" (Good and Brophy, 1987, p. 360). The three formats for individualized instruction allow considerable instructional flexibility. Option 1 is common in regular education and enables the more able student to progress at a faster pace than her less able peers. In regular education individualization often addresses the needs of the able or sophisticated student. In special education adjustments in the pace of instruction frequently involve a "slowing down" of instruction for students who are having trouble "keeping up" with their peers. In special education, the emphasis in individualized instruction is matching instruction to individual learning characteristics. Two important avenues to individualization in special education involve the search for aptitude treatment interactions and diagnostic prescriptive teaching.

Aptitude-Treatment Interactions

"Aptitude-treatment interaction refers to an educational phenomenon in which students who are dissimilar with regard to a particular aptitude perform differently under alternate instructional conditions" (Goodman, 1987, p. 117). The definition of aptitude treatment interaction formalizes the widely held belief that children learn differently, and implies the desirability of adapting instruction to meet individual student learning differences and instructional needs. The aptitude treatment interaction (ATI) paradigm separates children into instructional groups based upon measurement of a designated aptitude or characteristic, *e.g.*, auditory learners and visual learners, and provides differential instructional treatment in keeping with the measured aptitude. Students and methods are matched, *e.g.*, visual learners would receive reading instruction through a visual reading method and the auditory learners would receive reading instruction through an auditory reading method which emphasizes the auditory modality.

In accordance with the ATI model one would expect visual learners to do better under the visual reading method and the auditory learners do better with the auditory reading method. Such findings would support the ATI paradigm and the concept of individualized instruction embodied within it. If, however, the results indicated that one treatment was superior for both groups of students, then the results would be not supportive of the ATI model. Figure 6.2 depicts the three possible outcomes of ATI research. The hypothetical data in

Example A indicates that an ATI has occurred. Two groups of students who differ on a particular aptitude, one group being high and one group being low, performed differently under alternate treatments. Students with low aptitude performed better under treatment 1. Students with high aptitude performed better under treatment 2.

Figure 6.2. Aptitude Treatment Interaction Research Outcomes

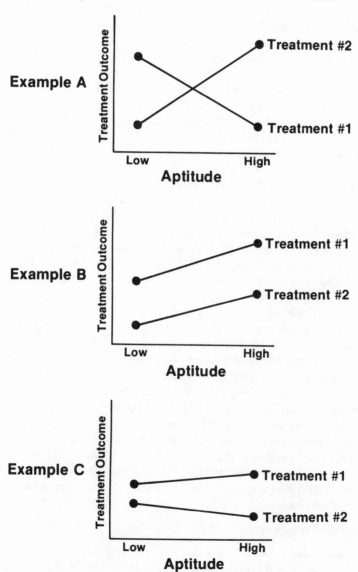

The hypothetical data in Examples B and C do not provide support for an ATI model. In both instances students performed better under treatment 1; the data do not support the use of differential treatments for these students. Rather, the data suggest the use of treatment 1 for all students or exploration of some other treatment.

The data cited above are hypothetical and used only for the purpose of illustration. What is the outcome of actual research endeavors? By and large research findings on aptitude treatment interactions have been disappointing. Bracht (1970) reviewed 90 ATI studies and found only 5 which offered supportive evidence of ATI effects. Ysseldyke (1973) reviewed and discussed 5 ATI students in which all of the subjects were handicapped students. In each study, instruction was matched to modality preference. No significant interactions between modality preference and reading method were found. In yet another review of modality based instruction, Arter and Jenkins (1977) reviewed 14 different studies and found only one (Bursuk, 1971) which reported a significant modality by instruction interaction. Reviews of modality based instruction continue to appear in the professional literature (Kavale and Forness, 1987), but the empirical picture has not changed. Aptitude treatment interaction research in the field of special education has primarily been concerned with the investigation of modality based instruction—with little positive results. ATI research has been attempted in other academic areas such as math (Holton, 1982) and reading (Blanton, 1971), and the aptitude dimension has involved a variety of learner characteristics including personality traits, anxiety, cognitive style, etc. (Lloyd, 1984), with equally disappointing results.

The ATI paradigm has a strong attraction for all educators, particularaly so for special educators who harbor a very strong commitment to individualized instruction and the quest for teaching adaptations to help handicapped learners. But based upon the results to date and increased understanding of the underlying complexity of the ATI phenomenon, Snow (1977) cautions educators that general theories of instruction are unlikely to evolve from ATI investigations, e.g., modality based reading instruction. ATI interactions are subtle, complex, content, and group specific and the effect, if it occurs at all, is not likely to generalize across students or instructional settings. ATI research is unlikely to lead to the discovery of "blanket treatments" (Snow, 1984). Therefore, despite its appeal, ATI investigations have not been, nor are they likely to be, fruitful avenues for instructional development.

Diagnostic-Prescriptive Teaching

Many definitions of diagnostic-prescriptive teaching can be found in the literature; the one put forth by Ysseldyke and Salvia

(1974) will be useful for furthering our discussion and understanding of individualized instruction. They define diagnostic-prescriptive teaching as "an attempt to identify the most effective instructional strategies for children who differ on any number of variables believed to be related to academic learning" (p. 181). They go on to say that diagnostic-prescriptive teaching includes: (1) identification of children who are experiencing learning difficulties; (2) diagnostic delineation of learner strengths and weaknesses; and (3) prescriptive intervention (specification of goals, methods, strategies, materials, etc.)

Ysseldyke and Salvia (1974) and Ewing and Brecht (1977) discuss diagnostic-prescriptive in terms of two theoretical models of instruction: (1) the ability training model; and (2) the task analysis model. According to Ewing and Brecht the ability training model "stresses the diagnosis of specific hypothetical constructs presumably related to the learning processes and the training of specific abilities in an effort to improve academic achievement" (p. 325). In contrast, the task analysis model "stresses assessment of academic skill development and prescribes instruction based on learners' observed behaviors in a hierarchial sequence of skill development" (p. 324).

It would appear that diagnostic prescriptive teaching could follow one of two paths: diagnosis of underlying process disabilities, e.g., visual perceptual skills, or diagnosis of specific skill or curricular deficits, e.g., decoding skills, math computation, time concepts, and then consequently provide the appropriate remediation. In the decade of the 1970s the dichotomization of instructional orientations among special educators into two theoretical models was, roughly speaking, an appropriate characterization of much of special education practice for the mildly handicapped. "Since the early 1970s, diagnostic-prescriptive teaching has taken on a meaning broader than the two theoretical models" (Timmermans, 1987, p. 509). Today many educators espouse a broader ecological perspective as well as integrative models which look at many aspects of the child's functioning—e.g., motivational, neurological, cognitive, cognitive academic, etc.—as well as the multiple environments in which the child lives and performs in order to help understand the nature of a child's disability and how to intervene most beneficially.

The approach one takes to diagnostic-prescriptive teaching will undoubtedly be influenced by one's experience, educational background, philosophical, and theoretical orientation. If one believes that the remediation of academic disabilities lies in correcting dysfunctional processes within the child, then the ability training model may be the method chosen. But the reader should remember that the ability training model is founded on the concept of aptitude treatment interactions and the quest for data to support the ATI effect has been illusive, in both regular and special education. If ATI can not be produced by researchers who set out to do so, what is the probability of ATI effects occurring in the far less controlled environment of the regular or special education classroom? On the other hand, if one believes that the appropriate approach to remediation of academic problems is to address academic, behavioral, or social skills deficits directly, then the task analytic model will be the method of choice.

Criticism of diagnostic-prescriptive teaching is strongest when the diagnostic-prescriptive teaching is associated with ability training (Arter and Jenkins, 1979; Ewing and Brecht, 1977). It might be beneficial to divorce the diagnostic process from both the task analysis and ability training models. This author and others (Deno, 1986) see no inherent distinction between the diagnostic process when applied to underlying processes or to curricular deficits. The diagnostic process (like the scientific method) is inherently neutral and is not irrevocably committed to either the task analysis model or the ability training model. Rather, educators are responding differently to the essential question, "What do we teach?" Proponents of ability training respond that underlying processes should be remediated. Proponents of the task analysis model respond that specific functional skill deficits should be the object of intervention and remediation. The process, as described by Ysseldyke and Salvia (1974), is the same. Of course, problems may arise regardless of one's orientation to intervention if the diagnostic process is not conducted with due care for the use of technically adequate tests and appropriate testing procedures, nonbiased decision-making, access to appropriate program and service options, etc.

A positive development regarding diagnostic-prescriptive teaching involves the expansion and refinement of the rather restricted diagnostic-prescriptive process as set forth by Ysseldyke and Salvia (1974) into the far-ranging and detailed assessment for instruction process. Zigmond, Vallecorsa, and Silverman (1983) discuss assessment for instructional planning in terms of a 12 step process leading from the initial decision of what to assess through assessment, planning, and implementation of intervention. In their detailed exposition of the 12 step assessment process, Zigmond and her colleagues have updated, refined and expanded diagnostic-prescriptive teaching, much to our benefit.

Diagnostic-prescriptive teaching based upon the knowledge base available to us may lack adequate empirical support. However, we need to distinguish between the diagnostic-prescriptive teaching process and the difficulties which stem from the application of the process, e.g., diagnostic focus, selection and use of test instruments, use of invalidated intervention techniques lacking in demonstrable relevance to academic growth, etc. As to ATI research, the lack of evidence of ATI interactions is an obstacle for those who would cling to modality-based instruction. Lloyd (1984), in the following quotation, encapsulates the current state of the art of diagnostic-prescriptive teaching and individualization:

At this time, our understanding of the characteristics of most special education students does not allow us to prescribe different methods of instruction for them. We do not know that certain kinds of programs are better for pupils labeled LD, ED, and MR, while other kinds of programs are better for nonhandicapped pupils. Further, we do not know that certain special education students benefit from one type of instruction while other special education students benefit from another type. In the future, we may discover that some characteristics of special education pupils (perhaps prior achievement and attributional style) can effectively guide our selection of instructional programs. At present, we can individualize instruction on the basis of the skills students need to be taught, and we can provide them the kind of instruction—structured, programmed presentations requiring frequent responding and rich in corrective feedback and reinforcement—that we can be reasonably sure is more effective than other methods (p. 14).

One-to-One Instruction

For many teachers, one-to-one instruction represents the ideal instructional group for handicapped learners. Upon closer inspection, however, the ideal may prove to be flawed. From the perspective of learning time and student engagement, one-to-one instruction in the classroom may be contraindicated.

In the classroom where one-to-one instruction prevails, the amount of teacher directed instruction received by each student will be very limited. Zigmond (1984, cited within Zigmond, Sansone, Miller, Donahoe, and Kohnke, 1986) determined that in secondary learning disabled resource rooms organized for one-to-one instruction, individual students received only 5 minutes of teacher-led instruction during each 45 minute class period. The remaining time was spent in independent seatwork activities. A student scheduled into the resource room 3 periods per week would receive a total of only 15 minutes of teacher led instruction per week! Zigmond recounts the experience of one high school special education teacher who reoriented her class to emphasize group rather than one-to-one instruction and by doing so was able to increase teacher directed instruction from 9 to 42 percent of student learning time. As to individual needs, the teacher felt confident that she could address individual needs during the practice portion of each lesson (cited in Zigmond, Sansone, Miller, Donahoe, and Kohnke, 1986).

Individualization which translates into students working or being instructed alone, *i.e.*, one-to-one, needs to be reconsidered in light of our knowledge about engagement levels under teacher-led instruction and independent seatwork conditions. A high level of one-to-one instruction generally entails a correspondingly high level of unsupervised seatwork. Teachers of the learning disabled (and presumably teachers of all mildly handicapped students) have a strong commitment to one-to-one instruction as the way to meet individual needs (Zigmond, Sansone, *et al.*, 1986). However, individualization as achieved through one-to-one instruction in reality provides handicapped learners far less instruction than they need and may represent an inefficient use of instructional time.

Cooperative Learning

An alternative to small groups based upon the number of students or student ability is a grouping structure deliberately intended to foster desirable patterns of student-student interaction. The type of student-student interaction which prevails in the classroom is undeniably related to student performance and the effects can be seen in measures of academic gains, and social and affective development.

Cooperative learning, a widely researched and applied approach to small group instruction, has received a great deal of attention from both researchers and practitioners, regular educators and, increasingly, from special educators as well. Cooperative learning is defined by the nature of the task structure and reward contingencies that operate within the small group structure (Stallings and Stipek, 1984). Task structure is the degree to which students interact with each other on learning tasks. Reward contingency is the degree to which the grade or reward for the work completed is based upon a total group effort. The combination of these two elements are reflected in Slavin's (1980) definition of cooperative learning: "the term refers to classroom techniques in which students work on learning activities in small groups and receive rewards or recognition based on their group performance" (p. 315).

Cooperative learning is seen as 1 of 3 alternatives for student-student interaction in the classroom; the other alternatives are competitive and individualistic learning. Johnson and Johnson (1987) have discussed the 3 interactive options in terms of the "goal structure" which each fosters among students. A goal structure is "the type of interdependence among students as they strive to accomplish their learning goals" (Johnson and Johnson, 1987, p. 3). The 3 goal structures which correspond to competitive, cooperative, and individualistic learning are described by Johnson and Johnson as follow:

1. Competitive goal structure: "students work against each other to achieve a goal that only one or a few students can attain" (p. 4). Student performance is assessed within a normative framework—one student achieves to the extent that other students fail. There are winners and losers as "negative interdependence" among students toward goal achievement prevails.

2. Individualistic goal structure: "students work by themselves to accomplish learning goals unrelated to those of other students" (p. 4). Student performance is generally gauged against a preset performance criterion; one student's performance has no impact on another.

3. Cooperative goal structure: "students work together to accomplish shared goals" (p. 6). Small heterogeneous groups of students work toward shared goals; achievement interdependence is a key to group success as all students must reach their goals in order for the total group to succeed. Criterion referenced evaluation is applied.

At the present time, competitive and individualistic learning dominate American classrooms; as much as 85 to 95 percent of classroom learning time passes under one or the other of these 2 instructional modes (Johnson and Johnson, 1987). Many researchers are advocating for a major shift in the status quo from competition and individualistic learning to cooperative learning. Johnson and Johnson (1987) recommend that cooperative learning activities take up 60 to 70 percent of instructional time with the remainder given over to individualistic and competitive activities. And Slavin (1980) sees cooperative learning as the desirable "dominant instructional mode" (p. 338) for American classrooms, a recommendation which he bases upon a firm foundation of empirical evidence and practical experience.

Moving beyond the questions of "why" to the issue of "how" to implement cooperative learning, we find that different authorities describe the instructional phenomenon in somewhat different ways. Slavin (1980) indicates that the essential elements of cooperative learning are task structure (the mix of activities that make up the school day), reward structure (how group performance is recognized and graded), and authority structure (the control that students exercise over their own learning). Cooperative learning involves changes in all 3 of the above. The major change must occur in task structure (competitive to cooperative); changes in reward and authority structure necessarily follow. Johnson and Johnson (1987) list 4 essential elements of cooperative learning: (1) positive interdependence (cooperation among student to achieve group goals); (2) face to face interaction among students; (3) individual accountability; and (4) interpersonal and small group skills. Slavin's, as well as Johnson and Johnson's perspectives on cooperative learning are different but not necessarily in conflict; the two approaches to cooperative learning have much in common. For example, Slavin's reference to reward structure and Johnson and Johnson's reference to positive interdependence address the same essential component, *i.e.*, the orchestrated cooperation among students necessary for the total group to reach its goal.

Sharan (1980) has categorized different approaches to cooperative learning including those of Slavin's and Johnson and Johnson's under the headings "peer-tutoring methods" and "group inquiry methods." He describes peer-tutoring methods as those which create interdependence among students by dividing a learning task among students within the group and structuring peer interaction within teams. Individuals within the group are held accountable for individual performance as well as the total group effort. Task completion demands mutual cooperation and team to team competition is an incentive to motivation. Sharan believes that this approach to cooperative group structure is well suited to basic skills acquisition as it provides the motivation needed for the drill and review activities needed to reach mastery on low level cognitive information and skills. In contrast, cooperative learning based upon group inquiry methods emphasizes data gathering, differentiated role assignments, and synthesis of individual contributions into a group project. Learning tasks are relatively complex involving high level cognitive processes. Individual accountability is achieved through role differentiation and individualized assignments. Evaluation of the group's effort is the culmination of the total cooperative undertaking.

Sharan (1980) believes the peer tutoring and group inquiry approaches to cooperative learning are complimentary methods that focus upon different aspects of classroom learning. He believes that different methods of cooperative learning "can be employed to activate different group processes and to achieve different goals" (p. 265). The teacher interested in pursuing cooperative learning with her students needs to appreciate the underlying methodological differences so that the method selected is the one that is suited to the nature of the learning tasks and the desired learning outcomes. The choice among different cooperative learning methods will also be influenced by the students' readiness for cooperative learning experiences and the degree of managerial complexity associated with different approaches. Group inquiry methods are decidedly more demanding of the teacher (Sharan, 1980; Schniedewind and Salend, 1987) in terms of prior training and on-going management. Group inquiry methods entail far greater adaptation of the on-going program of instruction and place greater demands upon the students for effective group process skills. For these reasons teachers, in particular special education teachers, are advised to introduce cooperative learning through the peer tutoring approach and to move on to the group inquiry approach after the students have had some experience with cooperative learning—good advice for any classroom teacher (Schniedewind and Salend, 1987).

Some different methods of cooperative learning will be briefly described. The various methods will be subsumed under Sharan's categories of group inquiry and peer tutoring methods.

TGT. Teams-Games-Tournaments is a peer tutoring approach to cooperative learning. It is intended to be a supplement to on-going instruction. TGT involves the creation of teams containing 4 or 5 student members. The teams are heterogeneous as to ability, age, sex, and other relevant characteristics. If the class group includes handicapped students they should be represented on all teams as well. Once or twice a week tournaments are held to test students' knowledge and mastery of specific academic material. Within teams, members help one another prepare for the tournaments; the entire team must be prepared. At the tournaments each team member is assigned to a tournament table with a mix of students from other teams but comprised of students of generally equal ability. Within the teams faster and slower students can take the roles of tutor and tutee respectively, thus facilitating students' helping one another. But the equal ability tournament groups gives every student the opportunity to contribute to a high or maximum score to their team score (Stallings and Stipek, 1984). Heterogeneous teams and homogeneous tournament groups could facilitate the involvement of mildly handicapped, mainstreamed students in cooperative learning activities (Slavin and Madden, 1983).

STAD. Student Teams and Achievement Divisions is similar to the TGT method just described. The major difference is that the teams prepare members for twice weekly quizzes rather than end of week tournaments (Stallings and Stipek, 1984). Team scores are derived from quiz scores. In addition to heterogeneous teams, students are organized into divisions which are roughly homogeneous. High scores within any division, regardless of the relative ability or achievement level of the division, earn the highest scores. "Thus, rewards are contingent upon performance within a group of children performing at about the same level, rather than upon children performing in a classroom of students achieving at very different levels" (Stallings and Stipek, 1984, p. 748). Each child's score takes into account his or her score on the last quiz. The student can also earn points for individual improvement. The scoring system is designed to motivate all students toward a maximal effort.

TAI. Team Assisted Individualization combines cooperative learning and individually programmed instruction; this method of cooperative learning has been used to great advantage in mathematics instruction (Slavin, Leavey, and Madden, 1984). As in the other peer tutoring cooperative learning methods, heterogeneous teams of 4 to 5 students are formed. Diagnostic pretests are administered to identify the students' performance levels in the subject matter to be taught; students then work on individualized curricular materials while helping and encouraging one another. The heterogeneous composition of the team makes it likely that assistance can be found among one's team members. A system for in-team monitoring of progress and mastery is created so that each student's work is checked at three points: team partners exchange papers; a checkout test is administered and scored by a teammate; and a final test is administered and scored by a designated "monitor" from another team. Each week team scores are determined by "the sum of the average number correct of all final tests taken by all team members (the accuracy score) and the average number of units covered by each team member times 10 (the progress score)" (Slavin, Leavey, and Madden, 1984, p. 413).

The individualized assignments based upon diagnostic testing has instructional possibilities for handicapped learners and low achieving students. But, as discussed earlier, individualization in regular education requires a degree of independence and self management which may be beyond the ability of many students in special education classes. For the handicapped and low achieving student more, not less, teacher directed and managed instruction is indicated. The peer tutoring component makes cooperative learning a viable strategy for increasing individualization and student support in the classroom. Cooperative learning and peer tutoring are complimentary strategies with much potential for the special education classroom. Peer tutoring is discussed at length in chapter 8.

JIGSAW. Jigsaw is a cooperative learning strategy first described by Aronson (1978). In jigsaw students are assigned to small heterogeneous groups as in TGT and STAD. Group interdependence is created by dividing the academic materials or tasks into as many parts as there are team members. Each team member gets his piece or share and must master his own portion of the overall assignment and teach or share it with the other members of the team. Team members are quizzed and individual scores given. Within jigsaw as originally set forth by Aronson (1978) there are no team scores. The jigsaw technique has been widely adopted and references to it are plentiful in the professional literature.

JIGSAW II. Jigsaw II is a variant of Aronson's Jigsaw developed by Slavin (1980). The team structure, task interdependence, and end of week quizzes are the same. However, Slavin (1980) added team scoring by aggregating individual quiz scores into team scores. Thus reward interdependence, i.e., group score dependent upon the individual scores of all team members, was added to the original jigsaw format.

Johnson and Johnson Cooperative Learning. Cooperative learning as described by Johnson and Johnson (1987) involves students in an activity over a relatively long period of time working toward the attainment of group goals. Group cooperation is essential as all succeed together or none succeed at all. Johnson and Johnson believe that any manner of instructional task can be assigned to the cooperative group; the more complex or conceptual the task, the more appropriate group inquiry methods are over peer tutoring methods of cooperative learning. Within the Johnson and Johnson cooperative learning approach the teacher fills a vital role, which involves 5 major functions:

1. To clearly specify the objectives of the lesson, and the academic and collaborative skills. The former involves the assignment of tasks appropriate to the students' abilities and instructional needs; the latter involves the inculcation of the specific collaborative skills that will be important to the group's activity and eventual successful completion of its assigned task.
2. To assign students to groups. By and large groups will be heterogeneous with regard to all important student characteristics. Groups should remain intact "long enough for them to be successful." Problem students may be assigned initially to particular groups wherein peers present a positive role model or counterbalance an individual's less than desirable traits. The teacher's response to a group which is experiencing difficulties should not be to disband and regroup. Rather, the teacher should assist the group to learn collaborative skills and thus achieve a major goal of cooperative learning. Ultimately all grouping decisions rest with the teacher.
3. Planning instructional materials to promote group interdependence. Johnson and Johnson employ the jigsaw concept of distributing resources, materials, and tasks among the groups' members in such a way that group cooperation is essential to successful completion of the task.
4. To structure positive goal interdependence. The teacher must create and communicate to the students that they are all in a

"sink-or-swim" learning situation. Students are responsible for themselves, each other, and for their group's completion of the assignment. Evaluation is criterion referenced and students know the criterion for success at the outset. Within the group individual members may be working toward differentiated criteria.

5. To monitor, intervene, and evaluate. The teacher will monitor, intervene, and evaluate as needed. Collaborative skills are a major concern for the teacher and are best taught as needed in the context of the group activity and functioning. Generalization of collaborative skills from one setting to another or one curriculum context to another cannot be assumed. The teacher will want to draw the students' attention to group processes through discussion. Emphasis is placed on the effectiveness of the group and the members' ability to work with one another. Evaluation will include the level of collaborative skills demonstrated by the students as well as the level of academic achievement.

Empirical Support for Cooperative Learning

A considerable body of empirical research has evolved with regard to the merits of cooperative learning. Although research involving regular education youngsters predominates, the potential of cooperative learning for the handicapped, and in general the mildly handicapped, has also received research attention. Overall, the weight of the research is supportive of the effectiveness and the benefits of cooperative learning on academic, social, and affective outcomes (Slavin, 1980; Sharan, 1980; Stallings and Stipek, 1984; Johnson and Johnson, 1987). Research findings are not consistently positive or supportive of every effort to implement cooperative learning; the exceptions help us to understand the dynamics underlying this instructional intervention. For example, DeVries and Slavin (1978) reported on a series of 10 studies of cooperative learning. Of the 10 studies, 7 produced significant effects for academic achievement (math and language arts, including reading, vocabulary, and grammar) for third, seventh, and twelfth grades. The 3 studies which failed to produce positive achievement gains all involved social studies content. Sharan (1980) has defined the differences between peer tutoring and group inquiry methods of cooperative learning, emphasizing the greater suitability of peer tutoring and cooperative learning approaches for low level task mastery, and of group inquiry approaches for content curricula and higher level cognitive functioning. In addition, Sharan sees a possible explanation for the split results of DeVries and Slavin in the mismatch between cooperative learning methods and the nature of the subject matter, and task demands of social studies curriculum. The TGT and STAD cooperative learning methods which were employed in the series of research studies by DeVries and Slavin (1978) may not have been suited to the content of social studies. The use of a group inquiry method might have produced different results. Other factors which may mediate between cooperative learning and student outcomes are socioeconomic background (Sharan, 1980), prior achievement level, and ethnic background (Stallings and Stipek, 1984). A specific example of the effect of mediating variables on cooperative learning outcomes is found in a study by DeVries, Mescon, and Schackman (1975). In this study the TGT approach was used to promote content reading skills among third grade students. Higher scores for 2 of the 3 performance measures under the TGT methodology were due primarily to gains made by the initially low-achieving students among the target student group. The results suggest that cooperative learning is particularly beneficial for the lower achieving student and that prior student achievement level intervened between intervention and outcome.

The generally positive and supportive tone of the literature pertaining to the use of cooperative learning methodologies with nonhandicapped students in regular education settings provides an auspicious introduction for consideration of the applicability of cooperative learning to handicapped students. Research involving handicapped and low-achieving students is of immediate concern. Cooperative learning techniques have been used in numerous attempts to increase interaction with and acceptance of handicapped students in mainstream classrooms (Madden and Slavin, 1983), and to increase the interaction among the handicapped and nonhandicapped in and out of school settings (Martino and Johnson, 1979; Johnson, Rynders, Johnson, Schmidt, and Haider, 1979). A major theme in the cooperative learning literature is its impact upon race relations, an area wherein cooperative learning has undoubtedly had positive and beneficial effects (Madden and Slavin, 1983; Sharan, 1980). Participation in cooperative learning experiences apparently neutralizes student differences based upon race and ethnic background. "It is through the medium of this intervention and communication process within small groups cooperating on academic tasks that these team-learning methods strive to influence pupils' cognitive learning, their attitudes toward learning and school, and their relations with members of other groups in ethnically heterogeneous classrooms" (Sharan, 1980, p. 242). The documented and beneficial impact of cooperative learning on race relations among ethnically and racially different groups of students bodes well for the possibility of a similar effect on relations among students divided by differences rooted in handicapping conditions. The benefits of cooperative learning go far beyond race relations.

Slavin (as cited in Madden and Slavin, 1983), in an extensive review of experimental field studies which contrasted cooperative learning with traditional group instructional methods, found that cooperative learning methods were "generally found to have more positive effects than traditional control methods on achievement, time on task, race relations, self esteem, and other outcomes" (p. 548). Madden and Slavin (1983) have discussed cooperative learning as a strategy to enhance mainstreaming experiences for mildly academically handicapped students. The strong research support and widespread use of cooperative techniques sets the stage for expanded use of cooperative learning as a means for facilitating the integration of mildly handicapped students into increasing numbers of regular education classrooms.

The brother and brother team of David and Roger Johnson are outspoken proponents of cooperative learning for handicapped learners. Like Slavin and his colleagues, Johnson and Johnson (1987) have been heavily engaged in the development of classroom applications of cooperative learning. The cooperative learning approach which they espouse falls into the group inquiry category as defined by Sharan (1980). Johnson and Johnson (1987) believe that "dramatically different learning outcomes result from the student-student interaction patterns promoted by the use of cooperative, competitive, and individualistic goal structures" (p. 34). With regard to achievement outcomes, Johnson, Maryama, Johnson, Nelson, and Skon (1981) conducted a meta-analysis of 122 studies which appeared in the literature from 1924 to 1981. The results indicated that cooperative learning tends to promote higher achievement than do either competitive or individualistic learning experiences. The authors found that the results applied across age levels, subject areas, and to a wide array of academic tasks, *e.g.*, concept attainment, verbal problem solving, categorization, spatial problem solving, etc.

As to the question of why cooperative learning is the most effective of the 3 learning modes in promoting achievement, Johnson and Johnson (1987) believe that the answer lies in the nuances of the group process; *e.g.*, discussion, debate, oral review and rehearsal, peer regulation, feedback, support, and the mutual liking which evolves from students working together toward shared goals. Others have also addressed this very question. Interestingly, it appears that the cooperative team structure in and of itself may not be the factor which accounts for the method's effectiveness and that reward interdependence—*i.e.*, group goal structure—may be the key to the effect (Sharan, 1983). Two recent studies in which students worked cooperatively but without a group goal resulted in lower achievement for cooperative learning than for individualistic learning (Johnson, Johnson, and Scott, 1978; Slavin 1980a). Studies in which cooperative learning was joined with a group reward produced superior academic gains for cooperative learning over competitive, individualistic learning or traditional control methods (Stallings and Stipek, 1984). The highly structured and focused schedule of teaching and testing which is an important aspect of cooperative learning is cited by Slavin (1978) as the important factor in the favorable achievement results produced by cooperative (STAD) learning methods. The underlying and intense structure of instructional activities (particularly in peer tutoring, cooperative learning methods such as TGT and STAD) emphasizes review, drill, learning to mastery and time-on-task. Instructional components such as these are important for the effective instruction of all students including the mildly handicapped and low-achieving student. It may be that cooperative learning works, in part, for the handicapped or low-performing student because it embodies many of the basic directive instructional methods that have been shown to be effective for this type of student.

Madden and Slavin (1983) point out one of the problematic aspects of cooperative learning: the failure of gains in interaction and acceptance patterns among students to be maintained over time, especially for studies of initially short duration. They cite 3 studies in which intervention phases varied from 2 to 5 weeks (intensity of treatment during that time varies also). All of the studies produced positive social effects, but the 2 studies which conducted follow-up activities found that the positive effects were not maintained. Slavin and Madden (1983) speculate that the environment of the regular classroom to which the students returned was not conducive to maintenance of the effects of the cooperative learning experiments. In the regular classroom where competition prevails the handicapped or slow learning students are at a disadvantage once again. In contrast, cooperative learning can be designed to "equalize" academically divergent students. Madden and Slavin (1983) observe that cooperative learning accomplishes this end in two ways: (1) group evaluation based upon each student's performance on individualized assignments; and (2) student evaluation based upon the student's improvement over her own past performance. Other evaluative strategies for motivating the slower student and encouraging the more able students to help their less able teammates are offered by Johnson and Johnson (1987); e.g., the group's score tied to the score of the lowest performing group member.

Cooperative learning will have to gain a better foothold in regular education classrooms if the balance between cooperative and competitive and individualistic instruction is to change (Johnson and Johnson,

1987). On the basis of the available research Slavin (1980) confidently states that cooperative learning can, or should, become the "dominant instructional mode" (p. 383) in American classrooms. Slavin (1980, p. 337) has summarized the instructional implication which can be drawn from the empirical literature on cooperative learning:

1. For academic achievement, cooperative learning techniques are no worse than traditional techniques, and in most cases they are significantly better.
2. For low level learning outcomes, such as knowledge, calculation, and application of principles, cooperative learning techniques appear to be more effective than traditional techniques to the degree that they use: a) structured, focused, schedule of instruction; b) individual accountability for performance among team members; and c) a well-defined group reward system, including rewards or recognition for successful groups.
3. For high level cognitive learning outcomes, such as identifying concepts, analysis of problems, judgment, and evaluation, less structured cooperative techniques that involve high student autonomy and participation in decision making may be more effective than traditional individualistic techniques.
4. Cooperative learning techniques have strong and consistent effects on relationships between black, white, and Mexican-American students.
5. Cooperative learning techniques have fairly consistent positive effects on mutual concern among students regardless of the specific structure used.
6. There is some indication that cooperative learning techniques can improve students' self-esteem.
7. Students in classes using cooperative learning generally report greater liking of school than do traditionally taught students.

Looking to the future, Slavin sees investigation of cooperative learning adapted for such specialized uses as mainstreaming, individualization of instruction, bilingual education, and remedial education. Since 1980 much research has, in fact, addressed these issues and more will no doubt be undertaken. Madden and Slavin (1983) believe that a shift in the balance between competitive and cooperative learning methodologies resulting in a greater proportion of cooperative learning would be beneficial for the regular education student, and greatly facilitate the academic and social integration of the handicapped student. "As a practical matter, a technique designed to benefit mainstreamed

MAH [mildly academically handicapped] students must also clearly benefit nonhandicapped students if it is to be used by many regular education teachers" (Madden and Slavin, 1983). The research evidence which supports the effectiveness of cooperative learning for both the regular and special education populations should dispel any objections that regular teachers might raise on this sensitive issue.

In Summary

The grouping of students for instruction can be based solely on sheer numbers, *e.g.*, whole group versus small group, or ability wherein students are "tracked" into homogeneous ability classes. Tracking is not beneficial for slow learning or low ability students; the negative consequences have been amply discussed and documented. As for handicapped learners, placement in special education effectively tracks these students out of regular education into the special education alternative. Thus ability grouping is not a pressing issue for the special education student until she tries to reenter regular education. Heterogeneously grouped classes will facilitate integration of the handicapped more readily than ability-based classes.

The option for grouping structures based upon number include whole group, small group, and one-to-one instruction. Whole group instruction is the easiest to manage; the teacher has only one preparation per subject area and can supervise all students at all times. Small group instruction entails greater management skill on the part of the teacher. But, small group instruction is more effective for subject matter which requires a high level of student-teacher interaction, *e.g.*, basic skills. One-on-one instruction facilitates individualization in that instruction can be matched to each child's unique learning needs and learner characteristics, *i.e.*, diagnostic-prescriptive teaching. Proponents of diagnostic-prescriptive teaching disagree on the focus of remedial instruction. Two schools of thought exist: one favors ability or process training, while the other focuses upon curriculum and the remediation of specific behavioral and skill deficits. The weight of the empirical literature and professional consensus support the latter approach, and yet, the best use of instructional time will not be achieved through either approach to individualization. Current research findings on effective instruction of basic skills supports active teaching within small group structures. Individualized instruction should supplement rather than preempt group instruction in basic skills.

Each grouping option impacts differently on student engagement. Student engagement is highest during teacher-led activities and drops sharply when students are working independently. This factor argues for whole group instruction. Small group instruction necessitates considerable independent student activity, *e.g.*, seatwork, with its attendant management problems. During one-on-one instruction student engagement is likely to be at its peak, but students receive the very least amount of teacher-led instruction within this teaching mode.

A third approach to grouping is based upon the interactive patterns among students; the options are competitive, cooperative, and individualistic learning. At present, competitive learning prevails in America's public school classrooms. Under competitive conditions some students succeed and some must fail. Competitive classrooms are not best for handicapped students who rarely if ever win the academic race. In contrast, cooperative learning fosters interdependence and cooperation among student toward achievement of group goals. Responsibility for the group's functioning resides with the students. Students learn to help one another because all win together or all lose together. Cooperative learning has been applied successfully to many different subjects, tasks and instructional situations. Properly organized and implemented cooperative learning can foster high levels of student engagement, interest, achievement, mutual respect, and cooperation.

Appendix 6.A. Anderson, Evertson, and Brophy's (1982)
Revised Principles for Small-Group Instruction in Beginning Reading

Programing for Continuous Progress

1. *Time.* Across the year, reading groups should average 25–30 minutes each. The length will depend on student attention level, which varies with time of year, student ability level, and the skills being taught.
2. *Academic focus.* Successful reading instruction includes not only organization and management of the reading group itself (discussed below), but effective management of the students who are working independently. Provide these students with appropriate assignments; rules and routines to follow when they need help or information (to minimize their needs to interrupt you as you work with your reading group); and activity options available when they finish their work (so they have something else to do).
3. *Pace.* Both progress through the curriculum and pacing within specific activities should be brisk, producing continuous progress achieved with relative ease (small steps, high success rate).
4. *Error rate.* Expect to get correct answers to about 80% of your questions in reading groups. More errors can be expected when students are working on new skills (perhaps 20–30%). Continue with practice and review until smooth, rapid, correct performance is achieved. Review responses should be almost completely (perhaps 95%) correct.

Appendix 6.A. Continued

Organizing the Group

5. *Seating.* Arrange seating so that you can both work with the reading group and monitor the rest of the class at the same time.
6. *Transitions.* Teach the students to respond immediately to a signal to move into the reading group (bringing their books or other materials), and to make quick, orderly transitions between activities.
7. *Getting started.* Start lessons quickly once the students are in the group (have your materials prepared beforehand).

Introducing Lessons and Activities

8. *Overviews.* Begin with an overview to provide students with a mental set and help them anticipate what they will be learning.
9. *New words.* When presenting new words, do not merely say the word and move on. Usually, you should show the word and offer phonetic clues to help students learn to decode.
10. *Work assignments.* Be sure that students know what to do and how to do it. Before releasing them to work on activities independently, have them demonstrate how they will accomplish these activities.

Insuring Everyone's Participation

11. *Ask questions.* In addition to having the students read, ask them questions about the words and materials. This helps keep students attentive during classmates' reading turns, and allows you to call their attention to key concepts or meanings.
12. *Order turns.* Use a system, such as going in order around the group, to select students for reading or answering questions. This insures that all students have opportunities to participate, and it simplifies group management by eliminating handwaving and other student attempts to get you to call on them.
13. *Minimize call-outs.* In general, minimize student call-outs and emphasize that students must wait their turns and respect the turns of others. Occasionally, you may want to allow call-outs to pick up the pace or encourage interest, especially with low achievers or students who do not normally volunteer. If so, give clear instructions or devise a signal to indicate that you intend to allow call-outs at these times.
14. *Monitor individuals.* Be sure that everyone, but especially slow students, is checked, receives feedback, and achieves mastery. Ordinarily this will require questioning each individual student, and not relying on choral responses.

Teacher Questions and Student Answers

15. *Focus on academic content.* Concentrate your questions on the academic content; do not overdo questions about personal experiences. Most questions should be about word recognition or sentence or story comprehension.
16. *Use word-attack questions.* Include word-attack questions that require students to decode words or identify sounds within words.
17. *Wait for answers.* In general, wait for an answer if the student is still thinking about the question and may be able to respond. However, do not continue waiting if the student seems lost or is becoming embarrassed, or if you are losing the other students' attention.
18. *Give needed help.* If you think the student cannot respond without help but may be able to reason out the correct answer if you do help, provide help by simplifying the question, rephrasing the question, or giving clues.

Appendix 6.A. Continued

19. *Give the answer when necessary.* When the student is unable to respond, give the answer or call on someone else. In general, focus the attention of the group on the answer, and not on the failure to respond.
20. *Explain the answer when necessary.* If the question requires one to develop a response by applying a chain of reasoning or step-by-step problem solving, explain the steps one goes through to arrive at the answer in addition to giving the answer itself.

When the Student Responds Correctly

21. *Acknowledge correctness (unless it is obvious).* Briefly acknowledge the correctness of responses (nod positively, repeat the answer, say "right," etc.), unless it is obvious to the students that their answers are correct (such as during fast-paced drills reviewing old material).
22. *Explain the answer when necessary.* Even after correct answers, feedback that emphasizes the method used to get answers will often be appropriate. Onlookers may need this information to understand why the answer is correct.
23. *Use follow-up questions.* Occasionally, you may want to address one or more follow-up questions to the same student. Such series of related questions can help the student to integrate relevant information. Or you may want to extend a line of questioning to its logical conclusion.

Praise and Criticism

24. *Praise in moderation.* Praise only occasionally (no more than perhaps 10 % of correct responses). Frequent praise, especially if nonspecific, is probably less useful than more informative feedback.
25. *Specify what is praised.* When you do praise, specify what is being praised, if this is not obvious to the student and the onlookers.
26. *Use correction, not criticism.* Routinely inform students whenever they respond incorrectly, but in ways that focus on the academic content and include corrective feedback. When it is necessary to criticize (typically only about 1 % of the time when students fail to respond correctly), be specific about what is being criticized and about desired alternative behaviors.

From *Handbook of Research on Teaching* (p. 346 by J. Brophy and T.L. Good, 1986, NY: MacMillan Publishing Company. Copyright 1986 by the American Educational Research Association. Reprinted by permission.

Chapter 7

Monitoring Student Performance

The monitoring of student performance is an essential component of the teaching process. Both regular and special education teachers will readily acknowledge and accept this responsibility. But, as with the time variable, there is a renewed appreciation for the contribution of the monitoring of performance to the outcomes of the instructional process. The need to monitor student academic engagement in addition to skill mastery and general achievement is a "new" idea which is pointing the way to more effective instructional practices in both regular and special education settings.

Monitoring of student performance is often cited as an essential component of the effective instruction. Edmonds (1979), noted for his work with disadvantaged children in urban schools, has identified frequent evaluation of student progress as one of 5 essential elements of successful and effective schools. He explains that

> there must be some means by which pupil progress can be frequently monitored. These means may be as traditional as classroom testing on the day's lesson or as advanced as criterion referenced system wide standardized measures. The point is that some means must exist in the school by which the principal and the teachers remain constantly aware of pupil progress in relationship to instructional objectives. (p. 32)

Rosenshine (1983) includes monitoring of student performance in a listing of essential instructional functions and urges teachers to monitor student performance on a daily basis and through weekly and/or monthly reviews. McKenzie (1983) in his review of the effective school literature has categorized the characteristics of effective schools under the 3 dimensions of leadership, efficacy, and efficiency. "continuous diagnosis, evaluation, and feedback" are cited within the efficiency dimension. In yet another review of the effective school literature, Purkey and Smith (1983) identified a system for the monitoring of student progress as one of 5 factors frequently cited in case study reports as contributing to effective schooling. In summation, Purkey and Smith state that "continual monitoring of individual pupil and classroom progress is a logical means of determining whether the school's goals are being realized and can serve to stimulate and direct staff energy and attention" (p. 445).

It is readily apparent that professional opinion views the monitoring of student performance as a condition of effective teaching. Monitoring has always been a part of the teacher's role; the current interest in student monitoring differs from earlier practices in focus and intensity, not intent. There is greater emphasis on monitoring individual students as well as group performance. Student engagement is a new focus for classroom evaluation and monitoring.

Regular education's renewed emphasis on monitoring student performance, especially at the individual level, is an affirmation of long standing special education practice. Special educators share the concern for student progress and performance, but for special education teachers, the monitoring of student performance is not "optional". Federal and state regulations prescribe monitoring as an essential component of every exceptional child's educational program. The Individual Education Program (IEP) is, in many respects, a monitoring device. The IEP document must contain annual goals and short term instructional objectives, an evaluation strategy, and time lines for the program's duration. These IEP components set the stage for the monitoring of the student's progress.

Monitoring Performance in Special Education

For special education teachers, the monitoring of student performance is encompassed in the larger activity of assessment, a primary area of professional responsibility. "Assessment" in special education is not the equivalent of "monitoring" in regular education; the former denotes a much larger scope of activity.

In the realm of special education, assessment is a process of data collection which provides the basis for decisions made about the individual child (Salvia and Ysseldyke, 1988; Ysseldyke and Algozzine, 1982; Zigmond, Vellacorsa, and Silverman, 1983; Wallace and Larsen, 1979). Although the definition of assessment is brief and to the point, the process itself is complex and demanding. Salvia and Ysseldyke (1988) take a broad encompassing view of the assessment process; they state that assessment fulfills 5 primary purposes: referral, screening, classification, instructional planning, and evaluating pupil progress.

Many authors have found it helpful to dichotomize the various assessment functions under the two categories of "assessment for classification" and "assessment for instruction" (Wallace and Larsen, 1979; Zigmond, Vellacorsa, and Silverman, 1983; Zigmond and Miller, 1987). The assessment functions of Salvia and Ysseldyke can be assigned to one or the other category:

Dichotomy of Assessment Functions

Assessment for Placement	*Assessment for Instruction*
Referral	Instructional Planning
Screening	Evaluating Pupil Progress
Classification	

Assessment for placement is heavily dependent upon the use of formalized and standardized tests and testing procedures. This assessment procedure usually culminates in designation of a categorical label, *e.g.*, mentally retarded, learning disabled, etc., and class placement, *e.g.*, resource room, self-contained class, etc. This arena of assessment activities and the labelling process which accompanies it has been the object of severe criticism (Hobbs, 1975, 1976; Hallahan and Kaufmann, 1977). From the teacher's point of view, the ultimate criticism of assessment for placement is that the testing activity results lack educational utility; that is, the test data, as well as the label affixed to the child, provide little if any useful guidance for the teacher in instructional planning or program development (Wallace and Larsen, 1979; Wallace and McLouglin, 1975).

In contrast, assessment for instruction has gained widespread support within the professional community. In this type of assessment, formal tests give way to informal testing wherein criterion referenced and teacher made tests are much preferred to formal norm referenced tests. Proponents of assessment for instruction stress the importance of the teacher's diagnostic function and the immediacy and relevance of curriculum relevant testing data for instructional planning and monitoring of student performance (Neisworth and Smith, 1979; Wallace and Larsen, 1979; Zigmond *et al.*, 1983).

Assessment for instruction provides information about the unique individual characteristics of the learner, *e.g.*, functional level, specific skill deficits, preferred learner style, attitudinal factors, etc., which enable the teacher to individualize curricular materials and task demands. Assessment entails the monitoring of student performance during ongoing instruction to determine if progress is being made toward specific

Time and Learning

instructional objectives and goals, to ascertain mastery of specific skills, and to determine when and if instructional or curricular changes are needed. Testing and teaching are so closely entwined in special education methodology, that a test-teach-test strategy is often espoused as an appropriate approach to daily instructional interaction between student and teacher. Finally, assessment provides the data for the important programmatic decisions that have to be made during the student's academic career; for example, decisions about mainstreaming, termination of special services, and/or transition into postsecondary options of employment, training and/or continued education.

The assessment process in special education places a strong emphasis on individualization; many special educators believe the essence of assessment in special education is to achieve the match between student characteristics and needs and instructional demands (Reynolds and Birch, 1977). The vital importance attached to individualization of instruction is a point of difference between special and regular education. This is not to say that regular education has turned its back on individualization of instruction; in fact, regular education has forged ahead in individualization approaches to meet the needs of the more able and sophisticated student through various forms of student managed and computer assisted instruction. It is the individualized needs of the less able, low-functioning and low-ability student that have received inadequate attention in the regular education classroom. Unfortunately, too often the regular education response to such students was to remove large numbers from the educational mainstream to the various special education placements. The persistent problems of vague definitions and loose, fluctuating placement criteria within special education have aided and abetted regular educators in this process. The magnitude of the overplacement and misplacement problem of slow or problem learners, but not handicapped students, in special education has come to light and is being addressed (Algozzine, Ysseldyke, and Christenson, 1983; Gerber, 1984). It is too early to tell if initiatives such as prereferral intervention strategies (Graden, Casey, and Christenson, 1985; Graden, Casey, and Bonstrom, 1985) and the regular education initiation which espouses a merger of regular and special services and the retention of handicapped youngsters in regular education (Reynolds, Wang, and Walberg, 1987; Will, 1986) will markedly stem the flow of excessive and inappropriate student placements to special education programs.

Setting Performance Standards

When teachers monitor student progress they do so with some end or outcome in mind. Targeted outcomes may be short-term, *e.g.*, mastery of daily instructional objectives, or long-term, *e.g.*, attainment of academic or vocational goals. Monitoring, therefore, necessitates the specification of goals and performance standards. What are appropriate performance standards for the mildly handicapped? What ultimate goals guide our educational efforts for these students?

The IEP process encourages teachers and parents to jointly plan and project the instructional program in terms of short-term objectives and annual goals. This timeframe, which is consistent with the year to year structure of public school programs, is important and useful for daily instructional monitoring. But in retrospect, one year is a relatively short period of time in a student's total academic career. We also need to take the long view, to set our sights on long range goals and gauge student progress toward those goals. We need to monitor student progress in terms of preparedness for postschool pursuits, and concomitantly we need to evaluate program effectiveness in terms of postschool adjustment. A future oriented perspective will do much to focus attention on not only the actual attainments of students, but the rate of progress as well. The critical monitoring questions then become: Is the student progressing? and is the student progressing at an adequate rate? Also, at this rate of progress, will the student reach her short-term objectives, annual IEP goals, and long-range goals?

Setting Long Range Goals

The common denominator which unites all students who fall within the mildly handicapped category is serious performance deficits (Meyen and Lehr, 1982). Remediation of academic deficits is the central focus of most special education programs, and monitoring of student performance is a key component of any remedial effort. But day to day progress without progress toward long-range goals may give the illusion of instructional effectiveness when, in fact, very little of substance is being accomplished. The author remembers the instance of a third grade special education classroom for mildly handicapped students in which the teacher pointed with pride to the number of reading books each student had read over the course of the school year. On first glance the numbers of books per child was impressive. Looking more closely at the books read, however, one realized that all the readers were at the approximately same reading level. The children had indeed been reading but not progressing toward higher levels of reading proficiency in materials of greater difficulty. Apparently the performance standard in this classroom was the number of books read—with no thought to moving the child forward in the attainment of higher performance goals. This classroom program is also problematic when viewed from the perspective of final outcomes. Had these children during the course of this school year made significant progress toward functional literacy and independent adult living? Unfortunately, the answer was no.

In another context, Schloss, Halle, and Sindelar (1984) offer a discerning observation about the "social validity" of instructional goals which is very relevant to this discussion of performance standards and instructional goals for the handicapped. They maintain that the multidisciplinary team has an obligation to consider the significance of the goals selected for handicapped students, and further, that the goals must be important to the learner and worthy of the time and effort devoted to their attainment. Schloss, Halle, and Sindelar state that "programs that produce substantial changes in trivial responses and programs that produce insignificant changes in critical learner behaviors are equally deficient" (1984, p. 42). One way to ensure substantive program content for handicapped students is to tie day to day instruction to meaningful long-range goals.

Education programs for mildly handicapped must be future oriented: elementary students must prepare for secondary school, and adolescents must prepare for postschool pursuits. In defense of norm referenced testing for mildly handicapped students, Goodman and Bennett (1982) state that the ultimate goal for mildly handicapped students is normalization. They believe that the "level of accomplishment of nonhandicapped students is the reference point against which the achievement of the mildly handicapped student is judged" (p. 259). The once raging debate over norm referenced versus criterion referenced testing (Ebel, 1978; Popham, 1978) has subsided. Special education classroom teachers and diagnostic personnel fully recognize that the greater classroom utility of criterion referenced tests and the consensus of professional opinion favor the use of criterion referenced and other informal classroom based tests for instructional planning. And yet, it appears that special educators still have not come to grips with the basic problem. Not only have special educators rejected the use of norm referenced test, but many resist a normative perspective on student performance as well. Goodman and Bennett (1982) remind us that the goals for mildly handicapped must be reintegration with the nonhandicapped, performance which meets normative standards and preparation of students for successful adult lives. A similar unwavering focus to the future is expressed by Meyen and Lehr (1980, 1982) who have serious doubts about the intensity of instruction to which mildly handicapped students are exposed during their academic programs. They cite the persistence of learning problems (despite remediation), and the failure of students in special education programs (particularly resource rooms) to perform better than similar students who remained in regular education as evidence of our failure to provide interventions of sufficient power to change the course of students' academic histories—histories, for the most part, of failure and frustration. Meyen and Lehr state that "throughout their educational histories, many, if not most, mildly handicapped students have not been subjected to intensive instruction, although they have been recipients of special education services" (1982, p. 99).

Meyen and Lehr (1980) are troubled by the implementation of the LRE (Least Restrictive Environment) requirement of P.L. 94-142, which they believe places priority on social integration rather than academic performance. They emphasize that the guiding principle for LRE ought to be "selection [placement] based upon knowledge of conditions that offer the highest probability for remediating academic performance deficits and not conditions that are socially least restrictive" (p. 96). When decisions are made regarding the restrictiveness of various educational placement, it is important to take into account the student's quality of life after leaving school as well as the quality of her academic and social life during the relatively brief years of formal schooling. It may be that the least restrictive environment during the school years can condemn the individual to a greater restrictiveness in adult life for lack of adequate literacy, vocational, and social skills. The retention of a normative perspective on the mildly handicapped, *i.e.,* how do these disabled learners perform in relationship to their non-handicapped peers, coupled with a mindset which clearly focuses upon the future, will help to keep programs for the mildly handicapped on the right track and moving forward.

The important consideration is the need to establish future oriented goals and norm referenced performance standards to guide us in program development and evaluation. We must gauge student performance not only in daily increments, but also by the degree and rate of progress toward long range goals and outcomes. The mildly handicapped have been enveloped in "a context of protectiveness" (Meyen and Lehr, 1980) which has shielded them from realistic performance demands. Our performance expectations for the mildly handicapped have been low. The insidious and destructive effect of low expectations on student performance is well documented. This is not to say that special educators are deliberately imposing low expectations; rather, existing special education standards simply do not demand enough. But the effect of low expectations and low performance standards, intended or not, has the potential to be harmful for the very children we seek to help.

"The personal costs of living a life inhibited by marginal performance are great" (Myen and Lehr, 1982). The literature on the postschool adjustment of mildly handicapped students who leave school ill prepared for employment, independent living, social interaction, family living, etc. paints a bleak picture of the future prospects for these students (Hasazi, Gordon, and Roe, 1985; McAfee and Mann, 1982). A normative perspective and performance standards that realistically reflect the demands of adult living would do much to help teachers and parents evaluate student progress, and adjust instructional programs when progress is inadequate, in a meaningful context.

A normative perspective from the early grades would also help parents in setting their expectations. Parental expectations sometimes have little relationship to the actual performance of the student. Expectations can be too low or too high, though Cummings and Maddux (1988) believe parental expectations for the mildly handicapped most often err toward the high side and are beyond the students' capabilities. It would benefit all concerned—teacher, parent, and student—to begin to view student performance in relation to the performance expectations and rate of progress held for the nonhandicapped. A temporal and normative perspective on student performance would help teachers in the monitoring process and in putting instructional years to best use.

In the day to day interaction of the classroom, teachers are constantly gauging student performance, deciding whether or not students have mastered the instructional objective(s) of the day's lessons. The validity of teachers' judgments is an important consideration, and we will return to this topic later in the chapter. For the moment, suffice it to say that teachers must make judgments about mastery and non-mastery of instructional objectives; that is, deciding if the student has learned the required knowledge or skills. It is also important that teachers attend to the rate of learning. Knowing that students A and B have mastered the instructional objectives is certainly important; knowing that student A required twice as much time to attain mastery is also important information for the teacher as she plans subsequent instruction. Student A will need additional instructional time to maintain a performance level commensurate with student B.

Mastery decisions are made by comparing student performance to a designated performance standard. In criterion referenced testing (commercial or teacher made) the student's performance is compared to a preset, fixed standard of performance. Attainment of the standard indicates mastery while failure to reach the prescribed performance level indicates nonmastery. How are performance standards set? Too often teachers apply one blanket performance criterion, *e.g.*, 80 or 90 percent across the board in keeping with the instructions found in countless commercial materials and textbooks (citations have been omitted to protect the guilty!). A degree of flexibility is needed. Performance standards should vary in response to the nature of the subject matter and pupil characteristics.

Subject matter and performance standards. Performance standards should reflect the nature of the subject matter being taught. We do not expect or require errorless performance when children are reading or doing reading related assignments. It is the nature of reading that the child is constantly reexposed to (and therefore has numerous opportunities to practice) the sounds, symbols, vocabulary, etc. of the reading material. If sufficient reading instructional time and guidance are provided and children are actively engaged in reading print material, a small percentage of word recognition errors and less than perfect comprehension should not be an obstacle to continued reading progress. Reading authorities do not, however, agree on the number of word recognition errors or percentage of comprehension errors that teachers should use to determine instructional reading level (Powell, 1971).

E.A. Betts, author of the *Temple Individual Reading Inventory*, the prototype for the development of many subsequent individual reading inventories (IRI), suggests 95 to 98 percent correct as the criterion for word recognition and 75 percent or better as the criterion for comprehension for identifying the student's instructional reading level. Many IRIs adhere to the Betts' criteria but others do not. Powell (1971) recommends that the performance criteria for word recognition need not be the same at all grade levels. He recommends instead that the word recognition requirement for grades 1 and 2 be 85 to 98 percent; for grades 3,4, and 5 it should be 91 to 98 percent correct; and for grades 6 it should be 94 to 98 percent correct. The criterion for comprehension is held constant at 70 to 95 percent correct for all grade levels. In effect, Powell allows more word recognition errors for younger children. He reasons that "if a child's comprehension score remained above 70-75 percent,the child could be assumed to tolerate whatever word recognition patterns accompanied that performance" (p. 638). Powell believes that the word recognition criteria for the instructional reading level should reflect both the difficulty of the materials and the grade level of the student.

Reading rate is increasingly being recognized as an important component of reading performance. Deno (1986) recommends that teachers strive for a reading fluency rate of 95 to 150 words per minute. Idol, Nevin, and Paolucci-Whitcomb (1986) suggest that criteria for reading rate as well as accuracy (word recognition) and comprehension be used to gauge students' reading performance. Interestingly, Idol-Maestas (1986) suggests varied criteria for reading rate based upon the difficulty level of the reading materials rather than the grade level of the student. For the preprimer level reading materials the suggested fluency rate is 25 correct words per minute (cwpm); for grade level 1 to 3 materials the suggested criterion is 30 cwpm; for grade levels 4 and up materials the suggested criterion is 50 cwpm. These criteria represent suggested initial reading rates, that is, the level at which instruction can begin, not the final or desirable reading proficiency rates for the students.

In the realm of mathematics Hasselbring, Goin, and Bransford (1987) make a strong argument for a performance criteria of 100 percent mastery of the basic math facts. They stress that students must attain "automaticity", that is, no more than a 1 to 2 second delay and perfect recall of all the math facts. The authors base this performance criterion on the belief that people have limited information processing capabilities; attention taken up by lower level skills is not available for performing higher order skills. Failure to achieve mastery of the basic number computations to this very high performance level may become an obstacle to future math achievement. They urge teachers to impose a stringent standard in their teaching of low level math skills. The reader is cautioned against overgeneralizing; this stringent performance standard should not be applied to all mathematics instruction. Some degree of error is to be expected (and allowed) when students are engaged in other types of math instruction. For those critical skills which must be mastered by all children to a very high level of proficiency, an extremely demanding performance standard is in order.

Within the realm of life skills instruction there are many examples of the need to set performance standards according to the nature of the subject matter. For all students there are some life skills which demand errorless performance as failure to perform adequately can place a student in jeopardy. The teacher of trainable mentally retarded (TMR) students who thought that her children should learn to cross the street safely 85 percent of the time—and included this performance standard in the students' IEP—wasn't as sensitive as she needed to be to the issue of performance standards. TMR students do not fall under the label mildly handicapped, but the TMR example certainly makes the point and has left an indelible impression on this author. A relevant example for the mildly handicapped was found in a current textbook which recommended a performance criteria of 75 percent in balancing a checkbook.

Student characteristics and performance standards. Performance standards will also be influenced by student characteristics. In suggesting varied word recognition criteria for the instructional reading level, Powell (1971) stated that the criteria should reflect both the difficulty of the materials and the age and grade of the student. Age and grade are clearly student characteristics.

Another instance in which student characteristics dictate accommodations in performance standards is found in the numerous classroom situations in which teachers employ a changing criterion design to meet the response capabilities of individual students. Within this format, performance criteria are initially set at a level far lower (or higher, depending upon the nature of the target behavior) than the level of performance desired by the teacher. As the student progresses and attains the preset criterion level, successively higher criteria are imposed until the level of performance is adequate. The changing criterion design is common in special education and uncommonly effective as well.

In summary, performance criteria should be selected to reflect the nature of the subject matter and the characteristics of the subject being taught. Blanket criteria rigidly applied should be avoided. The decisions teachers make with regard to performance standards are important in and of themselves; they impact also on the pacing of instruction and the use of instructional time. Performance criteria which are too stringent will hold children back; criteria which are too low will allow students to move forward without adequate mastery of prerequisite skills. It is important for the teacher to be aware of the impact of performance standards on instruction and instructional time.

Rate of learning. The IEP requires that special education teachers monitor student progress toward short-term objectives and annual goals. What the IEP so often lacks for the mildly handicapped student is a reference point which allows the teacher and the parents to gauge whether or not the student is progressing at an adequate rate.

To gauge progress, one must have a frame of reference or referent. Different referents can be used to judge student performance. *Norm referent* contrasts student performance to that of a larger group of representative students, frequently representing a national sampling of pupils, *e.g.*, a national sample of second grade students. *Criterion referent* contrasts student performance to a preset standard of performance irrespective of the performance of other students or classmates. *Self referent* contrasts the student's performance with his or her own past performance; improvement represents progress. And *peer referent* contrasts the student's performance to the performance of "average" age or classmates in the curriculum of the class or school. Criterion referencing and self referencing are widely employed in special education classrooms as they have much educational utility for the day to day instructional program. They are the frequently used referent points for the numerous mastery/nonmastery decisions that the teacher must make. Norm referencing for individual students is utilized most in the formalized assessment which precedes placement in special education. And district wide testing programs also rely heavily on norm referenced tests, as one would expect.

Peer referencing. Peer referencing encourages teachers to evaluate their students' rate of progress in comparison to their nonhandicapped peers. Peer referencing is actually a variation on norm referencing in that the student is compared to a small group of selected students. Peer referencing involves the use of nonhandicapped peers to set the performance standard against which the handicapped student is judged. The educational relevance of peer referencing is heightened by the fact that the performance standard is that of the peers performing in the curriculum of the school. By using "average" peers, not the best or worst students, the teacher is able to create a "norm group" that provides maximum and immediate utility for evaluating student progress. The reader may well object that the "average" peers in a subaverage school will be performing well below the national average. A similar objection could be raised in the case of an above "average" school where the "average" performance may fall well above national norms. The implication is that neither comparison is fair and that such evaluative comparison will result in a stilted perception of just how well or how poorly the student is performing. This objection has merit when one is comparing a student to formal normative standards. The "representativeness" of the norm group is an important issue. (Such comparisons are not valid or necessary for the day to day monitoring of pupil progress and performance in the classroom.) It is important to appreciate the fact that, on a day to day basis, teachers work within the context of their own classroom curriculum or the curriculum adopted for their school. Pupil performance is judged in terms of progress within a particular curriculum, and children are compared in terms of their relative progress within the curriculum of the classroom.

Peer referencing provides a normative perspective with immediate utility for instructional programming. It is important to remember also that it is the teacher who decides which children should be included in the peer referent group. The selection of peers will, indeed, should vary depending upon the evaluative question being asked. For instance, if one were seeking to determine if a particular child was functioning significantly below the other children in the class, one would compare the performance of the "slow" child with the performance of a group of his or her "average" classmates. If the question concerns a child's readiness for mainstreaming into a regular education classroom for reading instruction, the appropriate peer referents would be a selected group of average readers in the regular class in which the targeted child is to be mainstreamed. Idol-Maestas (1983) explores the issues surrounding mainstreaming of handicapped children from the perspective of the consulting teacher. She offers many examples of peer referencing (normative sampling is the term she prefers), using average students from regular classrooms as the peer referents. She indicates that normative sampling can be useful to the classroom teacher because it provides all of the following: (1) a specific behavioral description of how an average student performs a skill; (2) a clear idea of whether average students are meeting teacher expectations (and also a clear idea of what teacher expectations actually are for average students); (3) an indication of the degree of discrepancy between a poorly performing student and teacher expectations; and (4) a guide for setting goals, objectives, and criterial performance levels for students (Idol-Maestas, 1983).

Another application of peer referencing is found in the work of Sindelar (1981) who advocates the use of peer referencing in deciding about changes in placements for special education students. Sindelar (1981) believes that peer referencing offers an empirical basis for deciding if a student will be able to function in an alternative educational placement (possibly a less restrictive placement). He suggests that the performance of the student be compared to the performance of an age-matched peer group in the less restrictive setting being considered as a possible placement. If the student's behavior approximates that of the peer group in the less restrictive setting, the move to a less restrictive environment may be in order.

Another important instructional use for peer referencing is that it allows teachers to not only compare a student to his or her peers at one point in time but also to monitor the student's rate of progress in comparison to his or her peers over time (temporal perspective). Thus the teacher is able to determine if progress is adequate or if adjustments in the instructional program are indicated. If a teacher has comparable data on the level of performance for a particular student about whom there is concern, and a peer group who is performing and progressing adequately, the teacher can easily determine the degree of discrepancy between the student and peers. Perhaps more importantly the teacher can use peer performance to set a target performance level for the student in question. The discrepancy between the student and her peers represents the amount of catching-up that our student faces. The performance discrepancy divided by the amount of time available for instruction over the course of the school year yields the amount of progress per week which will be necessary to bridge the academic gap. Deno (1985) is an outspoken advocate of peer referencing and has discussed and described its application for handicapped students at great length. Deno gives us a specific example in the graph depicting performance data for a student named Rodney and his peers.

Figure 7.1. Curriculum Based Measurement

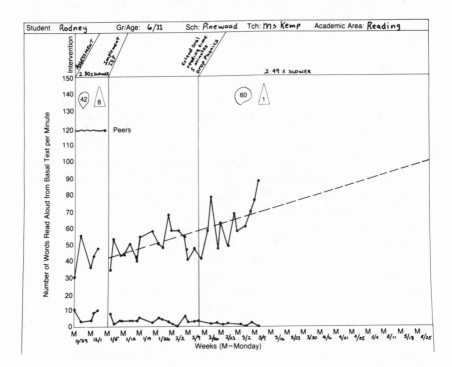

From "Curriculum based measurement: the emerging alternative," by S.L. Deno, *Exceptional Children*, 52, 1985, pp. 219-232. Copyright (1985) by the Council for Exceptional Children. Reprinted with permission.

Figure 7.1 displays reading performance data for Rodney and comparison performance data for a group of his peers. The baseline phase of the graph contains 3 series of connected data points: the 2 data series at the lower portion pertain to Rodney; the lowest data line represents the number of word reading errors, and the second lowest data line represents the number of words read correctly per minute (wpm). Rodney's error rate was 8 wpm of oral reading and his fluency rate was 42 wpm. The third and uppermost data series in the baseline phase indicates the reading rate of the group of classmates selected by the teacher to serve as a peer reference group. The baseline data strikingly presents the degree of discrepancy between Rodney's reading rate of about 42 wpm and the peer's reading rate of about 120 wpm. Rodney's oral reading rate is approximately 2.80 times slower than that of his peers. Regarding the degree of academic discrepancy, Deno (1986) suggests that student performance which falls 50 percent or more below that of the peer referent group is severe and should be evaluated further. The baseline data provides a very useful status picture of student performance and addresses the important issue of discrepancy. The utility of peer referencing is not limited solely to the identification of severe performance deficits; the stage is set for progress monitoring. To monitor Rodney's progress during the course of intervention it is necessary to set a performance goal and a goal date (Deno, 1986).

According to Deno (1986) goal setting involves a 3 step process: "(1) student performance is measured in the curriculum and contrasted with peer performance on the same measures; (2) a date is established as the day on which goal attainment will be reviewed formally; and (3) based on the student's and peers' current levels of performance, a judgment is made regarding a reasonable level the student might attain by the goal date" (p. 370). Having established a goal and goal date, a weekly performance objective can be determined. The weekly objective is "the average weekly increase in performance required to attain the goal level by the goal date" (Deno, 1986, p. 370). In Rodney's case, a goal of 100 wpm was selected and the goal date was set at May 26th. "The hatched line connecting Rodney's initial level of performance and his level on the goal date is the weekly objective; it represents the rate of increase required each week in order to attain the goal" (Deno, 1986, p. 370). Student performance is then monitored in relation to the weekly performance objective. Should the student's performance fall below the weekly objective (also referred to as the "aimline" or "goaline") on 3 consecutive days (Liberty, 1975, cited in Deno 1986), the teacher would be advised to consider changing the student's instructional program in some way to bring about a change in the student's performance level. Following 3 measurements which showed that Rodney's performance had fallen below the aim-line, we can see that Rodney's teacher adjusted his instructional program by extending his oral reading time by 5 additional minutes. Subsequent data indicate that the adjustment in instructional time apparently was effective in boosting Rodney's reading performance to an acceptable level. Had Rodney's reading performance not rebound-ed following the instructional adjustment, what should the teacher have done? Should the teacher have further modified instruction, or perhaps switched the curriculum? Each alteration in the instructional program should be treated as a hypotheses to be tested (Schloss and Sedlek, 1986). Schloss and Sedlek suggest that the teacher must contin-ue to alter and test the instructional process, and only after "all reason-able hypotheses have been tested and the learner is still performing below expectations" (p. 105) should the teacher consider altering (low-ering) performance objectives. The speed and ease with which curricu-lum based data can be collected and graphed makes the testing of instructional adjustments feasible for the classroom teacher.

Rodney's progress can be monitored on a continuing basis with data gathered at frequent intervals to help the teacher gauge his rate of progress and respond to problems quickly when the data indicates a need to do so. Rodney's progress will be monitored in relation to the goal set for him, in this instance 100 wpm by the 26th of May of the school year. A later notation on the graph indicates that Rodney is making progress toward bridging the gap which separates him from his peers. His rate of reading has improved and the degree of discrep-ancy has lessened. At this rate of progress he will be within range of his peers at the end of the school year. The "catch-up" game is indeed a difficult one for handicapped children.

Data-Based Decision Making

The monitoring of student performance entails a decision-making process. The teacher continuously makes decisions about the adequacy of student performance and the appropriateness of the instructional program. For example, has the student demonstrated mastery of the instructional objective(s)? Is the student's rate of progress adequate? Is there a need for program adjustments or modifications? Of course, one can make decisions in the absence of data, but we would hope that teacher refrain from this very questionable and risky practice! Educational decisions about children should be based upon valid, reli-able, and relevant information. According to Rosenberg and Sindelar

(1982), diagnostic-prescriptive teaching and direct instruction models of teaching (methods discussed and espoused in this and many other texts) require a data-based assessment methodology. Diagnostic-prescriptive teaching relies upon in depth knowledge of students' strengths and weaknesses to develop individualized intervention programs. Directive teaching relies upon frequently obtained data of observable, measurable student academic performance and behavior to monitor the appropriateness of instruction. Data-based assessment methods provide the "raw materials" for the decision-making process in both of these instructional approaches. Numerous textbooks and authorities tell us what teachers ought to do and how instructional decisions ought to be made, but recent research reveals that assessment practices in special education are often far from what are considered "best practices" in assessment (Ysseldyke, 1983; Ysseldyke, Thurlow, Graden, Wesson, Algozzine, and Deno, 1983). What, then, are the data and information sources that teachers rely upon as the basis for the many instructional decisions that have to be made?

Salmon-Cox (1981), in a study designed to explore elementary teachers' evaluation practices and use of standardized tests, found that teachers actually made little use of standardized achievement tests; test results were used primarily to confirm decisions reached by other means. In instances where the results of standardized testing conflicted with other data sources, *i.e.,*were lower than predicted, the standardized tests results were likely to be set aside. The author found that teachers overwhelmingly rely upon observations to assess the performance of their students; that is, the informal observations that take place during the give and take of instruction. In some related research Fuchs, Fuchs, and Warren 91982) reported that special educators base decisions about student mastery of instructional goals on unsystematic observations of student performance. The fact that teachers rely heavily upon unsystematic observations calls into question the accuracy and validity of their decisions. On this point, Fuchs and Fuchs (1984) found a tendency among teacher to overate student performance. They found that teachers' judgments about mastery were more consistent and accurate than their judgments about non-mastery. That is, the child was assumed to have attained mastery of particular objectives when she had not mastered the particular skills. In both studies teachers expressed confidence in the accuracy of their judgments. Teachers frequently use the results of individual reading inventories to make instructional placement decisions for their students. Fuchs, Fuchs, and Deno (1982) reported that teachers' actual placement of students within reading curricula diverged widely from the placements which were indicated by students' IRI scores. This finding suggests that teachers viewed the results of IRIs as equivocal. Once again, one must question how teachers make instructional decisions—what data base are they using?

Research evidence highlights the importance of on-going formative evaluation for handicapped learners. Cartwright and Cartwright (1989) define formative assessment as "the monitoring that takes place while instruction is under way" (p. 451). Deno (1986) maintains that formative evaluation is the "quality control" mechanism which indicates if our programs are succeeding or failing. Formative evaluation is cited repeatedly as an essential component of effective teaching of handicapped learners (Gersten, Carnine, and White, 1984; Rieth, Polsgrove, and Semmel, 1981; White and Haring, 1980; Fuchs, Deno, and Mirkin, 1984). The result of a meta-analysis of 21 controlled studies of the effects of formative evaluation on the achievement of mildly handicapped students led Fuchs and Fuchs (1986a) to report that the use of systematic formative evaluation procedures significantly increased students' school achievement. Systematic formative evaluation led to an achievement advantage of .7 standard deviation for students who were involved in formative evaluation in contrast to students who were not exposed to formative evaluation. In discussing the instructional implications of the research findings, Fuchs (1986) state that, "In terms of the standard normal curve and an achievement test scale with a population mean of 100 and standard deviation of 15, the integration of formative evaluation with instruction would raise the typical achievement outcome score form 100.00 to 110.50, or from the 50th to the 76th percentile" (p. 5). The results highlight both the statistical and potential practical significance of formative evaluation in the instruction of handicapped youngsters. It is apparent that assessment which accompanies the ongoing day to day instruction serves as a barometer for both student and program success. Formative evaluation is, in fact, part of the intervention (Deno, 1986).

A wide range of tests and testing procedures fall under the umbrella of formative assessment including criterion referenced commercial and teacher made tests, classroom observations, applied behavior analysis, etc. A relatively new and innovative approach to formative evaluation for the monitoring of student performance is termed curriculum based assessment (CBA). Gickling and Thompson (1985) define CBA as "a procedure for determining the instructional needs of students based upon the students ongoing performance within the existing course content" (p. 206). The appeal of CBA for teachers lies in the immediate educational utility of the testing results for instruction. CBA embraces a wide range of evaluative methods such as criterion referenced testing (Idol, Nevin, and Paolucci-Whitcomb, 1986), development assessments for very young children and infants (Bagnato, Neisworth, and Capone, 1986), and classroom observations (Blankenship and Lilly, 1981). The common characteristic which unites all CBA methods is the evaluation of student performance and progress in the curriculum of the classroom or school. Beyond this common feature, CBA methods divide along two avenues of development. One avenue builds upon the principles of criterion referenced testing (Idol, Nevin, and Paolucci-Whitcomb, 1986; Blankenship, 1985). The other avenue of development involves the combination of classroom observation techniques with student performance of specific and delimited academic tasks (Deno, 1985).

Criterion-Referenced Tests

According to Idol, Nevin, and Paolucci-Whitcomb (1986), CBA "is a criterion referenced test that is teacher constructed and designed to reflect curriculum content" (p. vii). The development and use of criterion referenced tests as part of the instructional process has been common practice in special and regular education for some time. The aspect of criterion referenced tests which comes under the CBM designation is the development of such tests to reflect the specific curriculum of the classroom or the school, rather than sampling items across a number of curricular programs, or keying test items to a standardized curriculum. The reader may object to so narrow a focus for selecting test items and setting performance standards. But one must bear in mind that teachers teach to the curriculum of the classroom. Without doubt there is value and a need to index local curriculum to national performance standards and, at some points along the way, to gauge student performance in terms of national norms (Goodman and Bennett, 1982). But for the day to day instructional activity, the classroom curriculum is the teachers' yardstick for gauging student progress and evaluating program effectiveness. CBA provides testing measures and procedures with maximum educational utility for the on-going instructional process.

Procedures recommended for the development of the CBM criterion referenced tests vary from one source to another. Blankenship (The Council for Exceptional Children, 1985) suggests the following 11 step process for the development and use of CBA measures:

(1) List the skills presented in the material selected.
(2) Examine the list to see if all important skills are presented.
(3) Decide if the resulting, edited list has skills in logical order.

(4) Write an objective for each skill on the list.

(5) Prepare items to test each listed objective.

(6) Prepare testing materials for student use, presenting the items.

(7) Plan how the CBA will be given.

(8) Give the CBA immediately prior to beginning instruction on the topic.

(9) Study the results to determine which students have already mastered the skills targeted for instruction; which students possess sufficient knowledge of the necessary prerequisite skills and are therefore ready to begin instruction; and which students lack mastery of the prerequisite skills.

(10) Readminister the CBA after instruction on the topic. Study the results to determine which students have mastered the skills and are ready to begin instruction in a new topic; which students are making sufficient progress but require more practice or continued instruction to achieve mastery; and which students are making insufficient progress, thereby requiring the teacher to modify some aspect of instruction.

(11) Periodically readminister the CBA throughout the year to assess for long-term retention. (Blankenship, 1985, p. 234).

However the teacher goes about the development of the testing instruments, the important points found in all methods are: analysis of curricular content, specification of teaching objectives, test item development to reflect teaching objectives, and the use of the testing results to monitor pupil progress and evaluate instructional effectiveness. The development of criterion referenced tests is a time consuming task, but the burden can be lessened by teachers pooling their efforts. The tests themselves, once prepared, will be used again and again and their usefulness for the teacher will amply justify the initial investment of time and effort.

Curriculum Based Measurement

Stanley Deno and his colleagues at the University of Minnesota pursued a different avenue in the development of curriculum based measurement (Deno utilizes the term curriculum based measurement in contrast to the more inclusive term curriculum based assessment). Distressed by teachers' apparent reliance upon informal observations rather than systematic observations and the degree of error found in teacher nondata-based evaluations of student performance, Deno (1985) and his colleagues sought to develop measurement procedures which could help to bridge the gap between measurement and instruction. The objective was to provide teachers with measurement procedures which were reliable, valid, simple, efficient, easily understood, and inexpensive (Deno, 1985). The result was the development of a set of generic measures—specific academic tasks—that were to be used formatively to evaluate student performance in the key academic areas of reading, written expression, spelling, and mathematics. The specific measures are:

Reading—one minute oral reading sample; all words whether correctly or incorrectly read, are scored.

Written expression—a 3 minute writing sample in response to a story starter or topic sentence; the number of words written or letter sequences is scored.

Spelling—a 2 minute spelling dictation test of words selected from the basal reading program or the classroom spelling curriculum; the number of correct letter sequences is scored[a].

Mathematics—a 2 minute test of math problems selected from the classroom curriculum; the number of correct digits[b] is scored (Deno, 1986).

The validity and reliability of the generic measures are an important issue. One is likely to ask if a mere 1 minute oral sample of reading is an adequate measure of reading performance, for isn't the essence of reading comprehension of the material? In response, Deno (1985) concurs that comprehension is the generally accepted goal of reading instruction, but points out that the writing of comprehension questions and the preparation of testing materials to assess comprehension does not satisfy the criteria of simplicity, efficiency, and economy. If an assessment method does not meet these criteria, teachers are unlikely to use it for formative evaluation, no matter how high the method's content validity. A series of reliability and criterion validity studies has revealed that reading aloud from text is a valid and reliable indicator of general reading performance and progress which can be used by teachers "as a 'vital sign' of reading achievement in much the same sense that heart rate or body temperature is used as a vital sign of physical health" (Deno, 1985, p. 224). An extensive review of the validity and reliability research pertaining to the CBM measures would take us far afield from the thrust of this discussion. For information on the underlying supportive research for CBM, the reader is referred to Deno, Mirkin, and Chiang, 1982; Fuchs and Deno, 1981; Deno, Marston, Shinn, and Tindal, 1983; Deno, Marston, and Mirkin, 1982.

At first glance, the brevity and simplicity of the generic measures may lead some readers to conclude that the measures are inadequate for the purpose they are intended to serve, *i.e.*, formative evaluation of student performance and progress. Quite the contrary, the generic measures have great utility for the teacher who desires to enhance her program with formative evaluation. So little time and effort on the teachers' part is required, that teachers can easily use the measures for on-going assessment of pupil performance over time (rather than rely upon informal observations). The data in graphic form readily reveals pupil progress (or the lack thereof) and the teacher can then respond accordingly (the reader may wish to refer back to Figure 7.1 at this point). Inadequate progress would signal the need for programmatic alterations. The effectiveness of an alteration in the instructional program can be determined quickly from the data display of student performance following the introduction of the instructional modification. If the student does not respond, the data will reflect a lack of improvement in performance and further alteration of the student's instructional program would be called for. Allowing weeks, months, even an entire school year to pass by without adequately assessing and responding to the student who is not benefiting from the instructional program cannot be considered acceptable special education practice when we have the means at hand to do better. Allowing students to continue on with ineffective instructional programs is an unconscionable waste of instructional time.

A word of caution is in order about the limits of CBM. The generic measures do not provide, and are not intended to be used for, in depth diagnostic evaluation of student performance. If one wishes to conduct an error analysis of student academic performance, *e.g.*, error analysis of a writing sample or inventory of a child's phonic or word analysis skills, the CBM measures espoused by Deno are inappropriate. The procedures recommended by Blankenship presented earlier in the chapter are an appropriate avenue for in depth diagnostic evaluation. The generic CBM measures are "vital signs" of general performance status and progress in 4 academic areas. Information on status and progress, frequently collected, is vital for appropriate and effective programs for handicapped learners. When pupil performance falters or progress is inadequate, the teacher is alerted that the instructional program is not meeting the student's needs. At this point, further in depth diagnostic assessment may be indicated and the time required to undertake and complete such a diagnostic process may be fully justified. In combination, the criterion referenced testing procedures of Blankenship (1985) and the performance and progress indicators of

Deno (1985) provide the teacher with formative evaluation techniques that meet most classroom diagnostic and assessment needs.

In Summary

Monitoring of student performance has been singled out in numerous research studies and research reviews as one of the essential elements of effective instruction. Monitoring is important to ensure the appropriateness and efficacy of instructional programming. Monitoring in special education is part of a broader activity of assessment. The monitoring of student performance at the individual level is a mandated responsibility for special educators; the IEP serves a monitoring function. The many evaluation functions encompassed under assessment fall into the 2 categories of assessment for placement and assessment for instruction. The former is concerned with the identification of exceptionality and the placement of children in appropriate special education programs; the latter, in contrast, is focused upon instructional planning and delivery in the classroom.

Monitoring of student performance necessitates the selection of performance standards. Appropriate performance standards tied to realistic long range goals can do much to ensure that instructional time is put to good use and toward the preparation of the mildly handicapped for their lives beyond high school. Performance expectations for the mildly handicapped which are too low and require too little of the student may be out of step with realistic expectations for adult living. Immediate performance standards for daily instruction should require both mastery and proficiency. Rate of performance needs to be recognized as an important dimension of mastery performance by special education teachers.

Monitoring of performance requires data for decision-making. The data we use as the basis for instructional decisions must be valid and reliable. A data based orientation to decision-making must replace the informal, unsystematic means that teachers currently rely on as the basis for their instructional decisions. Data based decision-making and formative evaluation have been shown to have a positive effect on student performance. New and innovative measurement approaches such as curriculum based assessment provide practical, reliable, and valid data to meet the pressing measurement needs of the classroom, namely, diagnosis of performance strengths and weaknesses, error analysis, and progress monitoring.

Chapter 8

Monitoring Student Engagement

To monitor student engagement it is necessary to observe student behavior during instruction. The monitoring of student engagement, therefore, requires that teachers have proficiency in classroom observation techniques. Classroom observations are a mainstay of instructional techniques employed with the more severely and moderately impaired. But many teachers of the mildly handicapped are less familiar with this data gathering method, as assessment for the mildly impaired has traditionally emphasized the use of pencil and paper tests. The need exists for teachers of the mildly handicapped to expand their testing and monitoring methods.

There are a variety of data sources and data collection methods available to be used in the monitoring of student behavior. Alberto and Troutman (1986) indicate that the 3 primary methods of data collection are: analysis of written records, observation of tangible products, and observation of a sample of behavior. Each method has value and utility, but no one method will satisfy all testing needs. In the selection of a data collection method, careful thought must be given to forming a logical match between the type of data needed and the method of data collection. Pencil and paper tests are not the most direct or appropriate measures of student engagement or nonengagement, even though the quality of performance that they record is, in part, influenced by the level of a student's engagement. Direct and immediate data on student engagement is derived by means of classroom observations. It is important to draw a sharp distinction between systematic observations and the unsystematic observations we know to be common to special education classrooms (and so dear to special education teachers: Salmon-Cox, 1981; Fuchs and Fuchs, 1984; Fuchs, Fuchs, and Warren, 1982). Systematic classroom behavior observations are objective, reliable, and valid (Sulzer-Azaroff and Mayer, 1977), and adhere to well established procedures for data collection, data display, and data interpretation. These established criteria for methodology and procedure apply to classroom observations in general. However, in keeping with the theme of this text and chapter, particular attention will be focused on the classroom observation and monitoring of student engagement.

Data Collection

The methods of data collection selected must be appropriate to the behavior being observed and to the kind of behavior change desired (Alberto and Troutman, 1986). The process of data collection begins with the statement of the target behavior. According to Schloss and Sedlak (1986), a clear and concise statement of the target behavior can enhance the learning process in three ways: by enhancing the reliability of the observation and data collection procedure, by helping the student identify the anticipated outcome of the educational program, and by assisting the teacher in carrying out the educational program. A clear, precise definition of the target behavior contributes to the effectiveness of the instructional process from the beginning phase of data collection through intervention.

The quality and utility of the target behavior will be greatly enhanced by avoidance of verbs which are ambiguous or vague in favor of action verbs which clearly indicate what the student is doing or is expected to do (Deno and Jenkins, 1967). For example, ambiguous verbs such as "to distinguish", "to appreciate", "to analyze", "to know", "to understand", "to demonstrate", etc., are problematic in that they lend themselves to varied interpretations and are not easily observed or measured. Action verbs that are directly observable such as "to number", "to label", "to tell", "to cross out", "to circle", etc., are preferred as they lead to clear, unambiguous statements of target behaviors which can be measured with greater reliability. Target behaviors need to be described or expressed in terms that are measurable, observable, and repeatable (Schloss and Sedlak, 1986). The reader will recall that the target behavior is but one component of an acceptable and complete behavioral objective. The other requisite components are the conditions under which the behavior is to be displayed, and the criteria for acceptable performance. With the description of the target behavior clearly in mind, the selection of a data collection method can be made.

According to Alberto and Troutman (1986) there are 4 common methods of data collection: event recording, interval or time sampling recording, duration recording, and latency recording. Both event and interval recording are relevant methods for monitoring engagement; duration and latency recording would not be applicable.

Event Recording

Event recording is the method of choice for data collection when the teacher desires to count the frequency of occurrence of a particular behavior. Event recording is appropriate for counting the frequency of occurrence of discrete behaviors; that is, behaviors which have a clear and discernible beginning and ending point. Examples of discrete behaviors are call outs, hand raising, asking questions, asking for assistance, the number of pages of homework completed, etc. Event recording readily applies to a host of academic behaviors. The end result of an event recording data collection procedure will be a frequency count (or rate) of the occurrence of the target behavior. When frequency data are obtained over observations sessions which vary in length of time (as may very well happen in the classroom), the data can be easily converted to a rate of occurrence by dividing the frequency of behavior by the length of time of the observation session:

$$\text{Rate} = \frac{\text{Number of Occurrences of Behavior}}{\text{Length of Observation Time}}$$

The format of the data collection sheets employed for event recording follow no set pattern. But there are important informational items which any event recording data sheet must include, *e.g.*, identifying information about the student and class, name of the observer, data, target behavior, observation time (beginning and ending time), frequency count, and total frequency. The reader is referred to Alberto and Troutman, (1986), Tawney and Gast (1984) and Schloss and Sedlak (1986) for numerous examples of data collection forms.

Event recording has great utility for the classroom and is probably the easiest of all the data collection methods for the teacher to use. Schloss and Sedlak (1986) point out that event recording can be applied to analysis of permanent products as well as directly to student behavior. While both permanent products and student behavior lend themselves to event recording, there is an important practical difference. Student behavior is transitory and therefore must be observed and counted as it occurs. Permanent products produce a tangible and lasting response which can be counted after the response (behavior) actually occurred. Because the students' every day work assignments are the source, the supply of permanent products is practically endless; for example, the number of words written, number of words correctly spelled, number of problems attempted and/or completed, etc. With a little forethought and planning, *e.g.*, making math assignments of comparable length to facilitate comparison from one instructional session to another, and structuring and collecting written assignments once per week for the purpose of analysis and event recording, the teacher can readily secure the permanent products from the ongoing instructional activities with little or no extra effort or, for that matter, intrusive or time consuming testing for the students.

The generic CBM measures proposed by Deno (1985), in effect, produce permanent products which are analyzed by means of event recording. The measures, brief as they are, have been shown to be reliable and valid indicators of student status and progress in the 4 academic areas of reading, math, spelling and written expression. The fixed format and set time limits of each CBM task make the measures extremely easy to use. The variation of curricular content, *e.g.*, selection of the reading materials from the classroom curriculum to match the given teaching or instructional situation, enhances the educational utility of the measurement procedure.

Interestingly, on-task behavior or engagement is not considered a discrete behavior. Therefore, event recording is not the appropriate data collection method for directly observing on-task or engaged behavior. A time sampling procedure is indicated. Schloss and Sedlak (1986) point out that engaged behavior is one of the more difficult behaviors to adequately define or reliably observe. However, engaged behavior, which may be difficult to define and observe, is related to the level of student performance and productivity, *e.g.*, number of problems done or sentences completed (Schloss and Sedlak, 1986). Event recording is readily applied to permanent products. Therefore teachers can monitor engagement through the productivity of their students by applying event recording to permanent products.

Interval Recording

Interval recording is the data collection method of choice for target behaviors which are not discrete; that is, lack a clear beginning and ending point. On-task or engaged behavior fits this description. When very high frequency of occurrence and duration are important dimensions of the target behavior, interval recording is more suitable than event recording for the purpose of data collection. Interval recording would be the data collection method of choice for the observation of student engagement.

To conduct interval recording, a specific period of time (observation session) is divided into intervals of equal length, *e.g.*, intervals of 10 to 15 seconds. Rarely do intervals exceed 30 seconds in length (Alberto and Troutman, 1986). Therefore, an observation session 10 minutes in total time divided into 10 second intervals would yield a total of 60 intervals. The observer then notes whether or not the target behavior occurs during each 10 second interval and marks a data sheet accordingly. Each interval would contain only one notation, generally a plus (+) to indicate that the behavior occurred, and a minus (-) to indicate that the behavior had not occurred during each interval. A variation on interval recording, termed "time sampling", involves the designation of a particular point during the interval when the behavior is to be observed and coded. For example, the first second of a 10 second interval may be designated as the moment within the interval when the observer must observe and code the student as engaged or nonengaged. The behavior which occurs before or after the designated moment can have no effect on the coding. The remaining time in the interval may be used for the recording of other behaviors such as hand raising (a discrete behavior), or for other observer tasks such as additional coding or repositioning within the classroom.

The format for the data collection sheet used in interval recording must minimally contain student and class identifying information, observer identification, date, target behavior, and the starting and ending times, and a means of coding the occurrence or nonoccurrence of the target behavior within each interval. The sources previously cited for event recording data forms also provide model forms for interval recording.

For interval or time sampling recording, data on student performance is gathered during observation sessions scheduled through the day. The amount of time devoted to observation need not be great; 2 or 3 observation sessions lasting 10 to 15 minutes over the course of the day may be adequate. A sufficient number of observation sessions (preferably randomly selected) of sufficient length will yield an accurate representation of student behavior (Schloss and Sedlak, 1986). The amount of time needed for interval recording is modest; nevertheless, interval recording will very likely necessitate the presence of someone other than the teacher to actually carry out the observations and data collection procedures. It is difficult, if not impossible, for the teacher to observe, record, and teach at the same time. Aides, volunteers, fellow teachers, can be enlisted to help.

Interobserver Reliability

An important issue related to classroom observations concerns the reliability of the observation process and the data which results. Interobserver (or interrater) reliability is the extent to which 2 observers agree on the occurrence, nonoccurrence or duration of the target behavior (Schloss and Sedlak, 1986). The procedure for determining interrater reliability involves two observers collecting data independently during the same observation session. The results are compared to determine the degree of agreement between the two data sets of the two observers. The exact procedures for determining interrater agreement will vary somewhat from one method of data collection to another (see Schloss and Sedlak, 1986). Authorities differ on the minimal acceptable level of interrater reliability for instructional purposes. Schloss and Sedlak (1986) hold to 70 percent; Alberto and Troutman (1986), and Sulzer-Azaroff and Meyer (1977) advise a minimal level of 80 percent. Interrater reliability percentages which fall below a designated level indicate the existence of problems in definition, coding procedures, training of observers, etc., all of which require immediate attention. The data are suspect until the problems are resolved and interrater agreement is raised to an acceptable level. Having gathered the data, the next step is to graph the data to facilitate interpretation.

Data Display

The task of graphing data is made easier by the existence of a set of standard conventions. Sedlak, Steppe-Jones, and Sedlak (1982) have distilled these conventions into 7 rules for the graphing of observational data. The rules are paraphrased below:

Rule 1:   all performance data must be in a common base or unit of measurement.

Rule 2:   the horizontal axis should represent the time dimension, *e.g.*, days, sessions, and weeks, while the spacings on the axis should be divided into units of equal length.

Rule 3:   the vertical axis should represent student performance, as well as be labeled appropriately and divided into spacings of equal size. The lowest performance level should not coincide with the horizontal axis.

Rules 4 and 5:   the graph should contain sufficient identifying information, *e.g.*, student names, school, dates, etc., so as to communicate information quickly and easily to the reader.

Rule 6:   the baseline and training phases of the graph should be clearly labelled; the phases should be separated by broken vertical lines.

Rule 7:   data points representing student performance are placed appropriately on intersecting lines, while data points within a phase are connected but not connected across a phase line.

The display of hypothetical data in the Figure 8.1 conforms to the seven rules of graphing. With very rare exceptions, all the graphs one is likely to encounter in textbooks and professional journals will adhere to these basic rules. Adherence to these rules of graphing greatly facilitates communication within the professional community. For the teacher, graphic displays of student data which adhere to these same conventions will facilitate interpretation, evaluation of performance, and the monitoring of student progress and program effectiveness. Graphic display of student performance data will go a long way toward inculcating a data based orientation to instruction among teachers.

Figure 8.1. Rules for Graphic Display of Observational Data

Student - John Doe   **Target Behavior** - Academic

Observer - Mary Smith   engagement during

School - Hillcrest Elementary   reading instruction

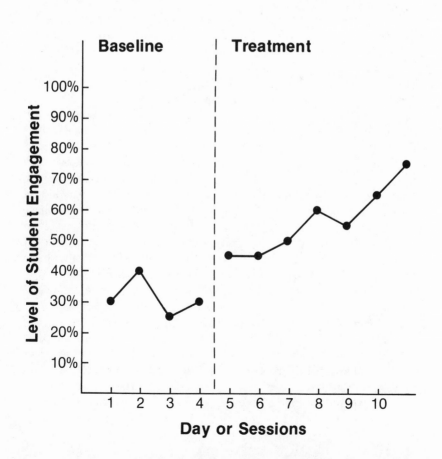

Data Interpretation and Analysis

There are 4 criteria which are generally applied to visually displayed data for the purpose of analysis and interpretation: mean, level, trend, and latency (Kazdin, 1982). The underlying purpose of visual inspection is to determine if the data provide evidence of a change in student behavior and concomitant evidence of a program or treatment effect. Schloss and Sedlak (1986) discuss the meaning and application of each of the visual inspection criteria.

They define the mean as "the average level of behavior during a given program phase" (Schloss and Sedlak, 1986, p. 160). The average performance level within the baseline phase and the average performance level within the treatment phase can be compared. A visually discernible difference would indicate a change in the student behavior being observed and measured. The magnitude of the difference would be an indication of the strength of the behavioral change and the power of the treatment.

Level is a "measure of the differences between program phases" (Schloss and Sedlak, 1986, p. 161). Level is gauged by comparing the last data point in one phase with the first data point in the next phase, e.g., the last data point under baseline conditions compared to the first data point under treatment conditions. Once again a visually discernible difference indicates of the presence and magnitude of the intervention effect. However, Schloss and Sedlak caution that the data points being compared must be representative of the total data within each phase. If this is not the case, more than one data point within a phase would be used for comparison purposes.

Trend (or slope) is defined as "the best fitting straight line between points in the baseline and intervention phases" (Schloss and Sedlak, 1986, p. 161). The trend line will clearly show the direction assumed by the data points within a phase. The trend of the data within one phase can be compared to the trend characteristic of the data in another phase in order to determine if the data provide evidence of a change in student behavior and treatment effect. For example, if the trend for data within a baseline phase was sharply downward and the trend for data in the following treatment phase was sharply upward, there would be strong evidence of a change in student behavior and treatment effectiveness.

Latency is "the period of time that elapses between the start of intervention to evidence of a performance change" (Schloss and Sedlak, 1986, p. 162). Latency refers to the amount of time which elapses between a change in instructional conditions and a change in student behavior. The student's response to a change in instructional conditions may be sharp and dramatic, slow and gradual, or even nonresponsive.

The 4 criteria are obviously interrelated. A marked change in one performance dimension of the graph will generally be reflected in changes in other dimensions of the graphed data. The 4 criteria for visual analysis are illustrated in Figure 8.2. The information imposed upon the graph in italics has been added for explanatory purposes only and would not appear in an actual graph. The mean level of behavioral strength during the baseline phase and intervention phases are substantially different from one to the other. The baseline data has a stable, flat trend.Under treatment conditions, the data display a marked upward trend. The difference between the last data point of the baseline phase and the first data point of the treatmentphase is quite pronounced. The data also indicated that the student responded quickly to the change in

Figure 8.2. Criteria for Visual Inspection of Graphed Data

Student - John Doe	**Target Behavior** - Academic
Observer - Mary Smith	engagement during
School - Hillcrest Elementary	reading instruction

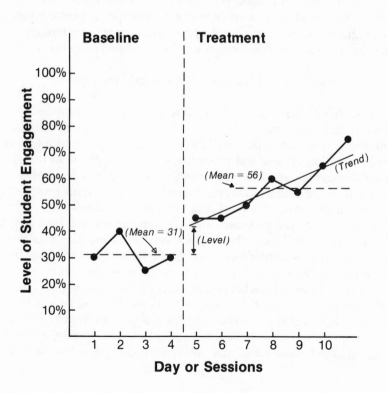

instructional conditions. The hypothetical example provides clear evidence of behavioral change on all 4 visual criteria. In actual practice, data for real students may or may not conform to this unequivocal pattern. With exposure to graphed data and experience in analysis and interpretation, teachers will quickly become adept at interpreting student performance data.

It is important to add that the teacher does not, indeed, should not, approach the task of visual analysis in a void. Analysis is guided by instructional objectives and goals. Are the results of the intervention consistent with the desired instructional outcomes as set forth in the objective and goal statements of the IEP? Is the pattern of student performance evident in the graphed data consistent with performance expectations based upon a peer referent group? Kazdin and Matson (1981) suggest that comparison of the handicapped student's performance with the performance of more able nonhandicapped peers (social comparison) will greatly aid the teacher in interpretation of student performance graphs. The process of social comparison espoused by Kazdin and Matson (1981) is similar in concept to peer referencing (Deno, 1985) and normative sampling (Idol, Nevin, Paolucci-Whitcomb, 1986) discussed previously. All 3 strategies embody the same recommendation, namely, that the appropriate performance of age or grade matched nonhandicapped students is the referent which must be applied to the performance of handicapped students.

Changing Teacher Attitudes and Practices

Teachers' often negative and nonreceptive attitudes toward observational and graphing techniques as well as their lack of familiarity with these procedures, pose formidable obstacles to the adoption and implementation of new and proven monitoring methods in the classroom. A major share of the responsibility for changing the status quo must fall to the teacher training institutions which train prospective teachers at the preservice level. Undergraduate students are a captive audience. As training programs and curricula are revised, new generations of teachers will exit school with at least a rudimentary knowledge and proficiency in instructional monitoring techniques, and in particular the data-based monitoring techniques discussed thus far.

The vast crop of teachers on the job at this time is of great concern and a challenge of considerable proportions. The research evidence clearly indicates that there is a need for change and improvements in many aspects of our instructional programs. The responsibility for bringing about meaningful and substantive change in teaching practices falls to the echelon of administrative and supervisory personnel who oversee programs and services for the mildly handicapped.

Within this context, in-service training for teachers takes on a particularly importance as it is the primary vehicle for upgrading teachers' knowledge and skills. Fortunately there is evidence of recent innovative approaches to in-service training which are proving to be effective. In addition to evidence of effectiveness, we have some reports of successful in-service training projects which raised student engagement levels by changing teaching behavior. The overlap of in-service training research and research on student engagement is of immediate interest and relevance.

Current teacher training research literature indicates that the components of effective in-service staff development programs are information sharing, skill demonstration, practice of new ideas and skills in actual classroom settings, and direct nonjudgmental feedback on teacher performance (Joyce and Showers, 1980; Smyth, 1984). When these elements are present in staff development programs, the probability of initial behavior change and long-term maintenance of desirable teaching behavior is enhanced.

Leach and Dolan (1985) published the results of an in-service training project which embodied many of these elements. Specifically, the authors' purpose was to design and assess the impact of a minimally intrusive low cost method for increasing student engagement (academic engaged rate, or AER). Two in-service formats were compared, one involved information sharing alone, the other involving information sharing plus direct nonjudgemental feedback on past performance. Three teachers participated in the study: 2 were randomly selected to receive information on instructional strategies to promote maximum AER and feedback on the AER of 3 target students within their classrooms, while the third teacher, serving as the control, received information only. Classroom observation data revealed that AER increased in the classrooms of the two teachers who received a combination of information and feedback. The AER level for the control class remained consistent throughout the study. An unanticipated finding revealed that the AER of nontarget students in the two experimental classrooms also increased. This generalized effect was most heartening and underscores the efficiency of the in-service model. In their discussion of the results, Leach and Dolan (1985) enumerate the pupil specific and non-pupil specific instructional strategies which the teachers employed, to great effect, to increase student AER: increased praise and attention, modification of task difficulty levels, greater teacher attention to quality of classroom preparation, more direct instruction, emphasis on academic goals, and minimization of external

Figure 8.3. On-Task Behavior During Small Group Instruction and Independent Seatwork

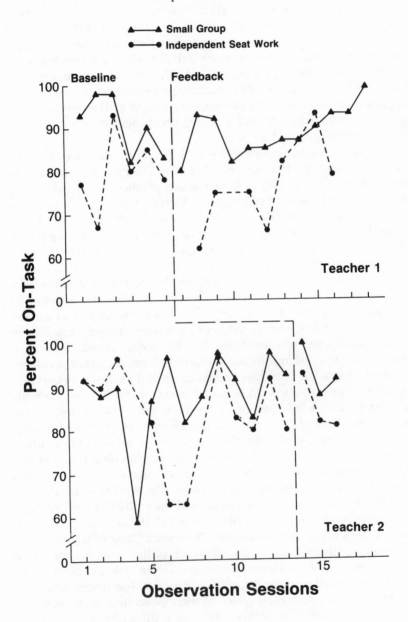

distractions. The experimental teachers, presumably as a result of the in-service training, made far better use of their instructional time with a resulting positive impact on student engagement.

A second study in a similar vein by Goodman, Shapiro and Bornstein (in progress) also focused upon the relationship between nonjudgemental feedback to teachers about student engagement and-subsequent levels of student on-task behavior. The study had two purposes: the first was to determine if teachers could effectively train their colleagues in classroom observational techniques; the second was to determine if nonjudgemental feedback to teachers would cause a change in the level of student on-task behavior. The authors found that teachers once trained in classroom observation techniques could effectively and efficiently train their fellow teachers in similar techniques up to a professionally acceptable level of performance, i.e., better than 80 percent inter-observer reliability. Regarding on-task behavior, data was gathered in 2 regular education and 2 special education elementary school classrooms. Data for the 2 regular education classrooms are presented in Figure 8.3. The data reveal the familiar pattern of higher on-task behavior during teacher led instruction (as occurs during small group instruction) as compared to the level of on-task behavior under independent seatwork conditions. Baseline data revealed a generally high level of on-task behavior from the outset. The potential for improvement in the level of student on-task behavior was limited by the initially high engagement rates. The data for teacher #1 indicates greater stability and attainment of very high levels of on-task behavior under The data also suggest that teacher sensitivity to feedback, particularly for those days when on-task behavior was uncharacteristically low, was acute. A sharp drop in student attentiveness invariably resulted in the classroom teacher seeking out the observer to discuss the problem and a strong rebound in student on-task behavior during the next observation session. The salient point in both the Leach and Dolan and Goodman et al. studies is the effectiveness of an in-service training model which relies heavily upon collegial interaction and judgmental feedback to teachers. The second salient point involved the designation of student on-task or engaged behavior as the criterion for success of the in-service training effort. It bears repeating that student engagement is being viewed as an index of teaching effectiveness.

The authors of both studies expressed concern about the intrusiveness of the training effort and observations on the ongoing classroom programs. Leach and Dolan (1985) made the point that many in-service studies which report positive results "generally involve complex procedures, were often expensive in time and resources, and

required a high degree of involvement and training by both consultants and teachers, which makes them difficult to adopt as regular ser-
vice-delivery strategies" (p. 57). They suggest that school personnel
could be trained to fulfill the functions so often done by consultants,
thereby decreasing both the expense and the degree of intrusiveness of
in-service training programs. Goodman *et al.* (in progress) addressed
this very issue and demonstrated that teachers could fulfill the training role associated with outside consultants, including the provision of
orientation and training to fellow teachers, planning and implementation of a training sequence complete with simulated and supported
observations prior to actual observations, and data collection and
graphing. Furthermore, the teacher-trainers in the Goodman *et al.*
study were able to do all of these in-service related tasks more efficiently, *i.e.*, in less time than outside consultants. Using teachers in
leadership roles in in-service programs opens up many possibilities
for positive collegial interaction and may go a long way toward over-
coming teacher resistance to important instructional innovations.

Monitoring methodology itself can be intrusive in the instructional process. Monitoring methods are time and energy consuming,
require a great deal of preparation, and can erode a considerable
amount of instructional time. It is no wonder that teachers do not
embrace such methodology with great enthusiasm. It is for this very
reason that the curriculum based measurement methods such as those
espoused by Deno (1985) are so attractive. The reader will recall that
the criteria for the development of the specific generic measures were
that they be reliable, valid, inexpensive, easily understood, and, regarding the issue of intrusiveness, simple and efficient (Deno, 1985). During
the initial conceptualization and development of the generic measures
every effort was made to ensure that they would be minimally intrusive and burdensome for the teacher. Wesson, Fuchs, Tindal, Mirking,
and Deno (1986) undertook a series of investigations with classroom
teachers in which the time required to carry out CBM and various
strategies for improving the efficiency of CBM were explored. The concern for efficiency, *e.g.*, the time and effort required to carry out CBM, is
well founded. The utility and value of CBM lies in its frequent use for
formative evaluation of student progress and instructional effectiveness. A monitoring method that is to be used frequently must place
minimal demands on teacher time while yielding highly useful instructional data. "With frequent curriculum-based measurement, a teacher
develops short, simple measures from a student's curriculum; adminis-
ters those measures about three times a week, or even daily; graphs
student performance data; and analyzes the graphed data to determine

the appropriateness of the student's program" (Wesson *et al.*, 1986, p. 166). The series of investigations conducted in close collaboration with classroom teachers revealed that the average amount of time required to do CBM (the 3 generic measures for reading, spelling and writing) was 6 minutes and 48 seconds once the teacher became familiar and comfortable with the testing procedures (the initial time requirement had been 15 minutes and 42 seconds). Subsequent investigations delved into the fine points of CBM techniques. For example, it was determined that a prescribed order of testing, *e.g.*, reading, spelling, then written expression, was superior to any other order of presentation as the teacher was able to score and graph the results of the reading and spelling tests while the student engaged in the 3 minute writing task thereby using time most efficiently. Other strategies which contributed to the efficiency of CBM included "precounting the words in oral reading passages, using mechanical devices to administer the measures, and teaching the student to score and graph their data" (Wesson *et al.*, 1986, p. 171). In other research on formative evaluation, Fuchs (1986) explored the 4 critical measurement dimensions: focus of measurement, frequency of measurement, data display, and data-utilization methods. The investigations provided support for the use of (a) "certain empirically validated key behaviors as the focus of monitoring activity, (b) long-term goal statements that may encourage teachers to focus not only on the immediate instructional content, but also on maintenance and generalization of skills, and (c) ambitious goals that support task persistence and striving" (Wesson *et al.*, 1986, p. 10). The literature also supports at least twice weekly evaluation of student performance, and the use of data-utilization rules to guide decisions about modifications in instructional programming.

Recent researcher endeavors which specifically confront the issues of efficiency are very encouraging. They reveal that the realities of the classroom and the concerns of teachers are being recognized and heeded. Teachers will resist monitoring approaches that are excessively intrusive or burdensome. If formative evaluation and data-based decision making are to become a mainstay of special education classrooms, methods must be developed which are highly efficient regarding time use and provide information of immediate and significant utility for the instructional process.

In Summary

Classes in which teachers closely monitor student progress and use this student performance data to keep instruction finely tuned to student needs yield higher achievement gains than classes where monitoring is less frequent and less intense. Formative evaluation provides the data which will alert the teacher to the need for adjustments when students are not progressing satisfactorily or affirm the effectiveness of instruction when students are doing well. Student performance data must be the basis for the data-based decision making process.

Student engagement has been identified as an important student performance variable and one which teachers should monitor. Engagement is both an indicator of student productivity and an index of management efficiency. High rates of student engagement are associated with higher levels of achievement and absence of disruption in the classroom.

Engagement is monitored by means of classroom observations. Two methods of data collection, event and interval recording, are applicable. Interval recording is appropriate for direct observation of engaged behavior; event recording is suitable for use with permanent samples of the students' work, *i.e.*, permanent products. Observation data is graphically displayed for visual analysis and interpretation. Adherence to commonly accepted guidelines for graphing and visual analysis of observational data facilitate communication among all parties with a legitimate interest in the data.

Teachers' resistance to formative evaluation and data-based decision making may stem from the intrusiveness of monitoring procedures. Teachers will rightly resist monitoring methods which intrude greatly upon instructional time. Innovative evaluative methods, *e.g.*, CBM, and research efforts to streamline evaluation strategies will hopefully help to change teacher attitudes toward monitoring. In-service programs which employ intercollegial experiences and informative yet nonjudgemental feedback on performance can be effective in changing teachers' in-class behavior.

Chapter 9

Increasing Instructional Effectiveness through Peer-Tutoring and Student Self-Management

In the day to day operation of the classroom the teacher is caught between competing time demands. On the one hand, there is the pressure for individualization to satisfy the unique and individual student needs. On the other hand, there are compelling research findings which highlight the need for more teacher directed group instruction. The situation facing the teacher is made more difficult by the research reports which reveal that the level of teacher attention to individual needs is negatively correlated with overall student achievement (Stallings and Kaskowitz, 1974) and indicative of less rather than more effective management skills.

There is little risk of over statement in the observation that the special education classroom is problem rich and resource poor. The resource in shortest supply may well be instructional time and the teachers' inability to give each student enough individual attention. A partial solution to the problem may lie in the use of "teacher surrogates". Wilson and Wesson (1986) use the term "teacher surrogates" to describe a variety of persons, other than the teacher, who can fill instructional roles in the classroom. Paraprofessionals and teachers' aides have been a mainstay of classroom operations for many years. The costs associated with the employment and maintenance of such quasi-teaching and supportive personnel have spurred on the search for other less costly alternatives. Wilson and Wesson (1986) include VISTA volunteers, foster grandparents, parent and community volunteers, university tutors, student teachers, and students in the role of peer tutors as potential surrogate teachers.

There is increasing interest in students as a primary instructional resource in the classroom. Research evidence that student tutors can be as effective as paraprofessionals in eliciting academic gains from their fellow students (Armstrong, Conlon, Parson, and Strahlbrand cited in Jenkins and Jenkins, 1985) has fueled interest in the use of students in instructional roles. The use of students as tutors for other students is seen as "a solution to the persistent problem of resource scarcity and the accompanying need for individualized instruction" (Gerber and Kauffman, 1981, p. 182). Jenkins and Jenkins (1985) suggest that teachers can increase academic engaged time through one-to-one instruction by recruiting students to increase their reserve of instructional personnel. They point out the many benefits associated with peer tutoring: for example, increased individualization, increased academic engagement time, increased productivity, increased effectiveness of lessons, instruction for individual students, freeing the teacher for group instruction or other necessary activities, and academic and affective gains for both student tutees and tutors.

Contrary to what some may believe, peer tutors are not a free resource. Gerber and Kauffman (1981) aptly indicate that existing resources must be allocated to the creation and maintenance of a peer tutoring program. The hours for training, the time for materials preparation, the ongoing monitoring of the tutoring program are "cost factors" which must be recognized. "Therefore, the choice to train one or more students as peer tutors is rational *if* the resulting educational outcomes are improved with the expenditure of the same amount of teacher time, or if the educational outcomes remain the same with an investment of less time" (Gerber and Kauffman, 1981, p. 162). To date the research literature has paid little attention to the costs of peer tutoring programs.

Another way in which students can enhance the efficiency of the instructional process is through self-management. There is a growing body of research which demonstrates that students, properly trained, are capable of fulfilling some instructional functions traditionally carried out by the teacher or teaching aides. The research shows that students are capable of self-management in the form of self-monitoring, self-recording (Blick and Test, 1987), and self-instruction and correction (Rosiewicz, Hallahan, Lloyd, and Graves, 1982). The training of students to assume a degree of responsibility for their own instructional self-management has the potential to enhance the management and operation of the classroom. Student self-management has also been investigated as a means of increasing on-task and engaged behavior and generally positive results have been reported.

Peer tutoring and student self-management have been identified as means toward better, more efficient use of instructional time in the classroom. The numerous benefits to students, teachers, and classroom operations associated with these instructional interventions further justifies the inclusion of these important topics.

Peer Tutoring

Peer tutoring involves students—one fulfilling the role of tutor and another in the role of the tutee—in instructional interaction in which one child assists another to acquire competence on specific tasks or skills. Historically, the role of the tutor was filled by a regular education teacher or a professional tutor, but today paraprofessionals (and, with increasing frequency and in increasing numbers, students) are fulfilling this role (Cohen, Kulik, and Kulik, 1982). Peer tutoring can involve students of the same age and in the same class or cross-age tutoring wherein an older pupil tutors a younger student. The variety of students who receive tutoring assistance is matched by the variety of students who have been recruited to serve as tutors. As one would expect handicapped or disabled learners are frequent recipients of tutoring assistance, but handicapped students in the role of tutors is also quite common (Cook, Scruggs, Mastropieri, and Castro, 1985-86; Scruggs, Mastropieri, and Richter, 1985; Scruggs and Richter, 1985). The focus for peer tutoring programs has been academic and affective outcomes for the students involved. The efficacy issues which surround the topic of peer tutoring involve the benefits which result for both the students being tutored and the students doing the tutoring (Gerber and Kauffman, 1981; Cohen, Kulik, and Kulik, 1982). The use of students as tutors can only be justified if it can be shown that tutors as well as tutees derive benefits from the tutoring experience. The tutorial experience is not justified solely by the improved performance or achievement gain of the tutee, nor is the experience justified by mere gains or absence of losses for the tutor. "It will not suffice to prove that some benefit, either social or academic, accrues to the tutor. Rather, it must be demonstrated that the tutor benefits in the way that serves his or her learning needs specifically" (Gerber and Kauffman, 1981, p. 181). This statement from Gerber and Kauffman sets a very stringent standard for peer tutoring programs, but one which underscores the ethical considerations which must be fully appreciated by those who would use students in teaching roles.

Student Outcomes

The literature pertaining to peer tutoring is comprised of both anecdotal and empirical studies. The former are of interest and useful in that they provide insight into the tutoring process and suggest avenues for research efforts. Unfortunately, conclusions about the effectiveness of tutoring programs or the dynamics of the tutoring process can not be drawn from this source. Rather, one must look to the empirical literature. Here we find that a variety of research designs have been employed. Quasi-experimental designs involving experimental students only and lacking a control group are common. The results derived from such studies must be interpreted with caution as we have no way of knowing if the observed effects, hopefully improvements in student achievement or attitudes, are the result of the treatment, such as peer tutoring, or the result of some other instructional or noninstructional variable, *e.g.*, another instruction intervention which occurred during the treatment period. Some studies in the absence of a contrasting control group have attempted to increase the credibility of their findings by projecting the degree of student gains against actual gains. When student improvement exceeds the projections the plausibility of a treatment effect is increased. However, this treatment of the data does not rule out all threats to internal and external validity. Studies which employed an experimental control group design, though fewer in number, are certainly stronger in experimental design. Given the presence of an experimental versus control group comparison, one can draw conclusions about treatment effects with a much greater degree of confidence. Additionally, research studies which contrast peer tutoring against other instructional interventions do much to establish the instructional value of peer to peer instruction. For example, Epstein (1978) compared the effects of peer tutoring in reading with 4 different control conditions: peer tutoring in math, self-instructional, teacher-instructed, and no-treatment. "Comparisons of this type, if carefully documented, could yield much information about the relative effectiveness of peer tutoring" (Scruggs and Richter, 1985, p. 287). Single subject designs are also included in the peer tutoring research literature. Studies incorporating a single subject design are revealing of individual learner performance under different conditions. Evidence of a treatment effect is demonstrated through the replication of the predicted (functional) relationship between peer tutoring and student performance on selected outcome measures.

A number of research reviews on the topic of peer tutoring are available (Cohen, Kulik, and Kulik, 1982; Cook, Scruggs, Mastropieri, and Castro, 1985-86; Devin-Sheehan, Feldman, and Allen, 1976; Fitz-Gibbons and Taylor, 1977; Gerber and Kauffman, 1981; Mohan, 1972; Rosenshine and Furst, 1969; Scruggs and Richter, 1985; Scruggs, Masteropieri, and Richter, 1985). The collective body of research provides invaluable information; however, some sources are more relevant than others. Some of the early reviews of peer tutoring pointedly excluded studies involving handicapped learners, *e.g.*, the research of Cohen *et al.* 1982. Despite this limitation, the review is useful as a point of reference to facilitate comparison of peer tutoring for the handicapped with peer tutoring for the nonhandicapped.

Cohen *et al.* reviewed the peer tutoring literature in regular education to determine the effects on both the student being tutored and the student in the role of tutor. Results were discussed in terms of achievement and affective outcomes. Regarding achievement outcomes for the tutored students, 45 of 52 studies reviewed indicated that children who received tutoring assistance performed better than untutored students in conventional classrooms. The student gains ranged from modest to strong. Further examination of the results revealed that stronger student achievement outcomes were associated with 6 programmatic features: structured programs; tutoring programs of short duration; teaching and testing of lower order skills; math rather than reading instruction; demonstration of stronger effects on locally developed tests, while weaker results were demonstrated on nationally standardized test measures; and the reporting of smaller effects in dissertations, and larger effects reported in published reports. Achievement gains were found for the tutors also: in 33 of 38 studies which tested achievement of the tutors, student tutors performed better than contrasting control students on examinations in the subjects being taught. In 5 studies achievement test results favored the students not serving as tutors. In the 10 studies which reported statistically significant achievement gains, all favored the student tutors. The results pointed to positive changes in students' attitude toward school and the subject being taught among both the tutees and the tutors. The number of studies which examined affective or attitudinal changes was much smaller than the bulk of the studies which investigated achievement gains. Regarding changes in students' self concept as a result of participation in the peer tutoring program, there were few relevant studies and these yielded little evidence of a generalized affective change such as improvement in self concept. The findings of Cohen *et al.* are generally consistent with the findings of earlier reviews, that is, academic performance gains for both the tutees and the tutors, improved attitudes toward school and subject matter taught, and little evidence of a generalized effect on self-concept or other social interaction patterns.

With the findings of Cohen *et al.* to serve as a backdrop, we turn to 3 recent research reviews devoted to examination and synthesis of the literature pertaining to peer tutoring with handicapped students. Scruggs and Richter (1985) examined peer tutoring for learning disabled (LD) students. In all, 27 studies were reviewed. Eleven of the studies employed learning disabled or reading disabled students as tutors. The subject taught was most often reading but spelling, math, and library skills were occasionally included. The ratio of studies which examined academic benefits for tutees only to studies which assessed effects for both the tutee and tutor was approximately 2 to 1 (20 to 9). Social outcomes were investigated in an equally small number of studies (5) for both the tutored and tutoring students. Scruggs and Richter categorized the research studies reviewed by their research design, *i.e.*, pre-posttest designs (absence of a contrasting control group) and experimental designs (contrast between experimental and control group). Seven studies involving a pre-post design reported positive academic gains as a result of the tutoring experience. In 4 of these studies actual achievement gains were contrasted with expected achievement gains based upon students' prior performance; in 3 instances actual achievement exceeded predicted achievement. These findings lend some strength to the positive achievement outcome, but still cannot fully rule out the possibility that other factors occurring within the same time frame were responsible for or markedly contributed to the observed improvements in achievement. Of the pre-post design studies, 3 employed handicapped students in the tutoring roles. The results reveal that both tutors and tutees made academic gains. In 5 out of 7 studies, there was evidence of social benefits for both the tutees and tutors. The types of social and behavioral gains reported included "fewer delinquencies, improved attitude toward school, cooperation, self-esteem, greater motivation, fewer anti-social acts, and less hostility toward authority figures" (Scruggs and Richter, 1985, p. 295). The reader is cautioned that these reported "findings" lack empirical support.

Sixteen of the studies in the Scruggs and Richter review included an experimental group versus control group comparison. Eight of these studies involved the comparison between peer tutoring and a no-treatment group. Although the authors reported successful outcomes resulting from the tutoring intervention, adequate descriptive information about the control group activities is lacking. Lack of information about the control group activities limits the conclusions that can be drawn from the data. The results suggest the superiority of peer tutoring, but we are left with the unanswered question: superior to *what*? All of the no-treatment control group studies reported group differences favoring the tutored students; only 3 out of 8 studies found statistically significant differences. These 3 studies involved secondary aged tutors working with younger learning disabled students. There is considerable evidence of the effectiveness of cross-aged tutoring (Maher, 1982, 1984; Maheady and Harper, 1987), and of added benefits accruing to tutors who participate in cross-age tutoring interventions (Scruggs and Osguthorpe, 1986).

The studies which involved a comparison of the effects of peer tutoring and alternative instructional interventions are most important. Six of the 24 studies reviewed involved such comparisons. Three of these reported statistically significant differences favoring the peer tutoring intervention. Superior effects for peer tutoring were found in contrasts between peer tutoring and 6th graders independently studying social studies materials (King, 1982), teacher instruction in reading skills for the learning disabled (Lamport, 1982), and teacher instruction and self-instruction in math for learning disabled students (Epstein, 1978). Two studies which employed single subject designs also claimed successful peer tutoring interventions (Higgins, 1982; Jenkins, Mayhall, Peschka, and Jenkins, 1974).

The research findings which have demonstrated the superiority of peer tutoring to the alternative of teacher instruction should not be misconstrued to suggest that peer tutoring is a desirable replacement for teacher directed instruction in general. These studies usually are of very short duration and involve the teaching of very limited and proscribed materials or skills. There are some who envision resource classrooms in which peer tutoring is the primary vehicle for instructional delivery and in which the teacher's role changes from instructor to manager (Jenkins *et al.*, 1974). This view is out of step with the current research supported emphasis upon group teaching and active teacher-directed instruction in the classroom. Peer tutoring is useful as a supplement to classroom instruction.

An important factor which bears upon all of the studies which contain a contrast between peer tutoring and alternative instructional conditions (whether or not those instructional alternatives are adequately detailed) has to do with the provision of equal instructional time for all instructional alternatives. If peer tutoring interventions added instructional time for the experimental students in excess of the amount of instructional time provided for the control students, then the superior gains reported for the peer tutoring alternative may merely be the results of extra time on task (Allen and Feldman, 1974; Devin-Sheehan, Feldman, and Allen, 1976; Scruggs and Richter, 1985). Some of the studies provide this crucial information; others do not.

On the basis of their research review, Scruggs and Richter concluded that children can effectively instruct other children, but they are reluctant to go beyond this general statement. The literature simply does not yet provide the specificity of information nor unequivocal data on many key issues which would warrant further firm conclusions about peer tutoring's effectiveness *vis a vis* other instructional alternatives, or the conditions under which peer tutoring is most effective or beneficial for handicapped students. The authors' reticence is well founded and accurately reflects the state of our knowledge about peer tutoring. On the basis of the research reviewed, it is safe to say that peer tutoring holds much promise as a supplemental instructional technique, but there is much to learn about the factors which contribute to its effectiveness and the conditions under which it will produce the desired improvements for the student tutees and tutors.

In another similarly structured research review, Scruggs, Mastropieri, and Richter (1985) studied the impact of being a tutor on the behavior and performance of behaviorally disordered students. Seventeen relevant studies were reviewed of which 6 employed single subject research designs, 5 were treatment group only pre-post investigations, 4 involved a no-treatment control group comparison, and 2 contrasted peer tutoring to alternative instructional interventions. Student performance on measures of social improvement and academic gains were assessed. The collective results revealed that the tutees, almost without exception, improved in academic performance. Academic gains were frequently, but not uniformly, reported for the tutors as well. Scruggs, Mastropieri, and Richter observed that tutors appeared to gain academically when the tutoring materials addressed the performance areas in which the tutors had need of improvement. If tutors have full mastery of the materials being taught then further academic gains are unlikely. In some instances, other than academic gains might justify the role of tutor for particular students, *e.g.*, behavioral or social gains for a behaviorally disordered student.

Scruggs, Mastropieri, *et al.* found that the consistency and strength of the achievement gains appeared to be related to the research design. Single subject investigations yielded more consistent findings of academic improvement than investigations involving experimental versus control group comparisons. The results on academic measures in the experimental control group designs were mixed, producing less evidence of successful peer tutoring interventions. The authors also reported that academic gains were more likely to be found when criterion measures which closely resembled the content of instruction during the peer tutoring sessions were used and were less apparent when standardized tests of achievement were employed as the outcome measures. Similar findings have been reported by Cohen, *et al.* (1982).

A major focus of the research review was the social benefits for the disabled students participating as tutors. Ten of the 17 studies yielded results regarding the social benefits for the tutors. The results revealed that tutors improved in their attitude toward the subject tutored and that positive interactions between tutor and tutee increased in number. However, generalized social gains as seen in enhanced self-esteem or improved sociometric ratings were not found; a similar pattern of social outcomes was revealed for both the tutors and tutees. The findings relative to social outcomes reported by Scruggs, Mastropieri, and Richter are consistent with the findings reported by other reviewers for both special education (Scruggs and Richter, 1985) and regular education students (Cohen *et al.*, 1982).

The third research review by Cook, Scruggs, Mastropieri, and Castro (1985-86) reported the results of a meta-analysis of research involving handicapped students as tutors for other students. Nineteen studies in which learning disabled (LD), intellectually handicapped (IH), and behaviorally disordered (BD) students acted as tutors were reviewed and their results aggregated and analyzed. Proceeding from the premise that the use of students as tutors requires the verification of academic and social benefits for the student tutors, the authors sought evidence of academic and social gains for both the tutors and tutees. In general the results of the meta-analysis confirm the findings of the research reviews already discussed. Involvement in peer tutoring benefits both tutees and tutors. Academic gains were about the same for all students irrespective of whether they were tutored or tutoring. The magnitude of the academic gains for all of the handicapped students were comparable to the academic gains reported for nonhandicapped students by Cohen *et al.* (1982). The data revealed that "being involved in a tutoring intervention raised the performance level of the handicapped tutor and tutee over one-half of one standard deviation above their respective control groups" (Cook *et al.*, 1985-86, p. 486). The findings consistent with the findings of other reviewers are that nonstandardized outcome measures produced stronger effects than standardized measures, and that there was little evidence of effectiveness on self-concept measures or other sociometric ratings. An interesting observation reported by these authors alone was the extent to which peer tutoring was a substitute or a supplement to the regular instructional program. In 31 percent of the cases, peer tutoring was a substitute for regular instruction and in 17 percent of the cases peer tutoring was provided as a supplement to the regular instructional program. Peer tutoring as a supplement versus a substitute to regular instruction had no apparent impact on the performance of the tutees but did appear to impact on the performance of the tutors. Tutoring students performed close to one standard deviation above the control group when tutoring was supplemental to regular instruction, but performed one-half standard deviation above the control group on academic measures when tutoring was a substitute for ongoing instruction. This finding is germane to the ethical issues involved in the use of students as tutors raised by Gerber and Kauffman (1981) and requires further study. It bears repeating that the use of students as tutors is only justified by the benefits to the tutors independent of the benefits to the tutees.

The collective results of all the research reviews discussed representing a significant body of special and regular education research literature supports the following conclusions:

- peer tutoring is academically beneficial for both tutees and tutors;
- benefits for tutees occur at a consistently high rate, and benefits frequently occur for tutors as well;
- social benefits are limited to attitudes toward school, the subject matter being taught and social interactions between tutors and tutees, while evidence of generalized social gains is scarce;
- handicapped students can function effectively as tutors for other students;
- the demonstrable effects of peer tutoring interventions are greater on criterion measures closely aligned to the materials being taught rather than on standardized test instruments;
- the outcomes of peer tutoring interventions are related to research design with experimental control group comparisons and single subject designs yielding stronger evidence of effectiveness than pre-post treatment only group designs.

Review of the literature also leads to the undeniable conclusion that the utility of the data base is restricted by the methodological weaknesses within the research literature. A considerable portion of the literature is anecdotal in nature and therefore of little empirical value and limited utility. Empirical research studies fall into 3 categories: single subject designs, one group pre-post comparisons, and experimental versus control group contrasts. The last category includes treatment control group comparisons and comparisons of peer tutoring with alternative instructional treatments. Studies which document controlled comparisons across competing instructional interventions, in this case peer tutoring and other small group or individualized instructional strategies, are particularly useful and are also definitely in the minority. Yet, it is the studies which contrast competing instructional interventions which most adequately address the issue of effectiveness. One group, pre-post designs, to a certain extent, give an exaggerated picture of peer tutoring effectiveness, although the consistency of positive findings supports the conclusion that peer tutoring impacts positively on student performance and behavior. Gerber and Kauffman (1981) assert that the true test of peer tutoring involves the demonstration of student gains in less time or student gains in the same time but at less cost. The issue is not whether or not peer tutoring works (the evidence suggests that it does), but rather whether it works better than a host of other available and educationally acceptable instructional alternatives.

Examples of studies which contrasted peer tutoring to other instructional interventions (while holding the total amount of instructional time constant across all instructional alternatives) are Epstein (1978) and Jenkins et al. (1974). Epstein contrasted intraclass peer tutoring for elementary LD students in reading with 3 competing instructional conditions: peer tutoring in math, self-instruction, teacher-instructed reading group, and a no-treatment control group. Peer tutoring in reading produced significantly better student performance than any of the other instructional alternatives. Jenkins et al. (1974), using multiple replications of a single subject design, compared the effects of peer tutoring and small group instruction for resource room students on measures of word recognition, oral reading, spelling, and multiplication. Student performance was, with one exception, superior under tutorial instruction across all academic tasks.

Peer tutoring is undoubtedly a viable instructional method which should be included in the teacher's repertoire of supplemental instructional techniques. Peer tutoring is applicable across a wide range of instructional settings for a variety of instructional tasks. Handicapped and nonhandicapped, tutees and tutors can derive benefits from the tutoring interventions. But despite the positive outlook for peer tutoring, we are hampered by the lack of specific information which details how to implement peer tutoring both effectively and ethically.

Guidelines for Peer Tutoring Programs

There are many resources which the teacher can consult if she wishes to develop and implement a peer tutoring program (Allen, 1976a; Argyle, 1976; Gartner, Kohler, and Reisman, 1971; Jenkins and Jenkins, 1985). Some general principles have emerged from the empirical literature which deserve special attention.

Researchers repeatedly stress the importance of structure in the peer tutoring program if the intended benefits are to be realized (Rosenshine and Furst, 1969; Cohen et al., 1982; Ellson, 1976). A variety of peer tutoring interventions have yielded positive results, but the stronger effects are associated with the more structured programs (Cohen et al., 1982). Sources of structure within a peer tutoring program are to be found in the training of tutors, the instructional materials and lessons formats, feedback and corrective procedures, etc. Despite the information available at this time, there are many unanswered questions about how one achieves optimally structured peer tutoring programs. For example, the training of tutors is critical to effective structure within the peer tutoring program but empirical evidence does not indicate which method of training is best (Allen, 1976b).

The classroom environment has much to do with the success for failure of a peer tutoring program. Gerber and Kauffman (1981) indicated that peer tutoring is more likely to succeed in the classroom environment when it "a) encourages cooperative behaviors through its reward structure, (b) provides clearly defined, hierarchially arranged learning objectives, and (c) maintains a systematic congruence and consistency between its behavior management and instructional procedures" (p. 175).

Regarding the students who are referred for peer tutoring, the research literature indicates that both the handicapped and nonhandicapped can receive help or function as tutors. The mildly handicapped are not categorically excluded from either role. Disability per se is not an obstacle to being an effective tutor. The important consideration is the tutor's competence in the subject matter to be taught vis a vis the tutee, not the tutor's academic status or class placement.

As to specific tutor-tutee pairings, researchers have studied factors such as sex, race, socioeconomic status, and age differential. No factors have yet come to light to indicate that certain "pairs" ought to be avoided or are clearly detrimental to the peer tutoring intervention. On the other hand, we lack information as to pairs that might be particularly effective. It appears that success for the tutee and tutor in their respective roles hinges upon the actual success encountered in the peer tutoring situation. Effective peer tutoring can involve students paired within the same class and age or involve cross-age tutoring in which an older student helps a younger child. Drawing upon the empirical literature, Gerber and Kauffman (1981) offer 3 general principles for selection and matching of tutees and tutors and guidelines for the training of student tutors: 1) responsiveness of tutees to peer modeling and peer-delivered reinforcement; 2) trainability of the perspective tutor including: a) familiarity with materials to be used in instruction; b) ability to reliably discriminate correct from incorrect responses and how to deliver reinforcement; and c) competence in instructional interaction behavior: and 3) absence of aversive or inappropriate behaviors on the part of either the tutor or tutee.

The magnitude and organizational demands which will face the teacher who undertakes the development and implementation of a peer tutoring program should not be underestimated. Time demands will be substantial and ongoing monitoring will be essential. It has been suggested that a full-time management position may be warranted as part of an extensive district-wide peer tutoring program (Jenkins and Jenkins, 1985). At the classroom level, the teacher can initiate peer tutoring on a modest scale which is compatible with the ongoing instructional program.

An Application of Peer Tutoring

An example of peer tutoring applied to ongoing classroom instruction is described below. One study, from the many available in the literature, was selected as a good example of how peer tutoring can be used as an instructional supplement to enhance student engagement and active responding, thus contributing to improved student performance.

A peer tutoring spelling game is described in detail by Delquadri, Greenwood, Stretton, and Hall (1983) as part of an empirical investigation designed to improve spelling performance through increased opportunity to respond. The peer tutoring spelling game was implemented in a self-contained third grade class of 24 children in an inner city, low-income, minority neighborhood. The majority of the children were performing below national norms in spelling. Six of the students were receiving help for learning disabilities in a special eduction resource room. The 24 children were categorized into 2 groups of low performers and average peers. The groups contained 6 and 18 students respectively. The teacher had requested help in the area of spelling for these 6 youngsters.

The peer tutoring spelling game was designed to satisfy five criteria: (1) to create no extra work for the teacher; (2) to benefit all students within the class; (3) to utilize materials in the current spelling program; (4) to supplement rather than supplant the ongoing spelling program; and (5) to be carried out during the existing time period available for spelling. In actuality, the peer tutoring spelling game used 15 minutes of instructional time per day. The fifteen minutes encompassed two 5 minute tutoring sessions and 5 minutes for determining and posting individual and team scores.

The essential components of the spelling game were team competition, peer tutoring and training, scoring and error correction procedures, and public posting of individual and team scores. At the beginning of each week children were randomly assigned to one of 2 teams and the teacher then assigned students to tutoring pairs. Teams and pairs remained intact for one week. All students were reassigned in the following week thus giving every student the opportunity to be on the winning team at some time. To train the children in tutoring the teacher took approximately 30 minutes during the first day of peer tutoring to outline and demonstrate the procedures for tutoring and scoring. An analogy to a basketball game proved helpful in that the students were told that they could score two points for baskets (correctly spelled words) and one point for foul shots (corrections of misspelled words).

The actual peer tutoring game involved two 5 minute tutoring sessions with the students in each pair reversing roles so that each child had the opportunity to be the tutee and the tutor each day. The students reviewed a list of 18 spelling words each week. A timer was used to signal the children to reverse roles and to proceed into final scoring procedures. During the tutoring sessions the tutee responded to directions from his or her tutor who indicated whether or not spelling responses were correct and provided corrective procedures if needed. While the students were engaged in peer tutoring, the teacher moved about the class checking individual pairs and giving bonus points for "good tutoring behaviors".

At the end of each daily session, the student pairs added up their individual scores. The teacher called for each child's score and subsequently determined the team score for the day. All scores were publicly posted. On Friday of each week, the children were tested on their list of 18 spelling words. Each student pair switched papers and determined their partner's score by assigning 3 points to each correctly spelled word. Individual and team scores were again posted by the teacher and the winning team was cheered by the class as "team of the week". The teacher randomly reviewed 10 students' scoring and point additions each day and all of the spelling tests on Friday. Errors in student scoring throughout the investigation were found to be less than 2 percent.

An experimental design consisting of an ABAB reversal design with concurrent baselines was used to determine the effect of the peer tutoring spelling game on student performance. The first baseline phase extended from week 1 through 18, during which time the children received instruction in a traditional spelling program. At the beginning of the week the children received a list of 18 words followed by discussion and workbook exercises. Each Friday there would be a spelling test. The first treatment phase of the investigation involved the implementation of the peer tutoring spelling game as described above. This phase lasted from week 19 through 24. During the 25th week, the teacher reversed back to the instructional conditions of the baseline period. The peer tutoring spelling game was reinstituted during the second treatment phase for the 26th and 27th weeks.

The results of the investigation indicated a dramatic increase in spelling performance for both the low performing LD and their average performing peers. During the baseline phase, the LD students averaged 9.8 spelling errors on their weekly spelling test. During the first treatment phase using the peer tutoring spelling game the average number of spelling errors for these students dropped to 2.5 on their weekly tests. The return to baseline conditions was accompanied by an increase in spelling errors to a mean of 11. When the spelling game was reintroduced the average number of spelling errors in the end-of-week spelling tests for the LD students fell to 3.0. As to the nonhandicapped students, their average number of spelling errors on the weekly test during baseline phase was 3.0. Their average fell to .5 under treatment conditions, increased during the reversal to baseline conditions, and fell once again to an average of less than one error following the reinstatement of the peer tutoring spelling game. The results demonstrated that the performance of the LD students was similar to that of average peers during baseline; that is to say, the peer tutoring intervention enabled the LD students to perform as well as nonhandicapped students under typical instructional conditions. It is important to emphasize that the peer tutoring intervention was beneficial for both the handicapped and nonhandicapped students. And both handicapped and nonhandicapped functioned well in both the role of tutee and tutor.

To what can we attribute the positive results? Instructional time was not increased; however, the students' active involvement and opportunity to respond was increased. Delquadri et al. (1983) view the increased opportunity to respond as the most important aspect of the intervention. They observed that during the peer tutoring spelling game, the slowest child in the class practiced the list of 18 spelling words an average of 2 1/2 times (10 practices per word each week prior to the Friday spelling test). In contrast, during baseline instructional conditions this same child would practice only 6 of the 18 words one time if all workbook activities were completed by Friday.

From a very pragmatic point of view, the ease with which the teacher was able to incorporate the peer tutoring spelling game into her instructional program is an important feature of the intervention. Both the teacher and the students were enthusiastic about the spelling game. In fact it was continued the following year and modified for use in math instruction as well. From an empirical point of view, the results of this study underscore the importance of instructional time, enhanced student engagement, active student responding, and feedback and correction to the students' improved performance.

Student Self-Management

Student self-management involves the transfer to students of a degree of responsibility for the conduct of their own instruction. Discussion of self-management strategies directs our attention to teaching functions such as monitoring performance, evaluating and reinforcing appropriate behavior, and recording and graphing of performance data as well as instruction itself. There is much research evidence which clearly demonstrates that students, under certain conditions and with appropriate training, can carry out instructional functions heretofore associated with the role of teacher or adult teaching assistants.

According to Cole (1987), the focus of self-management training in special education has been on teaching students to "become effective modifiers of their own behaviors through such procedures as self-monitoring, self-evaluation, self-consequation, and self-instruction" (p. 1405). Cole defines the four instructional functions in the following manner:

Self-Monitoring — "the observation, discrimination and recording of one's own behavior"

Self-Evaluation — "the comparison of one's own behavior against a preset standard to determine whether performance meets these criteria"

Self-Consequation — "the self delivery of positive consequences (self reinforcement) or aversive consequences (self punishment) following behavior"

Self-Instruction — "a process of talking to oneself to initiate, direct, or maintain one's own behavior"

There is no intent to suggest that the teacher abrogates her instructional responsibility to students by encouraging student self-management. Rather, experience in both clinical and special settings, with handicapped students of varying disabilities and ages, has shown that students are capable of performing these functions given training and supervision. As in the use of any intervention techniques, the primary concern is the benefits that accrue to the students; benefits to classroom operations are a secondary consideration. Research findings reveal that students benefit in multiple ways from self-management.

Self-Monitoring

Of the 4 self-management areas, self-monitoring has been the most heavily researched. Self-monitoring involves 2 components: self assessment, and self recording (Nelson, 1977). There are numerous research investigations of self-monitoring with handicapped students (Hallahan, Lloyd, Kosiewicz, Kauffman, and Graves, 1979; Hallahan, Marshall, and Lloyd, 1981; Hallahan, Lloyd, Kneedler, and Marshall, 1982; Lloyd, Hallahan, Kosiewicz, and Kneelder, 1982; Osborne,

Kociewicz, Crumley, and Lee, 1987; Rooney, Hallahan, and Lloyd, 1984; Rooney, Palloway, and Hallahan, 1985). On-task behavior is almost always targeted in this body of research. Measures of academic performance are frequently employed as well; academic measures may target rate, accuracy, and productivity in student performance.

In special education, self-monitoring is becoming an increasingly popular means of increasing on-task behavior (Snider, 1987). The procedure frequently used involves the student assessing her own attentiveness and marking a student recording sheet appropriately—"yes" for on-task and "no" for off-task (Hallahan, Lloyd et al., 1982)—in response to an audible tone at irregular intervals. The teacher provides appropriate training in self-monitoring by providing explicit examples of on-task and off-task behavior, directing students in the use of the recording sheet, modeling appropriate self-monitoring behaviors, and observing students in modeling appropriate self-monitoring behavior, etc. until the teacher is confident that the students are ready to proceed. Children readily acquire the necessary competence in monitoring techniques. The studies which reported the amount of training time typically indicated that training is accomplished in a matter of minutes (Kosiewicz, Hallahan, Lloyd, and Graves, 1982; Osborne, Kosiewicz, Crumley, and Lee, 1987). There may be a need for additional training for the lower functioning student (Rooney, Polloway, and Hallahan, 1985) and a need for corrective training for some students if there is evidence of confusion or misunderstanding. Generally, the training aspect of self-monitoring proceeds smoothly and requires only a small commitment of class time. As to the question of students' recording accuracy, researchers are divided on the importance of this factor for the effectiveness of self-monitoring procedures. Some researchers maintain that recording accuracy is essential (Bolstead, Johnson, and Nelson, 1977); others have found that accuracy of responding is less essential than consistency of student responding (Rooney, Hallahan, and Lloyd, 1984).

The research findings pertaining to self-monitoring with handicapped students has produced consistently positive results and a clear trend of improved on-task and attending behavior. The impact of self-monitoring on students' academic performance is less impressive. Snider (1987) has concluded that the results pertaining to academic performance are inconsistent and that self-monitoring appears to be more effective on drill, practice, and review activities than on new academic learning. She questions the value of improvements in attending without accompanying improvements in academic performance. She cautions that attending and learning are not the same and that on the basis of the research evidence to date, one cannot assume that improved attending is automatically followed by increases in academic performance. She states that "Current conceptualizations of attention support the position that academic gains will be forthcoming only when students know what to pay attention to. The goal can be accomplished through a curriculum in which tasks are well structured and carefully integrated" (p. 139). Snider's urging to teachers about the importance of both attending behavior and instructional variables in order to maximize the effectiveness of self-monitoring interventions is well founded and consistent with research indicating the dual importance of time and task dimensions for effective instruction.

In response, Hallahan and Lloyd (1987) note that there is value in improving attending behavior with or without accompanying academic performance gains. Greater conformity to teachers' expectations with an accompanying decrease in non-attending behavior, and possibly disruptive behavior as well, increases the likelihood that the classroom will become a more accepting and reinforcing environment for the student. Important points of agreement between Hallahan and Lloyd and Snider are that: (1) self-monitoring interventions are most appropriately used with those students who have attending problems which interfere with their ability to do independent work; and (2) self-monitoring is most appropriate for drill and practice activities, not initial acquisition of new skills.

Self-Instruction, Evaluation, Reinforcement

Self-management training has been successfully employed in ways other than self-monitoring. The literature contains numerous research reports of successful efforts to train handicapped students in self-instruction, evaluation, and reinforcement. The subjects in these research studies have varied from kindergartners to adults, have included the handicapped and nonhandicapped, and taken place in special education and regular education settings. A variety of behaviors including academic performance, disruptive behavior, attending behavior, impulsivity control, and general cognitive ability have been targeted in the research literature. Generally speaking, the results have been supportive of the feasibility of training and positive student outcomes.

Self-instructional interventions involve teaching the child to control and direct his or her behavior through verbal mediation. Meichenbaum and Goodman (1971) have developed a 5 step, self-instructional training strategy: (1) the adult models the task while the student observes; (2) the student performs the task as the adult verbalizes what is to be done; (3) the student performs the task while verbalizing aloud; (4) the student performs the task while whispering the self instruction; and (5) the student performs the task and self-instructs internally. Meichenbaum, in a study reported by Hallahan, Lloyd, and Graves (1982), illustrated the use of Meichenbaum and Goodman's 5-step strategy with some adaptation to improve the handwriting and math performance of a nine year old learning disabled boy. Robin, Armel, and O'Leary (1975) used self instruction to assist kindergartners to acquire handwriting skills. Self-instructional strategies are the focus of an entire curriculum for the secondary aged learning disabled adolescent developed by researchers at the Learning Disabilities Institute at the University of Kansas (Deschler and Schumaker, 1986). The strategies model seeks to teach disabled adolescents principles and rules for problem solving, completion of tasks, and independent work. The objective is to teach the student how to learn; in effect, to be a more competent learner able to work independently and to apply the strategies in many contexts and to different types of information and problems. Unlike many of the other self-management or self-instructional training efforts, the strategies model is embodied within a comprehensive curricular package which requires a significant amount of teacher training prior to presentation of the strategies model to students.

Other areas of self management in which students have assumed a measure of autonomy include self-evaluation (Robertson, Simon, Pachman, and Drabman, 1979) and self-reinforcement (Shapiro and Klein, 1980). These studies involved retarded and disturbed students in special class settings. Both studies reported improvement in attending, behavior, and academic performance.

By now there is extensive literature on self-management training for handicapped students. Self-monitoring and self-instruction have received the most attention to date, but research on self-evaluation and self-reinforcement, while far more limited, provides evidence of positive outcomes for students with serious and limiting disabilities. Self-management, in its various forms, undoubtedly can instill a measure of self-reliance and autonomy within handicapped students. In addition to the positive outcomes in attending, academic performance, and behavior which accrues to the students, there are secondary benefits for the teachers and classroom management. To the extent that students assume a measure of responsibility for managing and overseeing their own behavior, teachers are free to attend to other responsibilities and have greater latitude in directing their time and attention within the classroom.

Self-management clearly is a means to improve attending behavior. Self-management may be a particularly useful strategy for increasing engagement during independent seatwork activities. It remains to be seen if student self-management can be effective in maintaining engagement levels during independent seatwork which are in line with the engagement levels which occur under teacher-led or supervised instruction. However, a caution is in order. The reader will recall Snider's observation that increased attending does not automatically translate into increased academic performance or learning. "Attention is not an end in itself, the actual educational goal is learning" (Snider, 1987, p. 143). Teachers must direct their attention to both students' attending behavior and the appropriateness of the task and task demands.

In Summary

In the typical special education classroom the individual needs of students far exceed the teacher's ability to provide individualized instruction. The amount of instructional time available simply will not stretch that far. In classrooms in which teachers have attempted to individualize through one-on-one instruction, the amount of teacher directed instructional time received by each student is minimal, far less than the amount of time students receive through whole or small group instruction. Teacher surrogates—persons other than the teacher who can assist in the delivery of instruction—are commonly employed in our schools. Increasingly students themselves are being considered for and employed in instructional roles. Peer tutoring is gaining acceptance as a means to increase individualization and provide instructional assistance. The research literature is, by and large, supportive, indicating academic gains for both the tutees and the tutors. Social gains are more limited. Students of all types, ages, and varying handicapping conditions have been involved in tutoring interventions, with good results. Student tutoring pairs may consist of peers or classmates or may involve cross-age tutoring. Handicapped students have received tutoring assistance and functioned as tutors for others.

Peer tutoring programs require preplanning and on-going supervision. The more successful peer tutoring programs—those which produced greater student gains—were those which exhibited a high level of structure as evidenced in the training of tutors, lesson formats, corrective procedures, etc. There are ethical considerations involved in the use of students in instructional roles. Ultimately, peer tutoring programs must be of benefit to both students, tutee and tutor, in accordance with each student's needs. The data to date is encouraging and positive on this important point. It appears that peer-tutoring is a effective and beneficial supplement to the instructional program, one which enhances both engagement and opportunities for active academic responding.

Students are capable, given the proper training and supervision, of assuming a degree of instructional autonomy through self-management. Self-management may involve self-monitoring, self-instruction, self-evaluation, and self-reinforcement. As was the case with peer tutoring, a wide variety of students of different ages, handicapping conditions, and in different educational settings have been successfully trained in self-management techniques. Beneficial results have been documented for attending behavior, decreased disruptive behavior, and aspects of academic performance including rate, accuracy and productivity. The use of self-management techniques produces consistent and impressive results in enhanced student attending. The use of self-management techniques during independent seatwork as a means of maintaining high levels of student engagement needs to be further investigated. To the extent that students can self-manage aspects of their own instructional programs, teachers will have greater latitude in the use of their time for other tasks and for the most needy students.

Chapter 10

Direct Instruction and Mastery Learning

Discussion of direct instruction and mastery learning are included in this text because both instructional philosophies emphasize the importance of instructional time and the role of the teacher in effective use of time in the classroom. Both direct instruction and mastery learning espouse methods which are compatible and adaptable to special education teaching. Direct instruction will be discussed first.

Direct Instruction

In 1979, Barak V. Rosenshine referred to direct instruction as a relatively new concept. Rosenshine himself is credited with playing a major role in the development of the teaching methodology and popularization of the term (Carnine, 1987). Direct instruction merits our attention for a number of reasons: (1) the efficient and effective use of instructional time is a central feature of the direct instruction methodology; (2) student engagement is a critical component of the methodology intimately tied to its instructional effectiveness; (3) many other aspects of the direct instructional methodology are compatible with special education practices; and (4) direct instruction has yielded good achievement results for many types of handicapped and problem learners. We begin with Rosenshine's (1979) definition:

> Direct Instruction refers to academically focused, teacher-directed classrooms using sequenced and structured materials. It refers to teaching activities where goals are clear to students, time allocated for instruction is sufficient and continuous, coverage of content is extensive, the performance of students is monitored, questions are at a low cognitive level so that students can produce many correct responses, and feedback to students is immediate and academically oriented. In direct instruction the teacher controls instructional goals, chooses materials appropriate for the student's ability, and paces the instructional episode. Interaction is characterized as structured, but not authoritarian. Learning takes place in a convivial academic atmosphere. (p. 147)

In this admittedly "loose" definition, Rosenshine defines direct instruction through description. He goes on to expound upon the 5 essential components which delineate the philosophy and methodology of instruction. The five components are academic focus, direction of activities, grouping students for learning, verbal interaction, and major classroom activities.

Academic Focus.   Rosenshine states unequivocally that successful teachers are those who maintain a strong academic focus in the classroom. In the direct instruction classroom, the distribution of time between academic and nonacademic activities apportions the greater share of instructional time to academic pursuits. The extensive literature which documents the relationship between the time spent on academic activities and student achievement supports this use of instructional time. Rosenshine notes further that there is no evidence linking any nonacademic activity with achievement gains. As to the concern for affective outcomes in an academically focused classroom, Rosenshine indicates that one does not sacrifice affect for academic success. Classrooms with high levels of engagement and high achievement usually are found to be moderate to high on measures of "warmth" within the classroom environment. The least desirable instructional scenario with the worst prognosis for engagement and achievement is one in which teachers are high on affect and low in cognitive emphasis.

Direction of Activities.   In the direct instruction classroom it is the teacher who primarily selects instructional and learning activities; student autonomy in these areas is very limited. Classrooms in which the teacher assumes a strong role in the selection and organization of activities yield higher achievement gains. In contrast, classrooms which are characterized as student-centered yield lower achievement results. Rosenshine (1979) notes that such student-centered classrooms were typically lower in academically engaged time and achievement. He speculates that the explanation may be found in the fact that students who have many alternatives to choose from may be more susceptible to distraction. Student autonomy then is associated with less task orientation and engagement and lower achievement.

Grouping students for learning.   Direct instruction requires grouping structures which allow for adult monitoring and supervision, *e.g.,* whole group or small group instruction. The research data confirm that the level of student engagement differs markedly under the teacher-led versus independent instructional conditions. Individualized instruction which takes the form of one-on-one instruction in reality provides little adult supervision or interaction for the students. The teacher who works with only 1 or 2 students at a time ultimately spends very little time with any student. The level of student engagement is lower than that which is likely under group instruction and, as a consequence, achievement is lower.

Verbal Interaction.   Factual questions (lower-level or lower-order) and controlled practice will yield achievement gains on basic skills. Questions that are focused and direct and call for unequivocal answers drawn form the content materials are preferred to open ended, inferential, or opinion based questions. Controlled practice, a pattern of teacher-student interaction involving teacher questioning, student response, and feedback from the teacher, has been shown to be instructionally effective. Rosenshine (1979) discusses 2 patterns of controlled practice which correlate well with achievement. For low SES (Socioeconomic Status) students the pattern involves simple questions, a high percentage of correct answers, help when the answer is not known, and infrequent criticism. For high SES students the pattern involves harder questions, fewer (about 70 percent) correct answers, and calling on another child when the answer was not known.

Major Classroom Activities.   Rosenshine stresses the fact that students spend a major portion of instructional time working alone. The level of engagement during teacher-led activities is about 85 percent in comparison to the engagement level of 68 percent during independent activities (Rosenshine, 1981). The management issues confronting the teacher concern the optimal mixture of teacher-directed and student self-paced activities and how to keep students on-task during independent or seatwork activities. When kids work alone, most of their off-task behavior is due to "wait-time"—waiting for someone to correct their papers or tell them what to do next. A reduction in the amount of wait-time could help to reduce off-task behavior appreciably.

Through his numerous and extensive writings Rosenshine has done much to familiarize teachers with the general conceptualization of direct instruction. He has been an outspoken and prolific spokesperson for effective teaching and more specifically the methodology of instruction embodied in the direct instruction teaching model. He believes that teaching effectiveness and the principles of direct instruction go hand in hand. For a closer look at the actual methodology in application, we turn to the work of D. Carnine and J. Silbert who have discussed and detailed the direct instruction methodology as it applies to the areas of basic reading and mathematics instruction. In contrast to Rosenshine's work on "direct instruction", which is general and descriptive, Carnine's and Silbert's work on "Direct Instruction" is comprehensive, structured, and founded upon curricular theory.

Teachers may be most familiar with curricular exemplars of direct instruction such as DISTAR. The basic concepts and methods of direct instruction are discussed and dealt with to varying degrees of depth and intensity through the three modes of empirical and descriptive reports, textbooks, and curricular programs.

Direct Instruction in Reading and Mathematics

Direct instruction has evolved as an instructional orientation and methodology for instruction of the basic skill subjects. The methodology of direct instruction has been described in great detail for the disciplines of Reading (Carnine and Silbert, 1979) and mathematics (Silbert, Carnine, and Stein, 1981). Direct Instruction Reading (Carnine and Silbert, 1979) and Direct Instruction Mathematics (Silbert, Carnine, and Stein, 1981) are not self-contained curricular programs such as DISTAR, perhaps the best known exemplar direct instruction. Direct Instruction Reading and Direct Instruction Mathematics set forth the philosophy and principles of direct instruction and describe in great detail how the methodology is to be applied within the context of reading and Mathematics instruction. The direct instruction methodology is, in effect, imposed upon existing curriculum to enhance instructional effectiveness. According to Carnine and Silbert (1979), "Direct instruction reading is an orientation that identifies major skills, selects and modifies commercial programs that best teach those skills, appropriately places students in the classroom program, and presents lessons each day in the most efficient manner possible" (p. 11). The authors stress the appropriateness of direct instruction methods for teaching the instructionally naive student though they believe that direct instruction has broad applicability to other types of students as well. (On this point there is disagreement; this issue will be discussed later in the chapter.) Direct instruction rests upon the central premise that "much of the failure in schools can be attributed to the instructional system" (Carnine and Silbert, 1979, p. 23). Direct instruction can be viewed as a master plan for instruction which helps the teacher to be instructionally effective.

Direct instruction in the area of reading is structured on 3 key components: (1) organization of instruction; (2) program design; and (3) presentation techniques. Organization of instruction focuses upon the provision of adequate instructional time and maintenance of high levels of active student engagement. It is important that instructional time be devoted to priority instructional areas. The instructionally naive students may require more instructional time which may be scheduled even at the expense of less important subjects. Carnine and

Silbert have no definitive answer to the question, "Approximately how many minutes of reading instruction is required for an instructionally naive student of a given skill level to score at grade level on an achievement test by the end of the third or fifth grade?" However, their insistence on the provision of adequate, and even greater, instructional time for the less able student is supported by the research evidence which demonstrates that the slow learners need and benefit from added instruction (refer to chapter 3 for discussion of this issue).

Program design begins with the selection of a reading curriculum that is suited to the needs of the students. The curriculum will provide the content for instruction but may be weak in instructional delivery. Carnine and Silbert point out that direct instruction addresses the inadequacies of packaged curriculum programs in 6 areas: specifying objectives, devising problem-solving strategies, developing teaching procedures, selecting examples, providing practice, and sequencing skills.

Desired student outcomes need to be stated as clear and specific statements of instructional objectives. For example, the authors note that merely alluding to decoding as an outcome of first grade reading instruction is adequate. Objectives need to specify the types of words the student will be able to decode, the fluency and rate criteria, the way words are to be presented and, for passage reading, the complexity of sentence structure. Teaching objectives are evaluated according to their usefulness. Essential skills are taught first. Teaching stresses the students' acquisition of problem-solving strategies rather than rote memorization of facts or information. Although some students are able to deduce general strategies or rules from on-going instruction, the instructionally naive student requires explicit instruction. The teacher's task is to articulate and teach the strategies. Strategies are taught by means of formats which are in actuality scripted daily lessons. The format specifies the teacher behaviors, reactions, and/or responses to anticipated student responses. Having prepared the detailed format for the daily lesson beforehand, the teacher is able to focus her attention on the students and their performance (responses to instruction). The prepared formats structure and control the presentation of curricular content so that strategies are presented in optimal sequence, content is presented at the correct rate and in the correct amount, and students receive sufficient practice of strategies and skills to ensure initial acquisition and maintenance. Program design strives for controlled presentation of content, maximum student involvement, close monitoring, and correction of students' errors. The initial investment of time in preplanning and format development, which can be considerable, is an investment in effective instruction.

Presentation techniques are tailored to the age and/or level of the student and the nature of the materials to be taught. Carnine and Silbert (1979) point out that beginning reading is generally carried on within small groups with much oral responding from the students. The teacher monitors progress by attending closely to the oral responses of the children. Older students are typically involved in less group work and greater amounts of independent work and teachers rely far more upon written responses to monitor student performance and progress. Carnine and Silbert recommend small group structure for beginning reading instruction as this group structure facilitates frequent oral responding of the students and monitoring and feedback from the teacher. Even though one-on-one instruction might be considered the ideal, small group instruction leads to a better, more efficient use of instructional time. Homogeneous grouping is essential. The size of small groups should be varied to reflect the ability levels of the students. The instructional group for low functioning students would be smaller than the instructional group for the top level readers. During instruction, students should be seated in a semicircle (no desks or tables) facing the teacher with their backs to the remainder of the class. The teacher is positioned in front of the small group and is able to provide instruction to the group while maintaining visual supervision of the rest of the class.

Unison responding is a well known and very visible feature of direct instruction; its purpose is to bring about a high level of active student involvement while facilitating monitoring and feedback from the teacher. One might well ask how the teacher can monitor 6 to 8 children simultaneously, and though this might be an impossibility, the scripted format frees the teacher's attention from the details of the lesson to the children in the group. The numerous practice opportunities and high level of responding allows the teacher the time and opportunity to shift attention from one child to another. Carnine and Silbert stress the fact that "in monitoring the first priority is to test the instructionally naive children most often." Daily monitoring should be supplemented with "periodic comprehensive checks". Problems must be detected early to forestall the child's continued practice of incorrect responses, the need for unlearning and reteaching, and the waste of instructional time which such activities entail. Direct instruction requires that the pace of lessons be brisk in order to maintain student engagement and provide the maximum opportunities for responding and practice.

Diagnosis and correction procedures are important components of direct instruction. It is important for the teacher to determine if the student errors are due to a lack of attentiveness or a lack of knowledge. The teacher's response will be different in each case. If the problem is due to a lack of attentiveness than the teacher needs to work on motivating the student. On the other hand, if the problem is due to a lack of knowledge, the teacher must identify the specific skill deficits and provide remedial instruction. The corrective procedure recommended by Carnine and Silbert for use within small group instruction entails up to 6 steps: praise, model, lead, test, alternate, and delayed test. The teacher must strive for student mastery of each skill or strategy being taught. The authors emphasize that as many as 40 to 50 practice examples may be required to enable the instructionally naive student to reach criterion on a new skill the first time it is introduced (Carnine and Silbert, 1979). Thereafter the number of practice examples required to get or maintain a criterion level performance drops sharply and quickly. Failure to teach to criterion merely creates obstacles to further learning and progress.

In summary, Carnine and Silbert attribute the school failure of children to six possible explanations:

1. Many commercial reading programs do not adequately control the introduction of vocabulary.
2. The preskills of complex strategies are not taught prior to the teaching of the strategies, thus forcing children to cope with the prerequisite skills and strategies at the same time.
3. Programs embody "a little of a lot" philosophy and fail to provide sufficient practice and responding opportunities; consequently, students do not reach mastery.
4. Teachers are required to cover too many topics in each day; there is insufficient time provided for reading instruction, and student engaged time is inadequate.
5. Teachers frequently do not know how to place students at the appropriate instructional level within reading curricula.
6. Teachers believe that students should be instrinsically motivated to learn and are not prepared to instruct students who are not motivated.

Direct instruction reading addresses the deficiencies inherent in curricular programs—deficiencies of instructional strategy rather than content—and bolsters and sharpens the teacher's instructional skills. Direct instruction can help the teacher to provide effective instruction to precisely those students so often left behind by traditional materials and methods.

Direct Instruction Mathematics (Silbert, Carnine, and Stein, 1981) is a detailed exposition of the application of direct instruction philosophy and principles to the teaching of mathematics. Direct Instruction

Mathematics is very similar to Direct Instruction Reading in its philosophy of instruction and instructional methodology. The 3 components of organization of instruction, program design, and presentation techniques are repeated. The detailed discussion of each component and its focus and content varies somewhat from the prior treatment in relation to instruction in reading. The points of divergence represent differences in subject matter and possibly refinements of the methodology over time. The same emphasis on student engagement, efficient use of instructional time, active directive teaching role, active student involvement, formating and attendant instructional procedures (*e.g.*, monitoring, diagnosis, and correction, etc.) are emphasized in Direct Instruction Mathematics as they were in Direct Instruction Reading.

The brief description of the major components of direct instruction will not suffice for the teacher who wishes to implement direct instruction in her classroom. The teacher will need to consult the original sources in depth. But, even this brief description reveals the compatibility between direct instruction and the major instructional theme of this text, namely, the effective use of instructional time in the classroom. Many components of direct instruction, *e.g.*, engaged time, active student involvement in learning, structure of daily lessons, the directive and active instructional role of the teacher, monitoring, pacing, etc., are tied to efficient use of instructional time. Research findings support the use of direct instruction among disadvantaged and handicapped learners.

Direct Instruction and Compensatory Education: Research Findings

Direct Instruction emerged from the national experiments in compensatory education of the 1960s and 1970s. Head Start, the first nationwide effort at compensatory education, targeted impoverished urban and rural children at the preschool and kindergarten level for special education assistance. Project Follow-Through, started in the 1967-68 school year, picked up where Head Start ended and provided assistance for impoverished at-risk children during the early school years, grades 1 through 3. The intent of Project Follow-Through was to improve the grade school education of children from impoverished backgrounds.

The Direct Instruction Model developed by Engelmann and Becker was only one of many instructional models sponsored through Project Follow-Through. The national evaluation of Follow-Through conducted by Abt Associates (1976, 1977) produced impressive evidence in support of the effectiveness of the Direct Instruction Model. The Direct Instruction Model, perhaps more than any of the other sponsored programs, was successful in attaining its educational instructional goals: "to teach skills that would place Follow Through students above or competitive with national norms by the end of the third grade" (Becker, 1977, p. 526). The goal statement implies norm referenced comparison, that is, a comparison between the students within the Direct Instruction Model programs and a national standardization population. Results revealed that by the end of third grade the students who had participated in the Direct Instruction program were performing at the 41 percentile in total reading, at the 40 percentile in total math, at the 51 percentile in spelling, and at the 50 percentile in language (Abt Associates, 1976, 1977). The national evaluation data also revealed that the Direct Instruction Model produced more statistically and educationally significant differences on tests of basic skills, cognitive conceptual skills, and affective measures than any of the other 8 instructional models evaluated (Becker, 1977). The national evaluation of Project Follow-Through is a major source of the research literature on the effectiveness of Direct Instruction. Other research studies have added to the body of empirical literature which is supportive of direct instruction as an effective teaching methodology (Lloyd, Cullinan, Heins, and Epstein, 1980; Gersten and Carnine, 1984).

A key efficacy question concerns the lasting effects of the Direct Instruction Model. Becker and Gersten (1982) pursued an answer to this important question by assessing graduates of the Direct Instruction Model during their fifth and sixth year in school. The authors found that the direct instruction graduates performed better than local comparison groups but had lost ground in comparison to the national norm group. These findings, while adding to the evidence in support of Direct Instruction, indicates a need for a continuation of effective educational programs to help students retain and build upon the gains made during the first 3 years of compensatory education. Other studies of the long term academic effect (Meyers, 1984; Meyers, Gersten, and Guthin, 1984) have indicated that the length of exposure to direct instruction is a factor in the maintenance of academic gains. Studies reporting lasting effects found that the students who retained their early academic gains had participated in direct instruction for 3 or more years.

There is disagreement among educators as the type of student for whom direct instruction is most suitable. Some view direct instruction as appropriate for the instructionally naive student but not the instructionally sophisticated student (Peterson, 1979a, 1979b). Other criticisms of direct instruction include its focus on only narrow a range of educational goals (Peterson, 1979a), its insensitivity to individual student differences and use of one method of instruction for all students (McFaul, 1983), and its prescribed and mechanistic teaching methodology which devalues and deemphasizes the role of the teacher (McFaul,

1983). Carnine and Silbert (1979) argue that direct instruction, properly implemented, is effective for both naive and sophisticated learners. Evaluation data reveal that Direct Instruction Model was the only methodology among the Follow-Through Models effective for both low- and middle-income students (Guthrie, 1977). The debate has import within the context of regular education, but it has less relevance for special education where so many students are characterized by poor performance and low achievement overall. With this backdrop of empirical research in regular education, the pressing question for special educators concerns the effects of direct instruction for handicapped and problem learners.

Direct Instruction for Special Education Students: Research Findings

The research literature pertaining to the use of direct instruction methods with special education students is quite limited. Gersten (1985) has reviewed 6 studies involving special students. The type of students involved in these investigations varied greatly, e.g., high risk first graders (Serwer, Shapiro, and Shapiro, 1973), moderately and severely retarded (Maggs and Morath, 1976), intermediate level learning disabled (Lloyd, Cullinan, Heins, and Epstein, 1981), first graders with reading problems (Stein and Goldman, 1980), low-income students (Gersten, Becker, Heiry, and White, 1984), and adolescents and preadolescents in the high to moderate range of retardation (Gersten and Maggs, 1982). Gersten categorized the research studies by design rather than study population. Three studies were grouped under the heading of experimental design while 3 studies were discussed as quasi-experimental designs. The experimental studies embodied an experimental versus control group comparison with random assignment of subjects to the treatment or non-treatment control conditions. The quasi-experimental studies were those which lacked a control group. In place of an experimental versus control group comparison, these studies employed a non-equivalent comparison group, a norm referenced comparison, and a time series design.

Gersten explains the norm referenced comparison as a research design in which "students are pretested and posttested on the same form and level of a well-normed, reliable standardized achievement test, whose content matches the objectives of their curriculum program. The gain against the standardization sample is assessed for statistical and educational significance" (p. 48). The research design is noteworthy in terms of the performance standard selected for the between group comparison. The standardization populations of well known nationally normed achievement tests generally do not meet the require-

ment of representativeness, that is to say that the normative populations contain few if any handicapped students. Gersten contends that
the comparison of handicapped to the standardization population
imposes too stringent a standard for many handicapped students but is
applicable to "mildly handicapped students where normalization in
academic areas is an immediate goal" (p. 50). The study which
involved a non-equivalent comparison group necessitated careful articulation of the nature of the treatments (essential in any study), and verification that the 2 groups were comparable on all significant variables
at the outset of the investigation. The time series investigation involved
the repeated measurement of reading and math performance over time
for a selected group of target students. In the absence of a group comparison, evidence of a treatment effect would be found if the data veri-
fied a desirable change in student performance. Two of the 6 studies,
one experimental and one quasi-experimental study, will be discussed
in greater detail to demonstrate varied approaches to application and
evaluation of the direct instruction methodology.

Lloyd, Cullinan, Heins, and Epstein (1980) reported on the utility
of direct instructional methods in the remediation of oral language
and reading comprehension deficits among learning disabled pupils.
The 23 elementary learning disabled students in self-contained classrooms who participated in the study were randomly assigned to 2
experimental classes or 1 control classroom. In the experimental classrooms, applied behavior analysis techniques were combined with
direct instruction; the former was employed to monitor academic
progress under direct instruction and traditional teaching methodology. The Corrective Reading materials (Engelmann, Becker, Hanner,
and Johnson, 1978) were used for instruction in Reading and
Language Skills. The materials teach "specific critical skills and general case strategies for decoding and comprehension by means of carefully structured teacher-pupil interactions and independent pupil
exercises featuring extensive pupil responding and teacher feedback,
structured corrections for response errors, and exercises for skill discrimination and generalization" (Lloyd et al. 1980, p. 72). Students in
the control classroom were involved in language arts, arithmetic, per-
ceptual-motor training, and other psychological process training.
Activities specifically directed toward language and comprehension
instruction involved teacher-developed worksheets and chalkboard
activities. The teacher drew upon the basal reading series and a locally
developed Language Arts program.

Pupil progress in reading comprehension was assessed by testing
with the Gilmore Oral Reading Test; pupil progress in oral language
comprehension was assessed with the Slosson Intelligence Test. The

results showed that students in the experimental classes out-performed the control students on both reading and oral language; the
performance differences were statistically significant. The students in
the model classrooms scored about three quarters of a standard deviation higher on the measures of language comprehension than the control subjects. The authors contend that a difference of this magnitude
suggests educational significance as well as statistical significance.
Testing results did not yield evidence of an experimental versus control group difference in arithmetic achievement. As the experimental
instructional program was targeted to language and reading skills, not
arithmetic skills, the absence of a between group difference in mathe-
matic performance further substantiates the treatment effect. In summary, it appears that one can justifiably conclude that the direct
instructional methodology was instrumental in improving the language comprehension of these learning disabled students. However,
the authors qualify the results by pointing out that the children in the
experimental classrooms were exposed to decoding skills instruction.
It may be that enhancement of decoding skills contributed to the
improvement in comprehension skills. Further research would be
needed to assess the possible impact of interactive effects of decoding
on comprehending ability. Regarding the experimental intervention
program, the authors point out that further research is needed to
determine if the opportunity to respond, or the specific programmed
sequences, or a combination of either of these two intervention features contributed to the study outcome.

The study described above offers supportive evidence for the
efficacy of direct instruction techniques. Unfortunately, the reader
must accept the "whole package", as the results shed little light on the
specific features of direct instruction method which brought about the
performance improvement. It is just as important to know why and
under what conditions direct instruction works as it is to know that
direct instruction is an effective teaching method. Stein and Goldman
(1980) suggest that the insistence upon mastery performance is the
critical feature of direct instruction for handicapped learners. At this
point, we do not have conclusive answers to such questions.

In the second study to be discussed, Gersten, Becker, Heiry, and
White (1984) followed the progress of over 900 low-income students as
they advanced through the Direct Instruction Follow Through program for 4 years (kindergarten through third grade). The authors were
particularly interested in the effects of direct instruction on those students who entered the program with low cognitive skills as measured
by a pre-treatment test of intellectual status. All students were
grouped by IQ level: 70 or below, 71 to 90, 91 to 100, 101 to 110, 11 to

130, and 130 and above. All students were assessed using the Wide Range Achievement Test (WRAT) and the Metropolitan Achievement Test (MAT). The outcomes for the 2 lowest cognitive skills groups are most interesting. The lowest group, *i.e.*, initial IQ at 70 or below, entered kindergarten with performance skills significantly below average. By the end of the kindergarten year these students had advanced to the 47 percentile—just below the average. By the end of the third grade the students were performing at the 70th percentile. At this level their performance was equivalent to the 4.3 grade level. As the number of subjects in the lowest IQ group was quite small (N=8), some caution needs to be exercised in drawing conclusions. The second lowest IQ group contained a larger number of children (N=108). At entry, this group of students was also significantly below average in reading skills. By the end of the kindergarten year, the group was performing at the 53rd percentile and by the end of the third grade they were performing at the 66th percentile. The MAT test results indicated that the students in the 2 lowest IQ groups were advancing 1.0 grade equivalent for each year of instruction. Improvement in cognitive skills was also documented. The average IQ gain for the total student group was 8 points; the mean growth for the lowest IQ group was 17 points over the 4 year period. Overall the study demonstrated that direct instruction contributed to improvement in decoding skills, general language competence, and mathematics. The results for vocabulary concepts and word meaning were less promising. Many of the children who participated in the study could have qualified for special education placement, however they were maintained in the educational mainstream. The resulting data indicated that mainstreaming with direct instruction was effective for students clearly at risk for academic failure and special education placement.

The research on direct instruction applied to special education students and potential special education students is generally supportive of direct instruction methodology. Based upon his review of 6 special education applications of direct instruction, Gersten (1985) concludes that "involvement in reading or language curriculum programs based upon the model of direct instruction (Engleman and Carnine, 1982) tend to produce higher academic gains for handicapped children than traditional approaches" (1985, p. 53).

The research to date has assessed the effects of a "curriculum package" and tells us little about the individual components of direct instruction methodology and their relationship to student improvement. Two problematic issues that Gersten addressed in his review of direct instruction used with special populations concerns the definition of direct instruction and fidelity of implementation. The first issue points to the lack of clear definitions of the treatment provided to the experimental subjects. The reader is told that direct instruction is being utilized, but frequently is given insufficient information about what the treatment entails. One is left to speculate as to the exact nature of the direct instruction being provided. Researchers must do a more adequate job of defining the treatment variable. The second issue concerns the degree to which direct instruction methodology is faithfully followed during applied research. Are the programs being implemented as intended? If not, what is being evaluated?

The 2 issues are important concerns in evaluation research. For the teacher or administrator lack of adequate descriptive information leaves one to fill in the gaps as best one can. It also is a hindrance to replication and application of the results in classroom settings. Finally, the teacher who is impressed by the results of the research and wishes to pursue direct instruction methods in her classroom must accept the entire methodology. While it is safe to say that direct instruction appears effective for basic skills instruction with handicapped learners, it is difficult to explain how or why this is so. The teacher interested in direct instruction at this point in time must accept the methodology totally—and teachers may not be willing to do this. For the researcher, the prospect of teachers picking and choosing among direct instruction methods may also be unpalatable. Gersten (1985) calls for new lines of research—instructional dimensions research—which will determine exactly what teaching practices or curriculum are most effective in producing performance gains for handicapped learners. Such information would be invaluable to the teacher and/or administrator interested in pursuing or adopting direct instruction methodology.

Direct Instruction in Special Education

The review of research by Gersten (1985) and the work of other researchers (Englert, 1984; Leinhardt, Zigmond, and Cooley, 1981) is evidence that special educators are receptive to direct instruction in special learners. Schloss and Sedlak (1986), in a general methods textbook for special education, devote a section of their book to the "direct instructional approach". They define direct instruction as "a student-centered approach that links pupil performance data to systematic teaching procedures. Direct instruction involves a comprehensive set of educational principles that address the structure of the learning environment, the differentiation of teaching practices on the basis of learner characteristics, the effective use of motivating consequences, and the systematic articulation of instructional objectives" (p. 82). On the whole, the Schloss and Sedlak definition is compatible with other definitions of direct instruction presented earlier (Rosenshine, 1979; Carnine and Silbert, 1979). Schloss and Sedlak offer an instructional model which delineates a decision making process for facilitating the provision of systematic instruction. Some of the instructional principles associated with direct instruction are evident, *e.g.*, reinforcement, and specification of instructional objectives, but the focused, cohesive system of instructional principles with emphasis on curricular analysis and presentation techniques is not. As direct instruction, as a concept and methodology, is accepted and adapted into special education instructional practice, there is the danger that the unique methodology that is direct instruction will be diluted. If direct instruction becomes a generic term for structured, directive, teacher-centered instruction, there is the danger that the fine points of the methodology will be blunted, and that what teachers come to know and use under the label of direct instruction will be far removed from the original conceptualization, as well as the direct instruction interventions of proven effectiveness. There is a need to further study the applicability of direct instruction for handicapped learners to determine the elements of the instructional process responsible for positive performance outcomes and the conditions under which direct instruction produces positive learning effects. In the absence of such study the potential benefits of direct instruction for handicapped learners may be lost in causal and careless applications of isolated methods devoid of conceptual moorings.

Mastery Learning

Mastery learning as conceived and developed by B.S. Bloom is an application of Carroll's Model of School Learning. Through mastery learning, Bloom has translated Carroll's conceptualization and the five elements of learning which express the essential relationship between learning time and learning outcomes into applied instructional strategy and procedures.

The reader will recall that Carroll postulated that the degree of school learning is a function of the amount of time that the student spends in learning relative to the amount of time that the student needs for learning. Carroll, in contrast to the prevailing practice of the day, defined student aptitude in terms of the rate of learning rather than the predicted level of learning that the student could attain. Carroll also believed that the time spent and the time needed for learning were influenced not only by learner characteristics but also by the character and quality of instruction. "The degree of school learning of a given subject depends on the student's perseverance and opportunity to learn, relative to his aptitude for the subject, the quality of his instruction, and his ability to understand this instruction" (Block and Anderson, 1975, p. 2). Bloom transformed Carroll's conceptual model into a working model for mastery learning with the following logic:

> If aptitude was predictive of the rate, but not necessarily the level, to which a student could learn, it should have been possible to fix the degree of school learning expected of each student at some mastery performance level. Then, by attending to the opportunity to learn and the quality of instruction—variables under teacher control in Carroll's model—the teacher should have been able to ensure that each student attained this level. (Block and Anderson, 1975, p. 3)

Under normal instructional conditions, *e.g.*, students receiving similar amounts of the same instruction, students normally distributed with respect to aptitude for instruction in a particular subject will vary greatly in achievement, and only a minority of students will attain mastery. If, however, students receive instruction differentiated as to amount and quality to meet individual needs, then student achievement will vary slightly and many students will attain mastery. The mastery learning strategy translates this conceptualization into practice. The refinement and elaboration of the mastery learning strategy into workable classroom procedures was achieved, to a great extent, through the work of James Block (Block, 1971; Block and Anderson, 1975).

Under mastery learning conditions, in contrast to prevailing educational practices, students are provided with sufficient time and assistance to master important curricular content up to a preset performance standard. Under such instructional conditions, Bloom (1971, 1976) contends that most—fully 90 to 95 percent—of all students can achieve the high levels previously attained by only a minority of more able students. Mastery learning is seen as an alternative to "the most wasteful and destructive aspects of our present educational system which holds that only some students are able to learn well, others will learn less well, and still others will fail or just 'get by'" (Bloom, 1971).

Mastery learning founded on the fundamental belief that children can learn embodies a positive and optimistic view of students' learning potential. Unfortunately, despite much rhetoric to the contrary, prevailing educational practices frequently convey a different message to children and hold to policies and procedures which perpetuate less than optimal performance for many of them.

Teacher expectations influence behavior: teacher behavior toward students, and student behavior in response. Our existing educational system which views ability as varied across individuals and fixed within individuals sets the stage for a "pernicious self-fulfilling prophecy" (Bloom, 1971, p. 47), in which students fulfill the teachers' and system's expectations; consequently, large numbers of students do indeed fail to learn, or fail to learn up to their potential. Within such a system, grading is done on the basis of the normal curve. The results which mark some children for failure and others for success conveniently confirm the expectations which permeate the instructional system. In contrast to the above scenario, mastery learning seeks to make group instruction more responsive to individual student needs and to provide each student with sufficient time for attainment of predetermined levels of skill and knowledge.

Essential Elements of Mastery Learning

Mastery learning contains three essential instructional elements which provide the vehicle for its philosophy and the structure for its methodology. Mastery learning is not a self contained curriculum, rather it is a set of procedures which apply across curricular programs and subject disciplines.

Specification of objectives. At the outset, the teacher must define mastery for a course of study by formulating a set of course instructional objectives. The curricular content of the course or subject to be taught is broken down into smaller units requiring 1 to 2 weeks of instructional time. Subjects which have a basic hierarchial structure are best suited to mastery learning, though its application need not be limited solely to such curriculum. Performance standards are set (usually in the 80 to 90 percent criterion range); each student's performance is then gauged against this preset standard; in effect, a criterion referenced assessment. Students are not penalized in any way for requiring more time than their peers to reach mastery. All students whose performance satisfies the mastery criteria receive the same grade.

Formative evaluation. Diagnostic progress tests are given at the end of each unit of instruction. Not all students will achieve mastery after the initial instructional sequence. Formative evaluation will reveal those students who have mastered the curricular content of the unit and those students who require additional and/or remedial instruction. The frequency of formative testing can vary; testing is likely to be more frequent for the early units in an instructional sequence and less frequent for the later units. Students who have not achieved mastery participate in corrective learning procedures which provides them with the extra time and instructional assistance that they require. The provision of appropriate help to meet individual needs is central to the success of mastery learning. Bloom (1987) points out that it is the feedback-corrective process which truly distinguishes mastery learning from conventional instruction. In other respects mastery learning and conventional instruction are much alike. A variety of corrective procedures have been used in mastery learning experiments and applied programs: small-group study sessions, individualized tutoring, programmed instruction, audio visual methods, academic games, and reteaching (Block, 1971). "The sole function of the correctives was to provide each student with the instructional cues and/or the active participation and practice and/or the amount and type of reinforcement he required to complete his unit learning" (Block, 1971, p. 8). For those students who achieve mastery without additional corrective instruction, formative testing can reduce anxiety about end-of-course achievement and confirms the effectiveness of their learning and study habits. Formative tests fulfill a diagnostic purpose; therefore, they are not graded beyond the designation of "mastery" or "non-mastery". For the teacher, formative tests provide invaluable information about the source of a student's difficulty and indicate the type of corrective assistance required.

Summative evaluation. At the end of the learning sequence, students take a summative test to ascertain overall achievement in the series of instructional units. The results of the summative test are used for grading. Students who achieve the required level of mastery receive a grade of "A". A grade of "I", designating incomplete, is given to those who do not yet satisfy the performance requirement (Stallings and Stipek, 1986). Implementation of mastery learning will vary from one location to another. The teacher may or may not require that all students achieve mastery level performance before the class moves on to the new curricular materials. Essentially the teacher is faced with a trade off between mastery and content coverage (Slavin, 1987). A balance between the 2 is the responsible solution. Theoretically, the amount of time needed by the slower learners to achieve mastery should lessen as students progress through the learning units and become more efficient learners. Evidence of this effect is cited in the literature (Arlin, 1973; Anderson, 1973; Ozcelik, 1974; Block, 1970). Two other time related issues—how much time it takes for the majority of students to achieve mastery, and the degree to which mastery learning holds back the high achieving students—remain unresolved.

Critical Views of Mastery Learning

No one doubts that mastery learning has had an important and far reaching influence on instructional processes in both pure and applied research. But mastery learning is not lauded by all; it has its critics. One major focus of criticism is the impact of mastery learning on the pace of instruction. Critics maintain that mastery learning slows down the pace of instruction to accommodate the slower student at the expense of the more able and faster learner (Peterson, 1979; Smith, 1981). To a certain degree the imposition of mastery learning does impose some restriction on the learning pace of the high achieving students. However, the leveling effect, to which the critics object, apparently is an inherent feature of group instruction, not mastery learning *per se* (Slavin, 1987).

Dalhoff (1971), in his studies of grouping practices and achievement, found that teachers impose a uniform minimal level of achievement on their students. Teachers pace instruction so that all (or at least most) of their students reach this minimal level of achievement. They actually gauge and adjust the instructional pace to a sub-group of students functioning within the 10 to 25 percent range—hence the label "criterion steering group". The existence of a criterion steering group was confirmed in later research by Lundgreen (1972), and Arlin and Westburg (1976). Mastery learning may accentuate the leveling effect; it does not create it. Perhaps by increasing the level and rate of achievement of the initially slower students, mastery learning may mitigate the leveling effect for all students.

In response to the critics who assert that the interests of the more able students are sacrificed to the needs of the less able students under mastery learning conditions, it has been suggested that the fast learners (who finish their assignments) can pursue related enrichment activities that broaden their understanding and knowledge while the slower learners work toward initial mastery (Stallings and Stipek, 1986). Doubtless, this recommendation will do little to satisfy the critics. It is interesting that those who find the (presumed, not proven) sacrifice of high achievers to the interests of lower achieving students unacceptable apparently have no such concerns about the sacrifice of lower achieving students to the interests of the high achievers. The degree of failure and underachievement among students in our schools today is ample evidence that the schools best serve the needs of the few and not the needs of the majority. The important question is whether mastery learning truly imposes a hardship upon high achieving students. To date, there is no empirical evidence of any harm to high achieving students resulting from the use of mastery learning procedures (Slavin, 1987).

The question of how much extra time is needed to bring most students up to mastery level is a point of contention. Blocks and Burns (1976) indicate that 10 to 50 percent more study time is required for nearly all children to reach mastery performance level. Bloom (1984a), based upon a series of dissertation studies done at the University of Chicago, reported that 20 to 33 percent of additional instructional time for the mastery learning students—in excess of the amount of time allocated to the comparison group—was needed. The additional instructional time approximated one additional day per week. Bloom notes that all additional instruction was provided outside of class time. The provision of additional study time outside of regular class time helps to avoid unduly using class time for the benefit of only some students, while causing a loss of instructional time for other students, what Arlin (1984) calls the Robin Hood approach.

In theory, the extra time issue is mitigated by the increased learning efficiency among the less able, slower learning students (Bloom, 1976; Block, 1972). There is evidence that students who initially needed greater study time experienced a reduction in the amount of time needed to attain mastery level performance as they progressed under mastery learning conditions (Anderson, 1973; Arlin, 1973, Block, 1972; 1970; Arlin and Westbury, 1976; Merrick, Barton, and Wood, 1970). The research literature, however, does not yield wholly consistent research findings on this issue. Arlin (1984) conducted 2 investigations of students' time needs under mastery conditions in an effort to test the question of between student variability in learning time. The first of the 2 studies involved a 10 day instructional series of mastery learning comparing student time needs under mastery and conventional instructional. The second study involved a *post hoc* analysis of students' arithmetic achievement over a period of 4 years under mastery learning instruction. The second study lacked an experimental versus control group comparison. Instructional time data was analyzed for mastery learning conditions only.

Results of the first study revealed that the differences in amount of study time required remained the same for fast and slow learners, and that the amount of time needed by slow learners to reach mastery also remained stable over time. Data from the second investigation revealed that student time differences remained stable or increased over the course of 4 years. The contradictory results underscore the need for more research to determine under what conditions and for which students mastery learning does enhance learning efficiency. The issue is pivotal to the theoretical underpinnings of mastery learning and will impact on the appeal of mastery learning for the classroom teacher.

Another controversial point revolves about the issue of content mastery versus content coverage. Is it more beneficial for students to master all of the material that is presented, or to forego complete mastery for exposure to a greater amount of curricular content, albeit at a lower level of mastery? The mastery learning requirement that students master all curricular materials to a preset level, and that students not proceed to another unit of study until mastery has been attained in the prior unit of study, imposes some restrictions on content coverage. We know that more extensive content coverage is positively associated with achievement. It is doubtful that a unitary answer exists. The nature of the subject matter and student characteristics are also contributing factors. It would be most helpful to know when content mastery is preeminent and conversely when content coverage is indicated. Answers to such questions would also help in the setting of performance standards; lower standards when content coverage prevails, and higher performance standards when mastery of content is essential.

In special education practice, educators place a high value on content mastery. Special educators have encountered countless children who failed to master fundamental skills in the early grades and students with glaring gaps in their skill development. In either case the lack of mastery of essential skills and knowledge becomes a formidable obstacle to academic success. While the choice between content coverage and content mastery may pose a difficult choice for regular educators, the choice for special educators who deal with severe performance deficiencies is quite easy: content mastery must take precedence. For the special education student, mastery of essential skills and fundamental knowledge opens up the possibility of significantly increasing content coverage.

The main criticism of mastery learning have been summarized by Stallings and Stipek (1986). Mastery learning has been criticized for having too narrow a range of educational goals; espousing instructional procedures which are structured, rigid, and even mechanistic; placing unrealistic performance demands upon teachers; and encouraging a tendency among students to disregard or disdain information or skills on which they will not be tested. Some of the criticism stems from a fundamental clash of educational values and will defy resolution, *e.g.*, whether or not mastery learning strives towards too narrow a range of educational goals. Other criticism will be resolved in due time as a consequence of continuing research efforts, *e.g.*, whether or not mastery learning encourages students to be concerned only with curricular content on which they will be tested.

Instructional Effects of Mastery Learning

There is a large and far ranging body of literature which deals with various aspects of mastery learning in the theoretical and applied realms. However, for the practitioner a few key questions emerge: what are the achievement differences between students taught by mastery learning procedures and other instructional approaches, how does the retention of skills and content associated with other instructional approaches, does a reduction of achievement variance (and increase in learning efficiency) result from mastery learning programs, what are the affective outcomes for students who participate in mastery learning programs.

The research literature to date contains widely divergent assessments of the efficacy of mastery learning procedures. In an early review of mastery learning research Block and Burns (1976) concluded that there was strong support for the effectiveness of mastery learning. Stallings and Stipek (1986), reviewing the same 6 studies cited by Block and Burns, concluded that the data overall revealed "a positive trend for mastery learning but not a ringing vote of confidence for mastery learning students' superiority on standardized achievement tests" (p. 744). Slavin (1987) reports that the results of 2 recent meta-analyses by Kulik, Kulik, and Bangert-Drowns (1986) and Guskey and Gates (1986) yielded "extraordinarily positive effects of this method [mastery learning] on student achievement" (p. 176). But as a result of his own review of selected mastery learning research, Slavin (1987) reached a far different and far less supportive conclusion:

> The best evidence from evaluations of practical applications of group-based mastery learning indicates that effects of these methods are moderately positive on experimenter-made achievement measures closely tied to the objectives taught in mastery learning classes and are essentially nil on standardized achievement measures. These findings may be interpreted as supporting the "weak claim" that mastery learning can be an effective means of holding teachers and students to a specific set of instructional objectives, but do not support the "strong claim" that mastery learning is more effective than traditional instruction given equal time and achievement measures that assess coverage [content coverage] as well as mastery. (p. 202)

It appears that the research reviews of mastery learning differ greatly as to the actual research studies reviewed and that the differences in content have influenced the conclusions which emerge. An example is to be found in the different strategies for collection and selection of research studies employed by different reviewers. "Meta-analysis is simply the statistical analysis of a large collection of results from individual studies for the purpose of integrating the findings" (Cohen, Kulik, and Kulik, 1982, p. 238). Meta-analysis does not impose *a priori* criteria for the purpose of excluding methodologically weak or questionable studies. Typically, large numbers of research studies are contained in a meta-analytic analysis. In contrast, Slavin, in keeping with a "best-evidence synthesis" approach, imposed *a priori* criteria to identify studies for review and analysis which contained a high level of internal and external validity and strong experimental designs. The effect was to reduce the number of studies to be reviewed in depth to a mere seventeen investigations, some of which had not appeared in the professional literature. Slavin contends that the inclusion of these "unpublished studies" counters the "publication bias" against studies which report weak or negative results. Slavin points out that many of the studies included in his review could or would be included in a meta-analysis, but that many of the studies included in a meta-analysis would not have satisfied the criteria for inclusion in a "best-evidence synthesis". In fact, Slavin mentions several widely published and successful school improvement programs based upon mastery learning principles, but does not discuss them. *A priori* decisions regarding inclusion and exclusion will impact on the results of the review. Bearing this factor in mind, let us see if there are conclusions which transcend differences in the reviewers' methods.

Despite their difference, there is general agreement on the fact that mastery learning procedures yield more positive results on experimenter-made or teacher-made tests which closely parallel teaching objectives, and that mastery learning tends to yield weak or negligible results when instructional effects are assessed by means of standardized tests of academic achievement. In practical terms, in group comparisons of mastery versus nonmastery instruction, the results will tend toward mastery learning students when criterion referenced type tests are used to assess learning progress, but will demonstrate weak or negligible effects for mastery learning procedures when standardized achievement tests are used to assess learning outcomes. Though researchers may agree on the outcome, there is disagreement as to why this is so. Slavin (1987) contends that the use of experimenter-made or teacher-made tests to assess the outcomes of mastery learning instruction unfairly favors the experimental students. He maintains that a fair test of mastery learning versus conventional instruction would require that instructional time be held constant for both the experimental and control groups and that standardized achievement tests be employed to measure instructional effects. In a rejoinder to Slavin, Bloom (1987) rejects the use of standardized achievement tests to measure mastery learning effects. Rather, he holds that experimenter-made and teacher-made, *i.e.*, criterion referenced tests more accurately measure teaching objectives than standardized tests which encompass a broad range of school learning. Bloom contends that the disappointing results on standardized measures are what one would expect as a result of using inappropriate outcome measures. Bloom adds that much evidence in support of mastery learning is contained in the research literature—but not the restricted literature reviewed by Slavin.

Proponents of mastery learning claim that achievement variance among students, *i.e.*, the range of achievement form the lowest performing to the highest performing student, will be reduced under mastery learning conditions. A demonstrable reduction in achievement variance is, therefore, an important outcome of mastery learning investigations. Once again the research literature reveals conflicting results. In the Block and Burns (1976) review, 15 of 25 comparisons between experimental and control groups showed achievement variance among mastery learning students to be less than or equal to that of the control students. Contradictory findings are reported by Arlin (1984) as a result of 2 investigations of mastery learning. The first of the 2 studies involved a 10 unit instructional sequence taught in 4 elementary classrooms and embodied a comparison between mastery and nonmastery instructional procedures. The second study involved a *post hoc* longitudinal evaluation of the time needed for the mastery of arithmetic curriculum under mastery learning conditions over a period of 4 academic years (grades 1 through 4). The findings of the first study revealed that achievement variance between fast and slow learners remained stable over time and further that the amount of extra instructional time needed for the slower students to attain mastery also remained stable over time. In the second study, variability in student time to mastery either remained stable or actually increased over the 4 year period. More encouraging results regarding student learning efficiency were found in studies by Arlin (1973), Anderson (1973), and Block (1970), who reported that the time needed for student learning decreased under mastery learning conditions. In a discussion of his findings, Arlin 91984) points out that time differences may have been partially due to teachers pacing behavior rather than student time needs. On the other hand, Arlin suggests that a leveling effect, *i.e.*, teachers setting the pace of instruction to meet the needs of slower rather than faster students in the group, would artificially reduce achievement variance among the students. Under fast paced instruction, student achievement variance might very well increase. The related issues of achievement variance and variability in time needed for learning are central to mastery learning theory. The conflicting research findings highlight the need for a continuing research effort.

Regarding the question of retention, the research literature offers mixed results. Only 2 of the 6 studies reviewed by Block and Burns (1976) offer data on retention effects. Anderson (1976a) found that 3 out of 5 classrooms retained information significantly better than the control classrooms, and that in 2 additional classrooms retention favored the mastery learning students, though not to a significant degree. In the Burrows and Okey (1975) study, students in 3 mastery learning classrooms initially out-performed students in the control classroom and had a higher level of retention of curricular content when tested at a later date. But Slavin (1987) found little evidence of a positive retention effect in 6 comparisons drawn from 5 studies. The strongest retention effect was found in the Anderson (1986) study; the Burrows and Okey (1975) study was not among the studies he reviewed.

A less controversial but no less important research question concerns the affective outcomes of mastery learning among its student participants. Block (1974), in an early review of mastery learning, cites numerous studies which provide evidence that mastery learning has a positive effect on student interests and attitudes. Block admits that many of the studies are nonexperimental in design, but feels that the consistency of outcomes to a degree mitigates the lack of rigor in many of the early research efforts. The research findings indicate that students who participate in mastery learning programs are interested in school and have positive attitudes toward the school subjects learned under mastery conditions; they are also confident in their ability to learn, and generally enjoy learning within a mastery learning program. In a later research review, Block and Burns (1976) reiterate the general conclusion that mastery learning results in positive affective outcomes. More recently, Stallings and Stipek (1986) have reviewed the mastery learning literature and in general concur regarding the positive affective outcomes of mastery learning. They state that in comparisons of mastery and nonmastery learning programs the results tend to favor the mastery learning students; they characterize, however, the magnitude of the results as mildly positive in both achievement and attitudes. Stallings and Stipek call attention to a potentially negative consequence of mastery learning, that is, heightened test anxiety among students due to the all or nothing nature or the summative evaluation. In mastery learning programs, the student's grade hinges entirely upon her performance on the one summative evaluation. Of course, the student is given more than one opportunity to make the grade.

What ultimate conclusions can one draw from these disparate and conflicting research findings, and the conflicting points of view among eminent educators and scholars? Mixed, even conflicting results, are not reason for discouragement; rather, they signal the need for further research. Slavin (1987), despite the decidedly negative tone of his review and the minimal evidence supportive of mastery learning in the research studies he reviewed, does not call for an abandonment of research on mastery learning. Rather, he calls for a continued research effort to clarify the conditions under which mastery learning can be effective. There is evidence of mastery learning effectiveness on criterion referenced tests of instructional objectives specifically taught through mastery learning procedures. The evidence on retention, reduction of achievement variance, and time needed for learning is mixed. Evidence relating to affective outcomes are generally positive. There is demonstrable evidence and other indications that it is the low-functioning, slow learning students who benefit most from mastery learning. The utility of mastery learning for the low-functioning student is a compelling area for future research, one which may yield important findings for teachers who work with such students.

Mastery Learning and the Handicapped Learner

Mastery learning has much to offer special educators. Many of its instructional features are already part of special education methodology, *e.g.*, learning to mastery, formative evaluation, and corrective instruction based upon diagnostic testing. But the most important and most positive feature of mastery learning may well be the belief that all students can learn (Stallings and Stipek, 1986). This fundamental precept of mastery learning undermines the belief, widely held, that significant numbers of students cannot learn or cannot learn well and may force educators to reexamine established practices which contribute to the continued failure of large numbers of students within our schools. This fundamental precept may be the best antidote for the low expectations and the negative influence that low expectations exert on student performance, particularly the performance of students doubly handicapped by their own low achievement and an educational system which perpetuates inequalities in student performance.

Stallings and Stipek (1986) have identified the following features which make mastery learning beneficial for low ability and slow learning students: (1) its ability to foster a cooperative rather than competitive learning environment in which low achievers have little hope of success; (2) its ability to provide more time and supportive instruction for students who require it to attain mastery level performance; (3) its espousing of grading based upon criterion-referenced testing; and its ability to improve student motivation by enabling all students to succeed, and eliminating the embarrassment associated with making academic mistakes, which are no more than a natural part of the learning process. Additional features of mastery learning which enhance its applicability for the handicapped student and its use in special education settings are: (1) its positive view of individual differences, and its provision for corrective instruction suited to individual needs; (2) the stress mastery learning places upon the importance of full mastery of each step in the learning sequence; and (3) its stress upon the importance of sequential instructional objectives and formative evaluation of student progress.

There are many reasons why special educators should consider the potential benefits of mastery learning for handicapped learners. Research evidence of positive achievement gains for handicapped students under mastery learning conditions should further enhance mastery learning in the eyes of special educators. Fuchs, Tindal, and Fuchs (1985) compared the effectiveness of 2 approaches to mastery learning for the instruction of first grade students. Mastery learning procedures were compared to the "mastery learning" recommended by the publishers of a basal series used with the control students. The authors found that low achievers benefited from the mastery learning approach while high achievers benefited more from the traditional basal instruction. Wyckoff (1974) provided instruction in anthropology over a period of 9 weeks to sixth graders who had been randomly assigned to experimental and control conditions. The results revealed a statistically significant between group difference favoring the experimental subjects. Further examination of the results revealed that the positive outcome was due to the improved performance under mastery learning conditions of the low performance readers, not the high ability readers. In a third study conducted among Israeli junior high school students, very strong positive results for mastery learning were found for students whose fathers had not completed high school in comparison to students whose fathers had had more education (Mevarech, 1985). The collective results of these 3 studies are encouraging regarding the positive effect of mastery learning for both slow learners and low SES students.

In Summary

Both direct instruction and mastery learning are characterized by a strong emphasis on the use of instructional time and compatibility between their instructional methods and the methodology of special education. Neither approach is a curriculum *per se*; rather each embodies a set of instructional principles which is to be applied to existing curriculum to enhance teaching effectiveness..

Direct instruction has been popularized as a general orientation to basic skills instruction by Rosenshine, and as a highly structured and intensive methodology for teaching basic skills to young, instructionally naive students by Carnine and his colleagues. The "direct instruction" orientation and the "Direct Instruction" methodology share common elements; but there are differences as well, most notably the in depth analysis of curriculum and highly structured techniques for instructional delivery associated with the latter teaching approach.

Mastery learning focuses upon the amount of learning time provided to students and stresses the importance of providing sufficient time and appropriate initial and remedial instruction to every student. Given quality instruction, adequate time, and a willingness on the part of the student to spend the amount of time needed in studying, proponents of mastery learning fully expect that most pupils can attain the levels of achievement currently attained by only a minority of more able learners. Teaching methods emphasize specification of instructional objectives, formative and summative evaluation, and corrective instruction as needed.

Both direct instruction and mastery learning have been applied in special education with promising results. But the extent of the applicability of the methods for handicapped learners merits far more research effect. Both methods are prone to "splintered" application, in which teachers pick and choose the instructional elements they wish to use. In the process the integrity and power of the methods may be diminished or lost. There is a need for research to identify the critical components of direct instructionl and mastery learning and the conditions under which they are most effective for handicapped learners.

Chapter 11

The Future

Due to the works of theorists such as J. Carroll, B. Bloom, D. Wiley, and A. Harnischfeger, time has been recognized as a pivotal mediating variable between the student and learning outcomes. After a most fruitful quarter century of research it is possible to speculate from our current base of knowledge and understanding about the relationship of time to learning to future research directions likely to improve education for large numbers of mildly handicapped students in our schools.

Researchers have defined and quantified time in many different ways. Within the organizational and operational structures of our schools, time has been equated with exposure to schooling and delimited by the number of days in the school year and the number of hours in the instructional day. At the classroom level, exposure to instruction is equated with scheduled or allocated time which reveals the amount of class time designated for various activities. The more important definitions of time are concerned with the student's actual participation in the learning process. The critical dimension of instructional time for the student is engaged time, that is, the time in which students are actually attending to appropriate instructional tasks. One widely adopted definition extends the concept of engagement to include the dimension of task appropriateness by stating that students must be engaged in tasks in which they enjoy a high level of success, *i.e.*, academic learning time. Finally, the definition of time has been extended to reflect the nature of student participation during engaged time with the variable of interest being the degree of active attending and/or participatory behavior, *i.e.*, active academic responding.

In our current research time is viewed as both a mediating and outcome variable. An example of time as a mediating variable is found in the innumerable correlational studies which have explored the relationship between learning time and learning outcomes. Such studies reveal the magnitude of the correlational association between time and student performance and the proportion of achievement variance attributable to the time factor. An example of time as an outcome variable can be seen in the use of on-task behavior or engaged behavior to gauge the effectiveness of various instructional interventions. Presumably the interventions which result in the higher level of attending behavior represent the superior or more effective instructional approaches. According to Smyth (1984), "by utilizing the variable of time-on-task teachers have an immediate and utilitarian observational index of student involvement in substantive learning content which relates to overall achievement". Additionally, measures of engagement give teachers an efficient strategy for formative evaluation and monitoring.

Measures of time vary in their specificity and proximity to the actual learning behavior of students; in general, the closer the specific time measure is to actual student engagement, the stronger the resulting statistical relationships between learning time and student achievement. Scheduled or allocated time represents only the intended or planned use of learning time within the limits imposed by the daily school schedule. if the teacher allocates 1.5 hours per day for reading instruction, then the maximum time (opportunity) for reading instruction will not exceed that amount. Very likely the actual amount of reading instructional time will be far less than the amount allocated as some portion of school time must be used for managerial and other nonacademic activities. Engaged time focuses upon that portion of instructional time in which the student is actually involved in learning activities or tasks. Student involvement is optimal when the materials or tasks are appropriate in nature and difficulty level and when there are ample opportunities for active practice and responding. Within the limits of learning opportunity set by school district policies and regulations and the realities of the day to day operation of school programs, student time spent on appropriate instructional tasks is at the core of the learning process. The teacher's task then is to create, structure, manage, and maintain a learning environment which enables and encourages students to focus their attention and energy on appropriate learning tasks for significant portions of the school day.

The ferment of activity and interest in the relationship between learning time and learning outcomes has had both positive and negative consequences. On the negative side, Karweit (1983) maintains that "the view that time spent is equivalent to learning gained has become the newest myth to cloud our understanding of education" (p. 68), and that "more time produces more learning" (p. 73) is a fallacy which distorts our understanding of the educational process and represents a superficial awareness and understanding of the research findings. Undoubtedly some educators harbor this overly simplistic point of view, a point of view fostered by the reading of isolated articles or reports. The research literature on the whole, however, offers a broader perspective and a more balanced concern for both the time devoted to learning activities and the appropriateness of instructional tasks and activities—or, in Karweit's terms, "the simultaneity of engagement and appropriateness of instruction" (1983, p. 74). On the positive side, Karweit cites the extensive descriptive information about effective teaching practices and the illumination of future research possibilities among the beneficial outcomes of the interest and research in the time and learning relationship.

Patterns of Time Use

School time is divided between instructional and noninstructional uses with instructional time accounting for roughly half or less of the school day. The amount of time in which students are actively engaged represents a surprisingly small proportion of the total day or of total instructional time. The research findings to date reveal that the general patterns of time use are strikingly consistent across regular and special education classrooms. More normative studies are likely to reaffirm the patterns of time use already revealed. This pattern of time use is unlikely to change unless there are significant alterations in the scheduling and allocation of school time at the building or classroom level. That is not to say that we know all there is to know about the use of time in our schools. Though the research provides an invaluable picture of what currently exists, there are many gaps and fine details yet to be uncovered.

The literature on time use has a decidedly elementary bias; studies of the time use in secondary schools and classrooms is sparse. While the descriptive studies conducted in special education classrooms and programs for various types of handicapped learners reveals marked similarity in the utilization of school time across regular and special education settings, there are many questions yet to be explored with regard to the use of instructional time in special education classes, not the least of which concerns the patterns of time use for different types of handicapped students (the literature already hints at the possibility of differential treatment associated with different types of handicapping conditions (Sindelar, 1987)). In addition, the current practice of providing equal time to handicapped and nonhandicapped may satisfy social and/or legal requirements for equal treatment but may prove detrimental to handicapped students in the long run by denying the handicapped sufficient learning time to make a real difference in their learning deficiencies.

Optimal Level of Instructional Time

The research on time use for instructional purposes has shed light on the "average" but not the "optimal" use of instructional time. We know that engagement rates in the 70-85 percent range are characteristic of good students and that the engagement levels of poor students generally fall below this level. We know that there is a characteristic drop in engagement of approximately 15 percent from teacher-led to independent instructional situations for average, adequately progressing students. We do not know what the ideal or optimal engagement rates are for different types of students in different instructional settings. Nor do we know what engagement levels are possible given alterations in the instructional environment. The drop in engagement under independent seatwork conditions may reflect inadequacies in the instructional materials or setting, not an inevitable loss of student attention due to removal of direct instructional support from the teacher. We do not know how much time is optimal for all students to progress at a satisfactory pace in their school subjects. A unitary answer for all students is unlikely. This point is particularly germane for the atypical, non-average learner.

The need of the slower or disabled learner for more instructional time and the responsiveness of these students to instruction is a reoccurring theme within the research literature. But there is a limit to the amount of instructional time that can be provided and the amount of time that students can be expected to persevere at academic tasks. And, both in theory and practice, the addition of instructional time alone is insufficient to maximize learning outcomes. Greenwood, Delquadri, and Hall (1984) found that the mere addition of instructional time was ineffective in boosting achievement among inner city students. Other more substantive changes in the nature of instruction—in this instance, an increase in students' level of active participation—was needed in order to produce demonstrable improvements in learning and achievement. Further research must take into account teacher, student, and task variables, and the dynamic interactions among these variables. Continuing research to identify the most salient components of the instructional process and the conditions which favor optimal instruction is needed to reveal how the provision of more instructional time can be most effective in improving student performance. And a unifying conceptualization encompassing proven and effective instructional methods for mildly handicapped students is needed to focus teacher attention and effort much as "Direct Instruction" summarized the essential findings of the effective schools literature and focused regular educators attention on essential teaching functions.

In the near future, we are also likely to see the focus of research shift from description to experimental manipulation of the instructional time variable. Demonstration of the extent to which manipulations of instructional time and instructional variables produce the desired instructional outcomes is a logical next step for research endeavors.

Within Class and Within Subject Research

Normative studies have provided invaluable insight into how time is used in our schools. The need for descriptive studies continues particularly for special education students who should not be viewed or treated as a unitary student population. More relevant and revealing research on time use will emerge from probing investigations of time use within classrooms and subject areas. Numerous authors have documented the extreme variability that exists between and within schools, from class to class, even from child to child. The variability underscores 2 important facts: the first is the considerable control which teachers exercise over the expenditure of their time resources, and the second is the realization that children within the same school, at the same grade level, and even within the same class can experience very different instructional programs when instructional time and exposure to particular instructional activities vary.

More classroom level research is needed to explore the finer and more subtle dimensions of time usage and the concomitant impact of varying patterns of time use on students who differ in their backgrounds and learning characteristics. Rosenshine (1979) foresaw future studies of engagement for different activities within subject areas such as reading and writing and studies of engagement in different contexts such as students working alone and during supervised seatwork.

Research into patterns of time use within specific subject areas is underway, *e.g.*, research in the areas of language arts (Roehler, Schmidt, and Buchman, 1979), math (Good and Grouws, 1979) reading (Durkin, 1978079; Leinhardt, Zigmond, and Cooley, 1981; Haynes and Jenkins, 1986). Not surprisingly, the discipline of reading has received the most attention. Durkin's (1978-79) work focuses upon the nature and extent of comprehension instruction. Unfortunately her results reveal that minimal instructional time is devoted to substantive instruction of comprehension skills. The Leinhardt *et al.* (1981) and Haynes and Jenkins 91986) investigations utilized similar observational methods to explore the content and nature of reading instruction and included systematic observation of both teachers' and students' behavior. Both investigations sought to identify reading instructional variables which were most predictive of reading achievement.

A revelation of these and other studies which have explored time used for reading instruction is that the use of instructional time is inconsistent with our stated instructional goals and priorities. If the actual use of instructional time is taken as a measure of our commitment to often stated goals and priorities, the initial studies of time use in reading reveal serious inconsistencies between our espoused goals and our actual teaching practices. Continuing research on instructional practices and patterns of time use will bring this issue into sharp focus and, hopefully, provoke the educational community to correct the imbalances which exist. Educators must ensure that our limited resources of school and instructional time are invested in the most appropriate and important learning activities.

Research studies which compare and contrast instruction under different instructional conditions is limited. Most of the research to date has compared instruction and time use across different instructional settings, *e.g.*, regular education classroom versus the special education resource or self-contained classroom time use across different special education placements. Within classroom research has established the differential level of student engagement under teacher-led and independent working conditions. The characteristic decline in engagement which accompanies the removal of teacher or adult supervision is well documented. We do not know, however, if the loss of attention is the result of removing the adult presence or the result of inadequacies or weaknesses in the seatwork assignments, management factors, etc. The issue of effective seatwork—that is, seatwork which sustains student engagement and involvement in worthwhile academic activities—is important because of the significant amount of class time that children spend working independently, and because seatwork is a necessary accompaniment to small group or individualized instruction. Independent work, *e.g.*, students working alone with specially prepared materials, teaching machines, etc., is common practice in special education and consistent with special education's emphasis on individualization. Maintaining learning efficiency during seatwork activities is an important topic in need of serious study.

Student Characteristics

Regarding the handicapped learner, consideration must be given to the impact of individual student characteristics on the efficiency of the learning process. Handicapped learners often exhibit behavioral characteristics which are antithetical to efficient learning. Studies of student behavior which bear directly upon engagement and use of learning time have yielded important results. McKinney, Mason, Perkerson and Clifford (1975) studied the relationship between specific attending and work oriented behaviors and achievement among second graders. They found that patterns of student behavior related to achievement at the beginning of the school year were also predictive of the level of achievement at the end of the year. Passive responding, dependency, and distractibility were significant negative predictors of later achievement. "Knowledge of the child's classroom behavior patterns significantly enhanced the predictive value of paper-and-pencil tests which measure ability level" (McKinney et al., 1975, p. 202). The authors recommend that teachers intervene early in the school year to alter student's behavior patterns which are likely to hinder academic performance. Interestingly, the target behavior may not be those which traditionally are bothersome to teachers but rather those behaviors with a strong predictive relationship to achievement. The teacher is advised to inculcate behaviors most characteristic of effective learners among the less able and less motivated students.

Gettinger (1983, 1984a, 1984b, 1985), in a series of related research studies, has explored the relationship between time spent in learning (TSL) and time needed for learning (TTL).Gettinger's work is closely tied to Carroll's "Model of School Learning" and her results are very supportive of the model's central conceptualizations. In addition to demonstrating that TTL and TSL are indeed interrelated, Gettinger's (1984a) work establishes TTL as a critical mediating variable between time spent learning and achievement. Her research shows that spending less time than needed to learn a task to criterion level has a negative impact on initial achievement and retention (Gettinger, 1985). Lower functioning students, therefore, need and ought to spend more time to achieve preset learning goals. This factor may help to explain the greater benefits derived by the lower functioning student from the provision of additional instructional time and attention. Gettinger (1984b) believes that dynamic measures such as time-to-criterion, which reveal the student's ability to profit from instruction, can be used to identify those students who require more attention and assistance for optimal learning to occur. Teachers can then respond appropriately with remediation, added practice, more instructional time, etc.

An important and related question concerns those student attributes which contribute to a discrepancy between TTL and TSL. Both cognitive and noncognitive variables were investigated. Gettinger (1983) found that attention deficits account for a significant portion of the TTL-TSL discrepancy. Other noncognitive variables, e.g., loss of control, low self-esteem, and interest level accounted for a small but significant amount of the variability in the TTL-TSL discrepancy scores. Thus Gettinger and McKinney *et al.* concur on the need for intervention with the specific intent of altering noncognitive student characteristics. Though much has been said about effective teachers, Gettinger, McKinney, *et al.* remind us that we must also invest time and effort in developing effective and competent learners.

Our knowledge of time and the use of learning time has grown significantly over the course of the twentieth century; the explosion of knowledge and expansion of our understanding of time and the learning process has been most dramatic in just the last few decades. The research to date, while providing invaluable data and answering many questions, has outlined a research agenda for the future that will take years of study. Hopefully, special educators will be attuned to research developments in regular education as they occur and quickly translate important and relevant findings into practice in special education classrooms. A parallel agenda of research for special education should also be a priority which hopefully will yield important findings for the special classroom.

Time is the common denominator for both special and regular education teachers. The instructional clock starts ticking when the child enters school; it challenges teachers to make the best use of the finite amount of time that each and every child is placed within our charge and in our care.

Notes

Chapter 2

Special educators' persistent concern for attending problems is seen in the explosion of interest in the child with an attention deficit disorder (O'Brien and Obrzut, 1986). When dealing with a hypothetical construct such as attention deficit disorder, problems of definition, identification, and assessment methodology are unavoidable. The current ferment of activity surrounding the construct of attention deficit disorder is reminiscent of special education's sojourn with process and/or ability training the the 1960s and 1970s. That episode in special education produced few if any demonstrable benefits for handicapped children. The primary avenue of application for process/ability training was modality based instruction. The research overwhelmingly was unsupportive of such intervention approaches for disabled learners (Arter and Jenkins, 1977; Bracht, 1970; Kavale and Forness, 1987; Ysseldyke, 1973). One cannot help but be concerned about the intervention strategies which will evolve from the current interest and activity surrounding attention deficit disorder. Unfortunately, it is already evident that a primary intervention strategy for children diagnosed as having attention deficit disorder is the use of stimulant medications (O'Brien and Obrzut, 1986). Drug therapy was very prevalent in the 1960s and 1970s for children diagnosed as hyperactive. At that time there was serious concern about the potential physiological and psychological side effects of drug treatment for young children (Adelman and Compas, 1977; Clampit and Perkle, 1983) Many educators, past and present, have stressed the importance of exploring alternate nonchemically based interventions (Ayllon, Layman, and Kandel, 1975; Walden and Thompson, 1981), and similar discourse is currently being heard. It appears that our knowledge of the side effects of various medications has increased, but there is still concern about the long term effects of drug therapy with young children, and serious reservations about the extent of medical supervision and educational follow-up being provided to these children and their families (Hutchens and Hynd, 1987).

There are alternatives to drug therapies. There is evidence in the research literature of instructional, curricular, and environmental interventions which are effective in altering the behavior patterns of students with attention and behavior problems (Ayllon and Roberts, 194; Edwards, 1980). In some instances curricular/instructional modifications have been effective in controlling the behavior of problem learners who previously had required medication to enable them to perform satisfactorily in the classroom setting (Gickling and Thompson, 1985). Interventions involving modifications of curricular, reinforcement, and situational variables with sufficient power to bring the disruptive, disordered, and/or non-attending student into compliance with acceptable standards of behavior must be preferred to drug-based interventions which at best create a compliant but not a competent learner (Ayllon, Layman, and Kandel, 1975). With the specter of drug therapies overhead, the growing awareness of and interest in intervention based upon manipulation of the instructional process is most heartening. The convergence of special education and regular education interest in instructional time and student engagement should help to focus our attention on the learning process and our remedial efforts upon non-drug related interventions.

Chapter 3

1.   This study involving low achievers was included in the synthesis of studies which compared time usage across handicapped and nonhandicapped because of our inability to distinguish between the learning disabled and underachieving students (Ysseldyke, Algozzine, Shinn, and McGue, 1982; Warner, Schumaker, Alley and Deshler, 1980).

Chapter 7

a.   A letter sequence is every pair of letters that is written in correct order in the word being spelled, with blank spaces before and after the word: (Deno, Mirkin, and Wesson, 1983, p. 101). For example, the word cat has 4 letter sequences: space C, CA, AT, and T space. Letter sequences are used as a measure of performance because they are more sensitive to growth than total words spelled correctly.

b.   Correct digits refer to the number of correct numerals in the answer to a math problem. For example: 8+8=16, the answer of which has 2 correct digits. Correct digits are used as a measure of performance because they are more sensitive to performance change than total problems correct.

References

Abt Associates (1977). Education as experimentation: A planned variation model. (Vol. IV). Cambridge, MA: Abt Associates.

——— (1976). Education as experimentation: A planned variation model. (Vol. III). Cambridge, MA: Abt Associates.

Adelman, H. S., and Compas, B. E. (1977). Stimulant drugs and learning problems. *Journal of Education, 11*, 377-416.

Alberto, P. A., and Troutman, A. C. (1986). *Applied behavior analysis for teachers,* 2nd ed. Columbus, OH: Merill Publishing Company.

Algozzine, B., Ysseldyke, J. E., Christenson, S. (1983). An analysis of the incidence of special class placement: The masses are burgeoning. *Journal of Special Education 17* (2), 141-147.

Allen, V.L. (1976a). *Children as teachers.* NY: Academic Press.

——— (1976b). The helping relationship and socialization of children: Some perspectives on tutoring. In J. L. Allen (Ed.), *Children as teachers* (pp. 9-25). NY: Academic Press.

Allen, V. L., and Feldman, R. S. (1974). Learning through tutoring: Low-achieving children as tutors. *Journal of Experimental Education, 42*, 1-5.

Allington, R. L. (1983). The reading instruction provided readers of differing abilities. *The Elementary School Journal, 83*, 548-559.

——— (1980a). Teacher interruption behaviors during primary grade oral reading. *Journal of Educational Psychology, 72*, 371-377.

——— (1980b). Poor readers don't get to read much in reading groups. *Language Arts, 57*, 872-877.

——— (1977). If they don't read much, how they ever gonna get good? *Journal of Reading, 21*, 57-61.

Ames, R. (1983). Teachers' attributions for their own teaching. In J. Levine and M. Wang (Eds.), *Student and teacher perceptions: Implications for learning.* NY: Erlbaum.

Anderson, L. W. (1973). *Time and school learning.* Unpublished doctoral dissertation, University of Chicago.

Anderson, L., Brubaker, N., Alleman-Brooks, J., and Duffy, G. (1985). A qualitative study of seatwork in first grade classrooms. *Elementary School Journal, 86,* 123-140.

Anderson, L. M., Everston, C. M., and Brophy, J. E. (1982). Principles of small-group instruction in elementary reading. Michigan State University: The Institute for Research on Teaching (Occasional Paper No. 58).

—— (1979). An experimental analysis of effective teaching in first-grade reading groups. *Elementary School Journal, 79,* 193-223.

Anderson, L. W. (1981). Instruction and time-on-task: A review. *Curriculum Studies, 13*(4), 289-303.

—— (1984). Attention, tasks and time. In L. W. Anderson (Ed.), *Time and school learning* (pp. 46-68). NY: St. Martin's Press.

—— (1976). An empirical investigation of individual differences in time to learn. *Journal of Educational Psychology, 68*(2), 226-233.

Argyle, M. (1976). Social skills theory. In V. L. Allen (Ed.), *Children as teachers,* (pp. 57-71). NY: Academic Press.

Arlin, M. (1984). Time variability in mastery learning. *American Educational Research Journal, 21*(1), 103-120.

—— (1979). Teacher transitions can disrupt time flow in classrooms. *American Educational Research Journal, 16*(1), 42-56.

Arlin, M., and Westburg, I. (1976). The leveling effect of teacher pacing on science content mastery. *Journal of Research on Science Teaching, 13,* 213-219.

Arlin, M. N. (1973). *Learning rate and learning rate variance under mastery learning conditions.* Unpublished doctoral dissertation, University of Chicago.

Aronson, E. 91978). *The jigsaw classroom.* Beverly Hills, CA: Sage Publications.

Arter, J. A., and Jenkins, J. R. (1979). Differential diagnosis-prescriptive teaching: A critical appraisal. *Review of Educational Research, 49*(4), 517-555.

Averch, H. A., Carroll, S. J., Donaldson, T. S., Kiesling, H. J. and Pincus, P. (1974). *How effective is schooling? A critical review of research.* Englewood Cliff, NY: Educational Technology Publications.

Ayllon, T., Layman, D., and Kandel, H. J. (1975). A behavioral-educational alternative to drug control of hyperactive children. *Journal of Applied Behavior Analysis, 8,* 137-146.

Ayllon, T., and Roberts, M. D. (1974). Eliminating discipline problems by strengthening academic performance. *Journal of Applied Behavior Analysis, 7,* 71-76.

Bagnato, S. J., Neisworth, J. T., and Capone, A. (1986). Curriculum-based assessment for the young exceptional child: Rationale and review. *Topics In Early Childhood Special Education, 6*(2), 97-110.

Barr, R. (1975). How children are taught to read: Grouping and pacing. *School Review, 83,* 479-499.

Becker, W. C., and Gersten, R. (1982). A follow-up of Follow-Through: The later effects of the direct instruction model on children in fifth and sixth grades. *American Educational Research Journal, 19*(1), 75-92.

Becker, W. C. (1977). Teaching reading and language to the disadvantaged: What we have learned from field research. *Harvard Educational Review, 47*(4), 518-543.

Berliner, D. (1979). Tempus educari. In P. Peterson and H. Walberg (Eds.), *Research on teaching: Concepts, findings, and implications.* Berkeley, CA: McCutchan.

Berliner, D. and Pinero, V. C. (1984). Instructional time: How can teachers manage it better? *Instructor, 94,* 14-15.

Berliner, D. C. (1981). Academic learning time and reading achievement. In J. Guthrie (Ed.), *Comprehension and teaching: Research reviews.* Newark, DE: International Reading Association.

Bickel, W. E., & Bickel, D. D. (1986). Effective schools classrooms, and instruction: Implications for special education. *Exceptional Children, 52*(6), 489-500.

Blankenship, C., and Lilly, M. S. (1981). *Mainstreaming students with learning and behavior problems: Techniques for classroom teachers.* NY: Holt, Rinehart and Winston.

Blankenship, C. S. (1985). Using curriculum-based assessment data to make instructional decisions. *Exceptional Children, 52*(3), 233-238.

Blanton, B. (1971). Modalities and reading. *Reading Teacher, 25,* 210-212.

Blick. D. W., and Test, D. W. (1987). Effects of self-recording on high-school students' on-task behavior. *Learning Disabilities Quarterly, 10,* 203-213.

Block, J. H. (1974). Mastery learning in the classroom. In J. H. Block (Ed.), *School, society, and mastery learning.* NY: Holt, Rinehart and Winston.

——— (1972). Student learning and the setting of mastery performance standards. *Educational Horizons, 50,* 183-191.

——— (1971). *Mastery learning: Theory and practice.* NY: Holt, Rinehart, and Winston.

——— (1970). *The effects of various levels of performance on selected cognitive, affective, and time variables.* Unpublished doctoral dissertation, University of Chicago.

Block, J. H., and Anderson, L. W. (1975). *Mastery learning in classroom instruction.* NY: MacMillan Publishing Co.

Block, J., and Burns, R. B. (1976). Mastery learning. In L. S. Shulman (Ed.), *Review of research in education,* Vol. 4. Itasca, IL: F.E. Peacock Publishers.

Bloom, B. S. (1987). A response to Slavin's mastery learning reconsidered. *Review of Educational Research, 57*(4), 507-508.

———— (1984). The 2 sigma problem: The search for methods of instruction as effective as one-to-one tutoring. *Educational Researcher, 13*(6), 4-16.

———— (1984). The search for methods of group instruction as effective as one-to-one tutoring. *Educational leadership, 41*(8), 4-17.

———— (1980). The new direction in educational research: Alterable variables. *Phi*

———— (1976). *Human characteristics and school learning.* NY: McGraw-Hill.

———— (1974). Time and learning. *American Psychologist, 29*(19), 682-688. *Delta Kappan, 61,* 382-385.

———— (1971). Mastery learning. In J. H. Block, (Ed.), *Mastery learning: Theory and practice.* NY: Holt, Rinehart and Winston.

Bolstead, O. D., and Johnson, S. M. (1972). Self-regulation in the modification of disruptive classroom behavior. *Journal of Applied Behavior Analysis, 5,* 443-454.

Borg, W. R. (1980). Time and school learning. In C. Denham and A. Lieberman (Eds.), *Time to learn* (pp. 33-72). CA: National Institutes of Education.

Bracht, G. H. (1970). Experimental factors related to aptitude-treatment interactions. *Review of Educational Research, 40,* 627-645.

Brophy, J. E., and Evertson, C. M. (1974). Process-product correlations in the Texas teacher effectiveness study: Final report. Austin, TX: Texas University Research and Development Center for Teacher Education. (ERIC Reproduction Service No. ED 091 394).

Brophy, J. (1981). Teacher praise: A functional analysis. *Review of Educational Research, 51*(1), 5-32.

Brophy, J. E., and Good, T. L. (1986). Teacher behavior and student achievement. In M.C. Whittrock (Eds.), *Handbook of research on teaching* (3rd Ed.). NY: MacMillan.

———— (1984). Teacher behavior and student achievement. In M.C. Wittrock (Ed.), *Handbook of research on teaching: third edition.* NY: MacMillan Publishing Co., 328-375.

Brown, B. W., and Sax, D. H. (1979). Research issues concerning the production and finance of schooling. Research Series No. 65. East Lansing, MI: The

Institute for Research on Teaching, Michigan State University (ERIC Reproduction Service No. 187 001).

Bryan, T., and Wheeler, R. (1972). Perception of learning disabled children: The eye of the observer. *Journal of Learning Disabilities, 5*, 484-488.

Burns, R. B. (1984). How time is used in elementary schools: The activity structure of classrooms. In L. W. Anderson (Ed.), *Time and school learning* (pp. 91-127). NY: St. Martin's Press.

Burrows, C. K., and Okey, J. R. (1975). The effects of a mastery learning strategy on achievement. paper presented at the Annual Meeting of the American Educational Research Association, Washington, D.C.

Bursuk, L. A., (1971). Sensory mode of lesson presentation as a factor in the reading comprehension improvement of adolescent retarded readers. (ERIC Document Reproduction Service No. ED 047 435).

Caldwell, J. H., Huitt, W. G., and Graeber, A. O. (1982). Time spent in learning: Implications from research. *The Elementary School Journal, 82*(5), 471-480.

Carlberg, C., and Kavale, K. (1980). The efficacy of special versus regular class placement for exceptional children: A meta-analysis. *Journal of Special Education, 14*, 295-309.

Carnine, D. W. (1976). Effects of two teacher presentation rates on off-task behavior, answering correctly, and participation. *Journal of Applied Behavior Analysis, 9*, 199-206.

Carnine, D., and Silbert, J. (1979). *Direct instruction reading.* Columbus, OH: Merrill Publishing Company.

Carnine, D. (1987). Direct instruction. In C.R. Reynolds and L. Mann (Eds.), *Encyclopedia of special education.* NY: John Wiley and Sons.

Carroll, J. B. (1984). The model of school learning: progress of an idea. In L. W. Anderson (Ed.), *Time and school learning.* NY: St. Martin's Press.

———— (1963). A model of school learning. *Teachers College Record, 64*(8), 723-733.

Cartwright, G. P., Cartwright, C. A., and Ward, M. E. (1989). *Educating special learners.* Belmont, CA: Wadsworth.

Cegelka, W. M., and Tyler, J. L. (1970). The efficacy of special class placement for the mildly retarded in proper perspective. *Training School Bulletin, 67*(1), 33-677.

Chow, S. (1981). A study of academic learning time of mainstreamed learning disabled students. Final report. San Francisco: Far West Regional Laboratory for Education Research and Development. (ERIC Reproduction Service No. ED 216 467).

Clampit, M. K., and Perkle, J. B. (1983). Stimulant medication and the hyperactive adolescent: Myths and facts. *Adolescence, 72,* 811-822.

Cohen, A. (1981). Dilemmas in the use of learner-response delivery systems. Paper presented at the Annual Meeting of the American Educational Research Association, Los Angeles.

Cohen, P. R., Kulik, J. A., and Kulik, C. L. C. (1982). Educational outcomes of tutoring: A meta-analysis of findings. *American Educational Research Journal, 19*(2), 237-248.

Coker, H., Lorentz, J. and Coker, J. (1976). Interim report on Carroll County CBTC project, Fall, 1976. Atlanta: Georgia State Department of Education.

Cole, C. L. (1987). Self-management. In C. R. Reynolds and L. Mann (Eds.), *Encyclopedia of special education.* NY: John Willey and Sons.

Cole, C. L. , Gardner, W. I., and Karan, O. C. (1985). Self-management training of mentally retarded adults presenting severe conduct difficulties. *Applied Research in Mental Retardation, 6,* 337-347.

Coleman, J. S., Campbell, E. Q., Hobson, C. J., McParthland, J., Mood, A. M., Weinfeld, F. D., and York, R. L. (1966). *Equality of education opportunity.* Washington, D.C.: U.S. Department of Health , Education and Welfare.

Conroy, M. (1988). Pass or fail: How teachers rate pullout reading programs. *Learning, 16,* 70-74.

Cook, S. B., Scruggs, T. E., Mastropieri, M. A., and Castro, G. C. (1985-86). Handicapped students as tutors. *Journal of special education, 19*(4), 483-492.

Csapo, M. (1976). If you don't know it, teach it! *Clearinghouse, 12,* 365-367.

Cummings, R. W., and Madux, C. D. (1988). *Career and vocational education for the mildly handicapped.* Springfield, IL: Charles C. Thomas.

Dahloff, U. (1971). *Ability grouping, content validity, and curriculum process analysis.* NY: Teachers College Press.

Delquadri, J. C., Greenwood, C. R., Stretton, K., and Hall, R. V. (1983). The peer tutoring spelling game: A classroom procedure for increasing opportunity to respond and spelling performance. *Education and Treatment of Children, 6*(3), 225-239.

Delquadri, J., Greenwood, C. R., Whorton, D., Carta, J. J., and Hall, V. R. (1986). Classwide peer tutoring. *Exceptional Children, 52*(6), 535-542.

Deno, S., and Jenkins, J. (1967). Evaluating preplanning curriculum objectives. Philadelphia, PA: Research for Better Schools.

Deno, S. L., Mirkin, P. K., and Wesson, C. (1983). How to write data-based IEPs. *Teaching Exceptional Children, 16*(2), 99-104.

Deno, S. L. (1986). Formative evaluation of individual student programs: A new role for school psychologists. *School Psychology Review, 15*(3), 358-374.

———— (1985). Curriculum-based measurement: The emerging alternative. *Exceptional Children, 52*(3), 219-232.

Deno, S. L., Marston, D., and Mirkin, D. (1982). Valid measurement procedures for continuous evaluation of written expression. *Exceptional Children, 48*(4), 368-371.

Deno, S. L., Marston, D., Shinn, M. , and Tindal, G. (1983). Oral reading fluency: A simple datum for scaling reading disability. *Topics in Learning and Learning Disabilities, 2*(4), 53-59.

Deno, S. L., Mirkin, D. K., and Chiang, N. (1982). Identifying valid measures of reading. *Exceptional Children, 49*(1), 36-45.

Derevensky, J. L., Hart, S., and Farrell, M. (1983). An examination of achievement-related behavior of high- and low-achieving inner-city pupils. *Psychology in the Schools, 20,* 328-336.

Deshler, D. (1978). Psychoeducational aspects of learning disabled adolescents. In L. Mann, L. Goodman, J. L. Wiederholt (Eds.), *Teaching the Learning Disabled Adolescent* (pp. 47-74). Boston, MA: Houghton-Mifflin.

Deshler, D. D., and Schumaker, J. B. (1986). Learning strategies: An instructional alternative for low-achieving adolescents. *Exceptional Children, 52*(6), 583-590.

Devin-Sheehan, L. Feldman, R. S., and Allen, V. L. (1976). Research on children tutoring children: A critical review. *Review of Educational Research, 46*(3), 355-385.

DeVries, D., Mescon, I., and Shackman, S. (1975). Teams-games-tournaments (TGT) effects on reading skills in elementary grades (Rep. No. 200). Baltimore, MD: Johns Hopkins University, Center for Social Organization of Schools.

DeVries, D., and Slavin, R. (1978). Teams-Games-Tournaments: A research review. *Journal of Research and Developmental in Education, 12,* 28-38.

DeVries, E. K., and Slavin, R. (1978). Biracial learning teams and race relations in the classroom: Four field experiments using teams-games-tournaments. *Journal of Educational Psychology, 70,* 356-362.

Douglass, V. I., and Peters, K. G. (1979). Toward a clearer definition of the attention deficit of hyperactive children. In G. A. Hale & M. Lewis (Eds.), *Attention and the development of cognitive skills* (pp. 173-174). NY: Plenum.

Doyle, W. (1979). Classroom tasks and student abilities. In P. Peterson and H. Walberg (Eds.), *Research on teaching: Concepts, findings, implications* (pp. 182-209). Berkeley, CA: McCutchan.

Dunkin, M., and Biddle, B. The study of teaching. NY: Holt, Rinehart, and Winston, 1974.

Durkin, D. (1978-79). What classroom observations reveal asbout reading comprehension instruction. *Reading Research Quarterly,* 14(4), 481-533.

Ebel, R. L. (1978). The case for norm referenced measurements. *Educational Researcher, 7,* 3-5.

Eder, D. (1982). Differences in communicative styles across ability groups. In L. C. Wilkinson (Ed.), *Communicating in the classroom.* NY: Academic Press.

———— (1981). Ability grouping as a self-analysis of teacher-student interaction. *Sociology of Education, 54*(3), 151-162.

Edmonds, R. R. (1979). Some schools work and more can. *Social Policy, 9*(5), 28-33.

Education of the Handicapped Law report, supplement 203, October 23, 1987.

Edwards, L. L. (1980). Curricular modifications as a strategy for helping regular classroom behavior-disordered students. *Focus On Exceptional Children, 12*(8), 1-11.

Ellson, D. G. Tutoring. (1976). In N. Gage (Ed.), *The psychology of teaching methods.* Chicago, IL: University of Chicago Press.

Emmer, E. T., Evertson, C. M., Sanford, J. P., Clements, B. S., and Worsham, M. E. (1984). *Classroom Management for Secondary Teachers,* Englewood Cliffs, NJ: Prentice-Hall.

Englemann, S., Becker, W. C., Hanner, S., and Johnson, G. (1978). Corrective reading. Chicago: Science Research Associates.

Englemann, S., and Carnine, D. (1982). Theory of instruction: Principles and applications. NY: Irvington Publishers.

Englert, C. (1984). Effective direct instruction practices in special education settings. *Remedial and Special Education, 5*(2), 38-47.

Epstein, L. (1978). The effects of intraclass peer tutoring on the vocabulary development of learning disabled children. *Journal of Learning Disabilities, 11,* 63-66.

Esposito, D. (1973). Homogeneous and heterogeneous ability grouping: Principal findings and implications for evaluating and designing more effective educational environments. *Review of Educational Research, 43,* 163-179.

Evertson, C. M., Emmer, E. T., Clements, B. S., Sanford, J. P., and Worsham, M. E. (1984). *Classroom Management For Elementary Teachers*. Englewood Cliffs, NJ: Prentice-Hall.

Evertson, C. M., (1982). Differences in instructional activities in higher- and lower-achieving junior high English and math classes. *Elementary School Journal, 82,* 329-350.

Evertson, C. M., Anderson, C. W., Anderson, L. M., and Brophy, J. E. (1980). Relationship between classroom behaviors and student outcomes in junior high mathematics and English classes. *American Educational Research Journal, 17*(1), 43-60.

Evertson, C., and Emmer, E. (1982). Effective management at the beginning of the school year in junior high classes. *Journal of Educational Psychology, 74,* 785-498.

Ewing, N., and Brecht, R. (1977). Diagnostic/prescriptive instruction: A reconsideration of some rules. The *Journal of Special Education, 11*(3), 323-327.

Fisher, C. W., Berliner, D. C., Filby, N. N., Marliave, R., Cahen, L. S., and Dishaw, M. M. (1980). Teaching behaviors, academic learning time; and student achievement: An Overview. In C. Denham and A. Lieberman (Eds.), *Time to learn* (pp. 7-32). CA: National Institutes of Education.

Fisher, C. W.; Filby, N. N., Marliave, R., Cahen, L. S., Dishaw, M. M., Moore, J. E., and Bliner, D. C. (1978). Teaching behaviors, academic learning time and student achievement: Final report of phase III-B beginning teacher evaluation study, Technical Report V-1. San Francisco, CA: Far West Laboratory for Educational Research and Development. (ERIC Document Reproduction Service No. ED 183 525).

Forness, S. R., and Esveldt, K. C. (1975). Classroom observation of children with learning and behavior problems. *Journal of Learning Disabilities, 8,* 382-385.

Fox, R. G. (1974). *The effects of peer tutoring on oral reading behavior of underachieving fourth grade pupils.* Unpublished doctoral dissertation, University of Kansas, Lawrence.

Franca, V. M. (1983). Peer tutoring among behaviorally disordered students: Academic and social benefits to tutor and tutee. Dissertation Abstracts International, 44, 459-A.

Frederick, W. C., and Walberg, H. J. (1980). Learning as a function of time. *The Journal of Educational Research, 73*(4), 183-194.

Frymier, J. (1981). Learning takes more than time on task. *Educational Leadership, 38*(8), 634, 649.

Fuchs, L. S., Tindal, and Fuchs, D. (1985). *A comparison of mastery learning procedures among high and low ability students.* Unpublished manuscript. Vanderbilt University, Nashville, TN. (ERIC Document Reproduction Service No. ED 259 307)

Fuchs, L. S. (1986). Monitoring progress among mildly handicapped pupils: Review of current practice and research. *Remedial And Special Education, 7*(5), 5-12.

Fuchs, L. S., and Fuchs, D. (1986). Curriculum-based assessment of progress toward long-term and short-term goals. *The Journal of Special Education, 20*(1), 69-82.

———— (1984). Criterion-referenced assessment without measurements: How accurate for special education? *Remedial and Special Education, 5,* 29-32.

Fuchs, L. S., Fuchs, D., and Warren, L. M. (1982). Special education practice in evaluating student progress toward goals (Research Report No. 82). Minneapolis: University of Minnesota Institute for Research on Learning Disabilities. (ERIC Document Reproduction Service No. ED 224 198)

Fuchs, L., and Deno, S. (1981). A comparison of reading placement based on teacher judgment, standardized testing and curriculum-based assessment. (Research Report NO. 56). Minneapolis: University of Minnesota, Institute for Research on Learning Disabilities.

Fuchs, L. S., Deno, S. L., and Mirkin, P. L. (1984). The effects of frequent curriculum-based measurements and evaluation on pedagogy, student achievement, and student awareness of learning. *American Educational Research Journal, 21*(2), 449-460.

Fuchs, L., and Fuchs, D. (1986). Effects of systematic formative evaluation: A meta-analysis. *Exceptional Children, 53*(3), 199-208.

Fuchs, L., Fuchs, D., and Deno, S. (1982). Reliability and validity of curriculum-based informal reading inventories. *Reading Research Quarterly, 18*(1), 6-25.

Gable, R. V., and Kerr, M. M. (1980). Behaviorally disordered adolescents as academic change agents. In R. B. Rutherford, Jr., A. G. Prieto, and J. E. McGlothlin (Eds.), *Severe behavior disorders of children and youth, Vol. 4.* Reston, VA: Council for Children with Behavioral Disorders.

Gage, N. L. (1978). *The scientific basis of the art of teaching.* NY: Teachers College Press.

Gallagher, J. J. (1984). Learning disabilities and the near future. *Journal of Learning Disabilities, 17*(9), 571-572.

Gartner, A., Kohler, M., and Reissman, F. (1971). *Children teach children: Learning by teaching.* NY: Harper and Row.

Gerber, M., and Kauffman, J. (1981). Peer tutoring in academic settings. In P. Strain (Ed.), *Utilization of classroom peers as change agents* (pp. 155-187). NY: Plenum Press.

Gerber, M. M. (1984). The Department of Education's sixth annual report to congress on P.L. 94-143. Is Congress getting the full story? *Exceptional Children, 51*(3), 20-224.

Gersten, R., Carnine, D., and White, W. A. T. (1984). The pursuit of clarity: Direct instruction and applied behavior analysis. In W. L. Heward, T. E. Heron, D. S. Hill, and J. Trap-Porter (Eds.), *Focus on behavior analysis in education*, (pp. 38-57). Columbus, OH: Merrill.

Gersten, R. (1985). Direct instruction with special education students: A review of evaluation research. *The Journal of Special Education, 19*(1), 41-58.

Gersten, R., Becker, W. C., Heiry, T. J., and White, W. A. T. (1984). Entry IQ and yearly academic growth of children in direct instruction programs: A longitudinal study of low SES children. *Educational Evaluation and Policy Analysis, 6*(2), 109-121.

Gersten, R., and Carnine, D. (1984). Direct instruction mathematics: A longitudinal evaluation of low-income elementary school students. *The Elementary School Journal, 84*(4), 395-407.

Gersten, R. M., and Maggs, A. (1982). Teaching the general case to moderately retarded children: Evaluation of a five year project. *Analysis and Intervention in Developmental Disabilities, 2*, 329-343.

Gettinger, M. (1985). Time allocated and time spent relative to time needed for learning as determinants of achievement. *Journal of Educational Psychology, 77*(1), 3-11.

———— (1984a). Achievement as a function of time spent in learning and time needed for learning. *American Educational Research Journal, 21*(3), 617-628.

———— (1984b). Measuring time needed for learning to predict learning outcomes. *Exceptional Children, 51*(3), 244-248.

Gettinger, M., and Lyon, M. A. (1983). Predictors of the discrepancy between time needed and time spent in learning among boys exhibiting behavior problems. *Journal of Educational Psychology, 75*(4), 491-499.

Gickling, E., and Thompson, V. P. (1985). A personal view of curriculum based assessment. *Exceptional Children, 52*(3), 205-218.

Gickling, E. E., and Armstrong, D. C. (1978). Levels of instructional difficulty as related to on-task behavior, task completion, and comprehension. *Journal of Learning Disabilities, 11*, 559-566.

Gilmore, J. V., and Gilmore, E. C. Gilmore Oral Reading Test. NY: Harcourt Brace Jovanovich, 1968.

Glaser, R. (1977). *Adaptive education: Individual diversity and learning*. NY: Holt, Rinehart and Winston.

Glynn, E. L., and Thomas, J. D. (1974). Effect of cueing on self-control of on-task behavior in an elementary classroom. *Journal of Applied Behavior Analysis, 7*, 299-306.

Glynn, E. L., Thomas, J. D., and Shel, S. K. (1973). Behavioral self-control of on-task behavior. *Journal of Applied Behavior Analysis, 6*, 105-118.

Good, T., and Beckerman, T. (1978). Time on task: A naturalistic study in sixth-grade classrooms. *Elementary School Journal, 78*(3), 193-201.

Good, T. L. and Brophy, J. E. (1987). *Looking in classrooms* (Fourth Ed). NY: Harper and Row.

Good, T. L., and Grouws, D. A. (1979). The Missouri Mathematics Effectiveness project. *Journal of Educational Psychology, 71*, 355-362.

Good, T., Grouws, D. and Beckerman, T. (1978). Curriculum pacing: Some empirical data in mathematics. *Journal of Curriculum Studies, 10*(1), 75-81.

Goodman, L. and Bennett, R. E. (1982). Use of norm-referenced assessment for the mildly handicapped: Basic issues reconsidered. In T. L. Miller and E. E. Davis (Eds.), *The mildly handicapped student* (pp. 241-262). NY: Grune and Stratton.

Goodman, L. (1987). Aptitude treatment interactions. In C. R. Reynolds and L. Mann (Eds.), *Encyclopedia of special education*. NY: John Wiley and Sons.

———— (1985). The effective schools movement and special education. *Teaching Exceptional Children, 17*(2), 102-105.

Goodman, L., Shaprio, E., and Bornstein, J. Teacher to teacher training in classroom observation of student on-task behavior. In progress.

Goss, S. S. (1984). Keeping students on task. In D. B. Strother (Ed.), *Time and Learning (pp. 169-172)*. Bloomington, IN: Phi Delta Kappa.

Graden, J. L., Casey, A., and Christenson, S. L. (1985). Implementing a preferral intervention system: Part I. The model. *Exceptional Children, 51*(5), 377-384.

Graden, J. L., Casey, A., and Bonstrom, O. (1985). Implementing a preferral intervention system: Part II. The data. *Exceptional Children, 51*(6), 487-496.

Greenwood, C., Delquadri, J., Hall, R. (1984). Opportunity to respond and student academic performance. In W. Heward, T. Heron, D. Hill, and J.

Trap-Porter (Eds.), *Focus on behavior analysis in education* (pp. 58-88). Columbus, OH: Merrill.

Greenwood, C. R., Delquadri, J., Stanely, S., Terry, B., and Hall, R. V. (1981). Allocating opportunity to respond as a basis for academic remediation: A developing model for teaching. In R. B. Rutherford, A. G. Prieto, and J. E. McGlothlin (Eds.), *Severe behavior disorders of children and youth, monograph in behavioral disorders*. Reston, VA: Council for Children with Behavioral Disorders.

Greenwood, C. R., Delquadri, J., and Hall, R. V. (1978). *Code for instructional structure and student academic response: CISSAR*. Kansas City, KS: Juniper Gardens Children's Project, Bureau of Child Research, University of Kansas.

Gump, P. V. (1974). Operating environments in schools of open and traditional design. *School Review, 82*, 575-593.

Guskey, T. R., and Gates, S. L. (1986). Synthesis of research on the effects of mastery learning in elementary and secondary classrooms. *Educational Leadership, 43*(8), 73-80.

Guthrie, J. T. (1977). Follow Through: A compensatory education experiment. *The Reading Teacher, 31*, 240-244.

Halasz, I. M. (1984). Finding time to teach basic skills. *Vocational Education, 59*, 15-16.

Hall, R. V., Delquadri, J. C., Greenwood, C. R., and Thurston, L. (1982). The importance of opportunity to respond to children's academic success. In E. Edgar, N. Haring, J. Jenkins, and U. Pious (Eds.), *Serving young handicapped children: Issues and research* (pp. 107-140). Baltimore, MD: University Park Press.

Hallahan, D. P., Marshall, K. J., and Lloyd, J. W. (1981). Self-recording during group instruction: Effects on attention to task. *Learning Disabilities Quarterly, 4*(4), 407-413.

Hallahan, D. P., Lloyd, J., Kosiewicz, M. M., and Graves, A. W. (1979). Self-monitoring of attention as a treatment for a learning disabled boy's off-task behavior. *Learning Disabilities Quarterly, 2*(3), 24-32.

Hallahan, D. P., and Kauffman, J. M. (1977). Labels, categories, behaviors: ED, LD, and EMR reconsidered. *The Journal of Special Education, 11*(2), 139-149.

Hasazi, S. B., Gordon, L. R., and Roe, C. A. (1985). Factors associated with the employment status of handicapped youth exiting high school from 1979 to 1983. *Exceptional Children, 51*, 455-469.

Hasselbring, T. S., Goin, L. I., and Bransford, J. D. (1987). Developing automaticity. *Teaching Exceptional Children, 19*(3), 30-33.

Hassinger, J., and Via, M. (196(). How much does a tutor learn through teaching reading? *Journal of Secondary Education, 44*, 42-44.

Hawley, W. D., and Rosenholtz, S. J. (1984). Effective teaching. *Peabody Journal of Education, 61*(4), 15-52.

Haynes, M. C., and Jenkins, J. r. (1986). Reading instruction in special education resource rooms. *American Educational Research Journal, 23*(2), 161-190.

Heath, R. W., and Nielson, M. A. (1974). The research basis for performance based teacher education. *Review of Educational Research, 44*(4), 463-381.

Higgins, T. S. (1982). A comparison of two methods of practice on the spelling performance of learning disabled adolescents. *Dissertation Abstracts International, 43*(8-B), 4021.

Hill, P., and Kimbrough, J. (1981). The aggregate effects of federal education programs. The Rand Publications Series. Santa Monica, CA: The Rand Corporation.

Hobbs, N. L. (1975). *The futures of children.* San Francisco, CA: Jossey-Bass.

Hobbs, N. L. (1976). *Issues in the classification of children* (Vols. 1 and 2). San Francisco, CA: Josey-Bass.

Holton, B. (1982). Attribute-treatment-interaction research in mathematics education. *School Science and Mathematics, 82*(7), 593-601.

Hutchens, T. A., and Hynd, G. W. (1987). Medications and the school-age child and adolescent: A review. *School Psychology Review, 16*(4), 527-542.

Idol-Maestas, L. (1983). *Special educator's consultation handbook.* Rockville, MD: Aspen.

Idol, L. Nevin, A., and Paolucci-Whitcomb, P. (1986). *Models of curriculum-based assessment.* Rockville, MD: Aspen

Jencks, C. (1972). *Inequality: A reassessment of the effect of family and schooling in America.* NY: Basic Books.

Jenkins, J., and Jenkins, L. (1985). Peer tutoring in elementary and secondary programs. *Focus on Exceptional Children, 17*(6), 1-12.

Jenkins, J. R., Mayhall, U. R., Peschka, C. M., and Jenkins, L. M. (1974). Comparing small group and tutorial instruction in resource rooms. *Exceptional Children, 40*, 245-250.

Johnson, D. W., Johnson, R., and Scott, L. (1978). The effects of cooperative and individualized instruction on student attitudes and achievement. *Journal of Social Psychology, 104*, 207-216.

Johnson, R., Rynders, J., Johnson, D. W., Schmidt, B., and Haider, S. (1979). Interaction between handicapped and nonhandicapped teenagers as a function of situational goal structuring: Implications for mainstreaming. *American Educational Research Journal, 16,* 161-167.

Johnson, D. W., Marayama, G., Johnson, R., Nelson, D., and Skon, L. (1981). Effects of cooperative, competitive and individualistic goal structures on achievement: A meta-analysis. *Psychological Bulletin, 89,* 47-62.

Johnson, D. W., and Johnson, R. T. (1987). *Learning together & alone.* (2nd ed). Englewood Cliffs, NJ: Prentice-Hall.

Jones, C. P. (1981). *A descriptive study of cross-age peer tutoring as a strategy for reading improvement in two selected middle schools of the Highland Park, Michigan School System from 1970 to 1978.* Dissertation Abstracts International, 47.

Joyce, B., and Showers, B. (1980). Improving inservice training: The message of research. *Educational Leadership, 37,* 379-385.

Kallison, J. (1980). *Organization of the lesson as it affects student achievement.* Unpublished doctoral dissertation, University of Texas.

Kapadia, S., and Fantuzzo, J. W. (1988). Training children with developmental disabilities and severe behavior problems to use self-management procedures to sustain attention to preacademic/academic tasks. *Education and Training in Mental Retardation, 23,* 59-69.

Karweit, N. L. (1983-84). Time on task: A research review. In D. B. Strother (Ed.), *Time and learning* (pp. 19-78). Bloomington, IN: Phi Delta Kappa.

———— (1982). Time-on-task: Issues of timing, sampling, and definition. *Journal of Educational Psychology, 74*(6), 844-851.

Karweit, N., and Slavin, R. E. (1981). Measurement and modeling choices in studies of time and learning. *American Educational Research Journal, 18*(2), 157-171.

Kavale, K. A., and Forness, S. R. (1987). Substance over style: Assessing the efficacy of modality testing and teaching. *Exceptional Children, 54*(3), 278-239.

Kazdin, a. E., and Matson, J. L. (1981). Social validation in mental retardation. *Applied Research in Mental Retardation, 2,* 39-53.

Kazdin, A. E. (1982). Single-case research designs. NY: Oxford University Press.

Kemmerer, F. (1979). The Allocation of Student Time, *Administrator's Notebook, 27*(8).

Keogh, B. K., and Margolis, J. (1976). Learning to labor and to wait: Attentional problems of children with learning disorders. *Journal of Learning Disabilities, 9*(5), 276-286.

Kiesling, H. (1978). Productivity of instructional time by mode of instruction for students at varying levels of reading skills. *Reading Research Quarterly, 13*, 554-582.

Knowles, C. J., Aufderheide, S. K., and McKenzie, T. (1982). Relationship of individualized teaching strategies to academic learning time for mainstreamed and nonhandicapped students, *Journal of Special Education, 16*(4), 449-456.

Kosiewicz, M. M., Hallahan, D. P., Lloyd, J., and Graves, A. W. (1982). Effects of self instruction and self correction procedures on handwriting performance. *Learning Disabilities Quarterly, 5*(1), 71-78.

Kounin, J. (1970). *Discipline and Group Management in Classrooms*. NY: Holt, Rinehart and Winston.

Krupski, A. (1985). Variations in attention as a function of classroom task demands in learning handicapped and CA-matched nonhandicapped children. *Exceptional Children, 52*(1), 52-56.

Kuehne, C., Kehle, T. J., and McMahon, W. (1987). Differences between children with attention deficit disorder, children with specific learning disabilities, and normal children. *Journal of School Psychology, 25*, 161-166.

Kulik, C. C., Kulik, J. A., and Bangert-Drowns, R. L. (1986, April). Effects of testing for mastery on students learning. Paper presented at the annual meeting of the American Educational Research Association, San Francisco.

Kulik, C. C., and Kulik, J. A. (1982). Effects of ability grouping on secondary school students: A meta-analysis of evaluation findings. *American Educational Research Journal, 19*, 415-428.

Lamport, K. C. (1982). *The effects of inverse tutoring in reading disabled students in a public school setting*. Dissertation Abstracts International, 44(03-A), 729.

Lana, M., and Smith, L. (1979). The effects of low inference teacher clarity inhibitors on student achievement. *Journal of Teacher Education, 31*, 55-57.

Landrum, J. W. (1970). When students teach others. *Educational Leadership, 27*, 446-448.

Lane, P., Pollack, C., and Sher, N. (1972). Remotivation of disruptive adolescents. *Journal of Reading, 15*, 351-354.

Leach, D. J., and Dolan, N. K. (1985). Helping teachers increase student academic engagement rate. *Behavior Modification, 9*(1), 55-71.

Leinhardt, G., Zigmond, N., and Cooley, W. W. (1981). Reading instruction and its effects. *American Educational Research Journal, 18*(3), 343-361.

Leinhardt, G., and Seewald, A. M. (1980). Student level observation of beginning reading. Pittsburgh, PA: University of Pittsburgh, Learning Research and Development Center.

Leinhardt, G., and Palley, A. (1982). Restrictive educational settings. Exile or haven? *Review of Educational Research, 52,* 557-578.

Lloyd, J., Cullinan, D., Heins, E. D., and Epstein, M. H. (1980). Direct instruction: Effects on oral and written language comprehension. *Learning Disabilities Quarterly, 3*(4), 70-76.

Lloyd, J. W. (1984). How shall we individualize instruction—or should we? *Remedial And Special Education, 5*(1), 7-15.

Lloyd, J. W., Hallahan, D. P., Kosiewicz, M. M., and Kneedler, R. D. (1982). Reactive effects of self-assessment and self-recording on attention to task and academic productivity. *Learning Disabilities Quarterly, 5*(3), 216-227.

Lovitt, T. C., Curtiss, K. (1969). Academic response rate as a function of teacher and self-imposed contingencies. *Journal of Applied Behavior Analysis, 2,* 49-53.

Lovitt, T. C., and Curtiss, K. A. (1968). Effects of manipulating an antecedent on mathematics response rate. *Journal of Applied Behavior Analysis, 1,* 329-333.

Luchow, J. P., Crowl, T. K., and Kahn, J. P. (1985). Learned helplessness: Perceived effects of ability and effort on academic performance among EH and LD/EH children. *Journal of Learning Disabilities, 18*(8), 470-474.

Madden, N. A. , and Slavin, R. E. (1989). In R. E. Slavin, N. L. Karweit, and N. A. Madden (Eds.). *Effective programs for students at risk.,* Boston: Allyn and Bacon.

Maheady, L., and Harper, G. F. (1987). A class-wide peer tutoring program to improve the spelling test performance of low-income, third- and fourth-grade students. *Education and Treatment of Children, 10*(2), 120-133.

Maheady, L., Sacca, M. K., and Harper, G. F. (1988). Classwide peer tutoring with mildly handicapped high school students. *Exceptional Children, 55*(1), 52-59.

Maher, C. A. (1984). Handicapped adolescents as crossage tutors. Program description and evaluation. *Exceptional Children, 51,* 56-63.

———— (1982). Behavioral effects of using conduct problem adolescents as cross age tutors. *Psychology in the Schools, 19,* 360-364.

Mackenzie, D. E. (1983). Research for school improvement: An appraisal of some recent trends. *Educational Researcher, 12*(4), 5-17.

MacMillan, D. L., Keogh, B. K., and Jones, R. L. (1986). Special educational research on mildly handicapped learners. In M. C. Wittrock (Ed.), *Handbook of research on teaching,* (3rd Ed). NY: MacMillan Publishing Co.

Madden, N. A., and Slavin, R. E. (1983). Mainstreaming students with mild handicaps: Academic and social outcomes. *Review of Educational Research, 53*(4), 519-569.

Maggs, A., and Morath, P. (1976). Effects of direct verbal instruction on intellectual development of instructionalized moderately retarded children: A 2 year study. *Journal of Special Education, 10*, 357-364.

Martino, L., and Johnson, D. W. (1979). The effects of cooperative vs. individualistic instruction on interaction between normal-progress and learning-disabled students. *Journal of Social Psychology*, 177-183.

McAfee, J. K., and Mann, L. (1982). The prognosis for mildly handicapped students. In T. L. Miller, and E. E. David (Eds.), *The mildly handicapped student*. NY: Grune and Stratton.

McKinney, J. D., Mason, J., Perkerson, K., and Clifford, M. (1975). Relationship between classroom behavior and academic achievement. *Journal of Educational Psychology, 67*(2), 198-203.

McWhorter, K. T., and Levy, J. (1971). The influence of a tutorial program upon tutors. *Journal of Reading, 14*, 221-224.

McFaul, S. (1983). An examination of direct instruction. *Educational Leadership, 40*(7), 67-68.

Medley, D. M. (1979). The effectiveness of teachers. In P. L. Peterson, and H. J. Walberg (Eds.), *Research on Teaching: Concepts, findings, and implications* (pp. 11-27). Berkeley, CA: McCutchan.

Meichenbaum, D., and Goodman, J. (1971). Training impulsive children to talk to themselves: A means of developing self-control. *Journal of Abnormal Psychology, 77*, 115-126.

———— (1969). Reflection-impulsivity and verbal control of motor behavior. *Child Development, 40*, 785-797.

Mellberg, D. B. (1981). *The effect of the handicapped and nonhandicapped tutor on the academic achievement of the economically disadvantaged adolescent tutor and the elementary age tutee.* Dissertation Abstracts International, 42(02-A), 659.

Mevarech, Z. R. (1985). The effects of cooperative mastery learning strategies on mathematical achievement. *Journal of Educational Research, 78*, 372-377.

Meyen, E. L., and Lehr, D. H. (1982). Evolving practices in assessment and intervention for mildly handicapped adolescents: The case for intensive instruction. In J. T. Neisworth (Ed.), *Assessment in special education*. Rockville, MD: Aspen.

———— (1980). Least restrictive environment: Instructional implementations. *Focus on Exceptional Children, 12*(7), 1-8.

Meyer, L., Gersten, R., and Gutkin, J. (1984). Direct instruction: A project follow through success story. *Elementary School Journal, 2*, 241-252.

Meyer, L. (1984). Longterm academic effects of direct instruction follow through. *Elementary School Journal, 4,* 380-394.

Mohan, M. Peer tutoring as a technique for teaching the unmotivated. Fredonia, NY: State University of New York, Teacher Education Research Center, 1972. (ERIC Document Reproduction Service No. ED 061 154)

Nelson, R. O. (1977). Assessment and therapeutic functions of self-monitoring. In M. Hersen, R. Eisler, and P. M. Miller (Eds.), *Progress in behavior modification*(Vol 5) NY: Academic Press.

Norris, M. S. (1978). *Utilization of peer tutors with the autistic child: An analysis of training procedures and academic outcomes.* Dissertation Abstracts International, 39(11-A), 6700.

O'Brien, M. A., and Obrzut, J. E. (1986). Attention deficit disorder with hyperactivity: A review and implications for the classroom. *Journal of Special Education,* 20(3), 281-295.

O'Leary, K., and O'Leary, S. (Eds.) (1977). *Classroom management: The successful use of behavior modification* (2nd Ed.). NY: Pergamon.

Osborne, S. S., Kosiewicz, M. M., Crumley, E. B., and Lee, C. (1987). Distractible students use self monitoring. *Teaching Exceptional Children, 19*(2), 66-69.

Ozcelik, D. A. (1974). *Student involvement in the learning process.* Unpublished doctoral dissertation, University of Chicago.

Peterson, P. L. (1979). Direct instruction reconsidered. In *Research on Teaching: Concepts, Findings and Implications.* P. L. Peterson and H. J. Walberg (Eds.) Berkeley, CA: McCutchan, 57-69.

Peterson, P. (1979). Direct instruction: Effective for what and for whom? *Educational Leadership, 37,* 46-48.

Peterson, N. (1982). On terms: Feedback is not a new principle of behavior. *The Behavior Analyst, 5,* 101-102.

Popham, W. (1978). The case for criterion-referenced measurements. *Educational Researcher, 7,* 6-10.

Powell, W. R. (1971). Validity of the IRI reading levels. *Elementary English, 48,* 637-642.

Powell, M. (1980). The beginning teacher evaluation study: A brief history of a major research project. In Denham, C., and A. Lieberman (Eds.), *Time to learn.* CA: NIE.

Time and Learning

Purkey, L. C., and Smith, M. S. (1983). Effective schools: A review. *Elementary School Journal, 83*(4), 427-452.

Quirk, T. J., Trismen, D. A., Weinberg, S. K., and Nalin, K. B. (1976). Attending behavior during reading instruction. *The Reading Teacher, 29*(7), 640-646.

Railsback, C. (1985). Learn to arrest the crime of wasted classtime. *The American School Board Journal, 172*(4), 32-33.

Reck, C. (1984). A measure of time. *Momentum, 15*(3), 64-65.

Reynolds, M. C., Wang, M. C., and Walberg, H. J. (1987). The necessary restructuring of special and regular education. *Exceptional Children, 53*(5), 391-398.

Reynolds, M. C., and Birch, J. W. (1977). *Teaching exceptional children in all America's schools.* Reston, VA: Council for Exceptional Children.

Rieth, H. J., and Frick, T. (1982). An analysis of academic learning (ALT) of mildly handicapped students in special education service delivery systems: Initial report on classroom process variables. Bloomington, IN: Center for Innovation in Teaching the Handicapped.

Rieth, H. J., Polsgrove, L., and Semmel, M. I. (1981). Instructional variables that make a difference: Attention to task and beyond. *Exceptional Education Quarterly, 2*(3), 61-71.

Rieth, H., Polsgrove, L., Okolo, C., Bahr, C., and Eckert, R. (1987). An analysis of the secondary special education classroom ecology with implications for teacher training. *Teacher Education and Special Education, 10*(3), 113-119.

Robertson, S. J., Simon, S. J., Pachman, J. S., and Drabman, R. S. (1979). Self-control and generalization procedures in a classroom of disruptive retarded children. *Child Behavior Therapy, 1*, 347-362.

Robin, A. L., Armel, S., and O'Leary, K. D. (1975). The effects of self instruction on writing deficiencies. *Behavior Therapy, 6*, 178-187.

Roehler, L., Schmidt, W., and Buchman, M. (1979). *How do teachers spend their language arts time?* (Research Series, No. 66). East Lansing, MI: Michigan State University, The Institute for Research in Teaching.

Rooney, K. J., Hallahan, D. P., and Lloyd, J. W. (1984). Self-recording of attention by learning disabled students in the regular classroom. *Journal of Learning Disabilities, 17*, 360-363.

Rooney, K., Polloway, E. A., and Hallahan, D. P. (1985). The use of self-monitoring procedures with low IQ learning disabled students. *Journal of Learning Disabilities, 18*, 384-384.

Rosenbaum, M. S., and Drabman, R. S. (1979). Self-control training in the classroom: A review and critique. *Journal of Applied Behavior Analysis, 12*, 467-485.

Rosenbaum, J. E. (1980). Social implications of educational grouping. In D. Berliner (Ed.), *Review of research in education, 8*, 361-401.

Rosenberg, M. S., and Sindelar, P. T. (1982). Educational assessment using direct continuous data. In J. T. Neisworth (Ed.). *Assessment in special education.* Rockville, MD: Aspen.

Rosenshine, B. V. (1981). How time is spent in elementary classrooms. *Journal of Classroom Interaction, 17*(1), 16-25.

Rosenshine, B. V. (1979). Content, time, and direct instruction. In P. L. Peterson, and J. H. Walberg (Eds.), *Research on teaching: Concepts, findings, and implications.* Berkeley, CA: McCutihan.

Rosenshine, B., and Furst, N. (1969). The effects of tutoring upon pupil achievement: A research review. Washington, D.C.: Office of Education, (ERIC Document Reproduction Service, No. ED 064 462).

Rosenshine, B. (1983). Teaching functions in instructional programs. *Elementary School Journal, 83*(4), 335-352.

Rosenshine, B. (1976). Recent research on teaching behaviors and student achievement. *Journal of Teacher Education, 27*, 61-64.

Rosenshine, B., and Stevens, R. (1984). Classroom instruction in reading. In P. D. Pearson (Ed.). *Handbook of Reading Research.* New York: Longman.

Ross, A. O. (1976). *Psychological aspects of learning disabilities & reading disorders.* NY: McGraw-Hill Book Company.

Ross, R. P. (1984). Classroom segments: The structuring of school time. In L. W. Anderson (Ed.), *Time and school learning.* NY: St. Martin's Press.

Rossmiller, R. A. (1983). Time-on-task: A look at what erodes time for instruction. *NASSP Bulletin, 67*(465), 45-69.

Rowley, G. L. (1976). The reliability of observational measures. *American Educational Research Journal, 13*(1), 51-59.

Salmon-Cox, L. (1981). Teachers and standardized achievement tests: What's really happening. *Phi Delta Kappan,* 631-634.

Samuels, S., and Turnure, J. (1974). Attention and reading achievement in first grade boys and girls. *Journal of Educational Psychology, 66*(1), 29-32.

Salvia, J., and Ysseldyke, J. E. (1988). *Assessment in Special and remedial education.*Boston, MA: Houghton Mifflin.

Schloss, P. J., Halle, J. W., and Sindelar, P. T. (1984). Guidelines for teachers' interpretation of student performance data. *Remedial and Special Education*, 5(4), 38-43.

Schloss, P. J., and Sedlak, R. A. (1986). *Instructional methods for students with learning and behavior problems*. Boston, MA: Allyn and Bacon, Inc.

Schniedewind, N. S., and Salend, S. J. (1987). Cooperative learning works. *Teaching Exceptional Children*, 19(2), 22-25.

Scott, J., and Bushell, D. Jr. (1974). The length of teacher contacts and students' off task behavior. *Journal of Applied Behavior Analysis, 7*, 39-44.

Scruggs, T. E., Mastropieri, M. A., and Richter, L. (1985). Peer tutoring with behaviorally disordered students: Social and academic benefits. *Behavioral Disorders, 10, 283-294*.

Scruggs, T. E., and Osguthorpe, R. T. (1986). Tutoring interventions within special education settings: A comparison of cross-age and peer-tutoring. *Psychology in the Schools, 23*, 187-193.

Scruggs, T. E., and Richter, L. (1985). Tutoring learning disabled students: A critical review. *Learning Disability Quarterly, 8*, 286-298.

Sedlak, R. A., Steppe-Jones, C., and Sedlak, D. (1982). Informal assessment: Concepts and practices. In T. L. Miller, and E. E. Davis (Eds.), *The mildly handicapped student*. NY: Grune and Stratton.

Serwer, B. L., Shapiro, B. J., and Shapiro, P. S. (1973). The comparative effectiveness of four methods of instruction on the achievement of children with specific learning disabilities. *The Journal of Special Education, 7*, 241-249.

Shapiro, E. S., and Klein, R. D. (1980). Self-management of classroom behavior with retarded/disturbed children. *Behavior Modification, 4*(1), 83-97.

Sharan, S. (1980). Cooperative learning in teams: Recent methods and effects on achievement, attitudes, and ethnic relations. *Review of Educational Research, 50*, 241-272.

Sharan, S., and Sharan, Y. *Small-group teaching*, (1976). Englewood Cliffs, NJ: Educational Technology Publications.

Shavelson, R., and Dempsey-Atwood, N. (1976). Generalizability of measures of teaching behavior. *Review of Educational Research, 46*(4), 553-611.

Shulman, L. S. (1986). Paradigms and research programs in the study of teaching: A contemporary perspective. In M. C. Wittrock (Ed.), *Handbook of research on teaching*. 3rd ed. NY: MacMillan.

Silbert, J., Carnine, D., and Stein, M. (1981). *Direct Instruction Mathematics*. Columbus, OH: Charles E. Merill Publishing Co.

Sindelar, P. T., and Deno, S. L. (1978). The efficacy of resource programming. *The Journal of Special Education, 12*, 17-28.

Sindelar, P. T., Smith, M. A., Harriman, N. E., Hale, R. L., and Wilson, R. J. (1986). Teacher effectiveness in special education programs. *The Journal of Special Education, 20*(2), 195-207.

Sindelar, P. T. (1981). Operationalizing the concept of the least restrictive environment, *Education And Treatment of Children, 4*(3), 279-290.

Sindelar, P. T. (1982). The effects of cross-aged tutoring on the comprehension skills of remedial reading students. *The Journal of Special Education, 16*(2), 199-206.

Singh, R. K. (1982). *Peer tutoring: Its effects on the math skills of students designated as learning disabled.* Dissertation Abstracts International, 42, 4793-A.

Slavin, R. E. (1980). Cooperative Learning. *Review of Educational Research, 50*(2), 315-342.

Slavin, R. E., Leavey, M. B., and Madden, N. A. (1984). Combining cooperative learning and individualized instruction: Effects on student mathematics achievement, attitudes, and behaviors. *The Elementary School Journal, 84*(4), 410-422.

Slavin, R. E. (1987). Mastery learning reconsidered. *Review of Educational Research, 57*(2), 175-213.

Slosson, R. L. *Slosson intelligence test.* New York: Slosson Educational Publications, 1971.

Smith, L., and Sanders, K. (1981). The effects on student achievement and student perception of varying structure in social studies content. *Journal of Educational Research, 74*(5), 333-336.

Smith, J. (1981). Philosophical considerations of mastery learning theory: An empirical study. Paper presented at the annual convention of the American Educational Research Association, new York.

Smyth, W. J. (1984). Time, achievement, and teacher development. In L. W. Anderson (ed.), *Time and school learning.* NY: St. Martin's Press.

Snider, V. (1987). Use of self-monitoring of attention with LD students: Research and application. *Learning Disabilities Quarterly, 10*, 139-151.

Snow, R. E. (1977). Individual differences and instructional theory *Educational Researcher, 6*(10), 11-15.

Snow, R. E. (1984). Placing children in special education: Some comments. *Educational Researcher, 13*(3), 12-14.

Soar, R. (1973). Follow-through classroom process measures and pupil growth. Final report. Unpublished report, Gainesville, FL: College of Education, University of Florida.

Solomon, D., and Kendall, A. J. (1979). *Children in classrooms.* NY: Praeger.

Spady, W. (1981). *Outcome-based instructional management: A sociological perspective.* Unpublished manuscript, American Association of School Administrators, Arlington, VA.

Stallings, J., Cory, R., Fairweather, J., and Needles, M. (1977). *Early childhood education classroom evaluation.* Menlo Park, CA: SRI International.

Stallings, J., Needels, M., and Stayrook, N. (1979). The teaching of basic reading skills in secondary schools. Phase II and Phase III. Menlo Park, CA: SRI International.

Stallings, J. D., and Kaskowitz, D. H. (1974). *Follow-Through Classroom Observation Evaluation, 1972-1973.* Menlo Park, CA: Stanford Research Institute. (ERIC Document Reproduction Service No. ED 104 969)

Stallings, J. (1981). What research has to say to administrators of secondary schools about effective teaching and staff development. (ERIC Document Reproduction Service No. 209 748)

————— (1980). Allocated academic learning time revisited, or beyond time on task. *Educational Researcher, 9*(11), 11-16.

————— (1975). Implementation and child effects of teaching practices in a follow through classrooms. *Monographs of the Society for Research in Child Development, 40* (7-8, Serial No. 163).

Stallings, J. A., and Stipek, D. (1986). Research on early childhood and elementary school teaching programs. In N. C. Wittrock, (Ed.), *Handbook of research on teaching*, 3rd ed. NY: MacMillan.

Stein, C., and Goldman, J. (1980). Beginning reading instruction for children with minimal brain dysfunction. *Journal of Learning Disabilities, 13*, 219-222.

Stowitschek, C. E., Hecimovic, A., Stowitschek, J. J., and Shores, R. E. (1982). Immediate and gerarative effects on instructional performance and spelling achievement. *Behavioral Disorders, 7*, 136-148.

Strauss, A. A., and Lehtinen, L. E. (1947). *Psychopathology and education of the brain-injured child.* New York: Grune and Stratton.

Sulzer-Azaroff, B., and Mayer, G. R. (1977). *Applying behavior-analysis procedures with children and youth.* NY: Holt, Rinehart and Winston.

Tawney, J.W. and Gast, D.L. 1984). *Single subject research in special education.* Columbus, OH: Merrill.

Thurlow, M. L., Graden, J., Greener, J. W., and Ysseldyke, J. E. (1983). Learning Disabled and non-learning disabled students' opportunities to learn. *Learning Disability Quarterly, 6*(2), 172-183.

Thurlow, M., Ysseldyke, J., Graden, J., and Algozzine, R. (1984). Opportunity to learn for Learning Disabled. *Learning Disabled Quarterly, 7*(1), 55-67.

———— (1983). What's so "special" about the special education resource room for learning disabled students? *Learning Disabilities Quarterly, 6*(3), 283-288.

Thurlow, M., Graden, J., Ysseldyke, J. E., and Algozzine, R. (1984). Student reading during reading class: The lost activity in reading instruction. *Journal of Educational Research, 77*(5), 268-271.

Timmermans, S. R. (1987). Diagnostic prescriptive teaching. In C. R. Reynolds, and L. Mann (Eds.), *Encyclopedia of special education.* NY: John Wiley and Sons.

Tobias, S., and Ingber, T. (1976). Achievement-treatment interactions in programmed instruction. *Journal of Educational Psychology, 68*(1), 43-47.

Torgeson, J. K. (1982). The learning disabled child an inactive learner: Educational implications. *Topics in learning and learning disabilities, 2,* 45-51.

Walden, E. L., and Thompson, S. A. (1981). A review of some alternative approaches to drug management of hyperactivity in children. *Journal of Learning Disabilities, 14*(4), 213-217.

Wallace, G., and Larsen, S. C. (1978). Educational assessment of learning problems: Testing for teaching. Boston: Allyn and Bacon.

Wang, M. C., Gennari, P., and Waxman, H. C. (1985). The adaptive learning environments model: Design, implementations and effects. In M. C. Wang, and H. J. Walberg (Eds.), *Adapting instruction to individual differences* (pp. 191-235). Berkeley, CA: McCutchan.

Warner, M. M., Schumaker, J. B., Alley, G. B., and Deshler, D. D. (1980). Learning disabled adolescents in the public schools: Are they different from other low achievers? *Exceptional Education Quarterly, 1,* 27-36.

Waxman, H. C., and Walberg, H. J. (1982). The relationship of teaching and learning: A review of reviews of process-product research. *Contemporary Education Review, 1*(2), 103-120.

Wesson, C., Fuchs, L, Tindal, G., Mirkin, P., and Deno, S. L. (1986). Facilitating the efficiency of on-going curriculum based measurements. *Teacher Education and Special Education, 9*(4), 166-172.

White, O. R., and Haring, N. G. (1980). *Exceptional Teaching*, Columbus, OH: Charles E. Merrill.

Wiley, D. E. & Harnischfeger, A. (1974). Explosion of a myth: Quantity of schooling and exposure to education, major educational variables. *Educational Researcher, 3*(4), 7-12.

Wiley, D. E. (1973). Another hour, another day: Quantity of schooling a potent path for policy. In W. H. Sewell, R. M. Houser, and D. L. Featherman (Eds.), *Schooling and achievement in American society* (pp. 225-265). NY: Academic Press.

Wilkinson, I., Wardrop, J. L., and Anderson, R. C. (1988). Silent reading reconsidered: Reinterpreting reading instruction and its effects. *American Educational Research Journal, 25*(1), 127-144.

Will, M. C. (1986). Educating children with learning problems: A shared responsibility. *Exceptional Children, 52*(5), 411-415.

Williams, S. O., and Highsmith, M. C. (1983). Feed computers the facts, and watch 'instructional downtime' waste away. *The American School Board Journal, 170*(5), 34-35.

Wilson, R. & Wesson, C. (1986). Making every minute count: Academic learning time in LD classrooms. *Learning Disabilities Focus, 2*(1), 13-191.

Wyckoff, D. B. (1974). *A study of mastery learning and its effects on achievement of sixth grade social studies students*. Unpublished dissertation, Georgia State University, Atlanta.

Ysseldyke, J. E. (1973). Diagnostic-prescriptive teaching: The search for aptitude-treatment interactions. In L. Mann, and D. Sabatino (Eds.), *The first review of special education*. Philadelphia, PA: JSE Press.

Ysseldyke, J. E., and Salvia, J. (1974). Diagnostic-prescriptive teaching: Two models. *Exceptional Children, 41*, 181-185.

Ysseldyke, J. E., Algozzine, B., Shinn, M. R., and McGue, M. (1982). Similarities and differences between low achievers and students classified learning disabled. *The Journal of Special Education, 16*(1), 73-85.

Ysseldyke, J. E., Thurlow, M. L., Christenson, S. L., and Weiss, J. (1987). Time allocated to instruction of mentally retarded, learning disabled, emotionally disturbed, and nonhandicapped elementary students. *The Journal of Special Education, 21*(3), 43-55.

Ysseldyke, J. E., and Algozzine, B. (1982). *Critical issues in special and remedial education*. Boston, MA: Houghton Mifflin.

Ysseldyke, J. E., Thurlow, M., Graden, J., Wesson, C., Algozzine, B., and Deno, S. (1983). Generalizations from five years of research on assessment and decision making: The University of Minnesota Institute. *Exceptional Education Quarterly, 4*(1), 75-93.

Ysseldyke, J. E. (1983). Current practices in making psycho-educational decisions about learning disabled students. *Journal of Learning Disabilities, 16*, 226-233. Annual Review of Learning Disabilities.

Zigmond, N., and Miller, S. E. (1986). Assessment for instructional planning. *Exceptional Children, 52* (6), 501-509.

Zigmond, N., Vallecorsa, A., and Silverman, R. (1983). *Assessment for instructional planning in special education*. Englewood Cliffs, NJ: Prentice-Hall.

Zigmond, N., Levin, E., and Laurie, T. E. (1985). Managing the mainstream: An analysis of teacher attitudes and student performance in mainstream high school programs. *Journal of Learning Disabilities, 18*(9), 535-541.

Zigmond, N., Sansone, J., Miller, S. E., Donahoe, K. A., and Kohnke, R. (1986). Teaching learning disabled students at the secondary school level: What research says to teachers. *Learning Disabilities Focus, 1*(2), 108-115.

Index